321
SERIOUSLY SMART THINGS
YOU NEED TO KNOW

Mathilda Masters
Illustrations by Louize Perdieus

321
SERIOUSLY
SMART THINGS
YOU NEED TO KNOW

CONTENTS

1

ANIMALS GALORE

HEE HEE! GOT IT! ???

1 THE THIEF ANT HAS EARNED ITS REPUTATION (BUT NOT ITS FOOD...)

Ants are tiny creatures, and **thief ants** are truly minuscule at a mere 1.5 millimetres long. The workers grow no larger than 2.5 millimetres, which is far smaller than many other 'ordinary' ants. And there's a good reason why.

Thief ants go in search of other ants' nests, building themselves a comfy home somewhere close by. Then the workers start digging tunnels to go and plunder the larger ants' nest, while their queen stays safe at home. The worker ants burrow into the walls of the other nest, and look for food to steal.

If the big ants try to fight back, the little thieves quickly scurry back through their tunnels, which are far too small for the larger guards to fit through. (See Fact 40 for more about ants.)

2 A DOMESTIC CAT CAN OUTRUN USAIN BOLT

Usain Bolt can run 100 metres in less than ten seconds. That's about 10 or 11 metres per second – pretty darn fast. It's no surprise that Usain's nicknames include the 'Lightning Bolt' and 'Thunderbolt'.

But did you know that your pet cat can run even faster? Ordinary **domestic cats** can easily sprint at 13.9 metres per second, making them ever so slightly faster than the Jamaican superhero.

Your cat's big cousin, the **tiger**, does even better at 23.9 metres per second. But having a cheetah hot on your heels is when you should really be worried: a cheetah can run at over 30 metres per second, making it the world's fastest land animal. It can even keep up with cars on the motorway!

3 MRS MANTIS IS A CANNIBAL

Praying mantises are weird animals. Some species grow no larger than 2.5 centimetres, while others can reach up to 25 centimetres. That's pretty big for an insect!

Even though their long, green bodies make them look like grasshoppers, mantises cannot jump and are actually more closely related to cockroaches. The 'praying' part in their name is a reference to the way they sit upright and hold their front legs together while searching for prey. Perhaps they should be called 'preying' mantises!

There are 2,400 different praying mantis species, most of which live in tropical regions. They all have a triangular head, a long neck and extremely long front legs. They also have at least five eyes: two enormous compound eyes and three smaller 'eye spots', or *ocelli*. These eyes are on top of their head, and are hard to see.

But perhaps the strangest thing about praying mantises is their ears. Each mantis has only one ear, and it's in the middle of its stomach, between its legs. Funnily enough, the older a praying mantis is, the better it can hear. The opposite is true for humans, as your grandparents could probably tell you!

Praying mantises generally eat other insects, but the larger species will sometimes gobble up a small bird or a frog.

Praying mantises are also cannibals, and sometimes even eat up members of their own families. The strongest nymph (that's what young praying mantises are called) will quickly devour its brothers and sisters until only a few remain, giving the nymph a greater chance of survival.

The females of the larger species will devour the male after mating. No wonder the males often take hours to approach the female, and never take their eyes off her during the act. They are literally risking their lives.

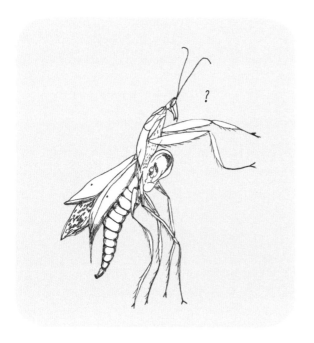

EXTRA-GRUESOME PRAYING MANTIS FACT

Sometimes the female praying mantis will start eating the male before mating is over. Even missing his head and half his body, the male will continue to work away until the job is done.

MMM MMM

POO POO

4 RABBITS EAT THEIR OWN DROPPINGS

If you keep **rabbits**, you've probably already noticed how they sometimes eat their own droppings. That's because rabbits can't digest all the nutrients in their food in one go.

Anything they can't digest is pooped out as hard droppings. The rabbits don't eat those.

But rabbits also leave a much softer type of droppings, which they immediately eat again afterwards. These softer droppings are produced by the appendix or caecum, and still contain various nutrients. Only a second trip through the intestines will release all the nutrients that the rabbits need. Rabbits that don't gobble up their appendix droppings can die of malnutrition.

5 ELEPHANTS CAN'T JUMP

And just as well, you may think! If all the world's **elephants** were to jump at the same time, the earth might spin out of its orbit!

But did you know that elephants actually can't jump? They are far too heavy, and would break their legs if they did. Elephants weigh between 1,500 and 7,000 kilograms, depending on the species. The lightest is the Borneo dwarf elephant, which – at 1,500 kilograms – still weighs more than the average car. But the West African and Savannah elephants are the real heavyweights, and are easily comparable to a large truck.

Despite their size, elephants are very good runners, and over short distances can reach speeds of up to 40 kilometres per hour.

But elephants aren't just big and heavy: they are also very intelligent, sociable creatures, sharing food and water with each other even when it becomes scarce.

They have very good memories, and can always find their way to anywhere they have already been before. They especially like running into family members along the way! When they do, there's always plenty of kissing and cuddling.

Whenever they come across the tusks or bones of another dead elephant, they usually know who they belonged to, and show respect by carefully stroking the remains with their trunks.

EVEN MORE FACTS ABOUT ELEPHANTS . . .

- Elephants don't need mobile phones to communicate over long distances. They make a grumbling sound with their throat that is so low, humans can't hear it. But it allows them to send messages across distances of up to 5 kilometres – telling their friends and family where to find food for example, or to warn other elephants about predators.

- A stampeding herd can often be sensed through the ground by other elephants grazing tens of kilometres away. That way they know that something's afoot, and stay on guard against poachers or other threats.

- The elephant's only natural predator is people. Elephant herds need vast areas to live in, which are gradually being eroded by humans. Not only that, but there are poachers who hunt elephants for the ivory in their tusks. In 1930 there were still around five million African elephants in the wild; now only 200,000 to 300,000 survive. Many countries run special environmental programmes to help protect elephants.

- Elephants are excellent swimmers, and use their trunks like snorkels to stay underwater for long periods.

- The elephant's long tusks eventually made eating difficult, and so it needed something to help bring the food to its mouth. That's how the elephant's trunk came to be, evolving from its upper lip into a kind of gripping arm.

- The elephant's trunk is an incredibly useful tool, allowing it to pick up anything from a coin to a tree trunk, to stroke or slap other elephants, or even take a shower. The old Indian word for an elephant was *hastin*, which means 'animal with a hand'.

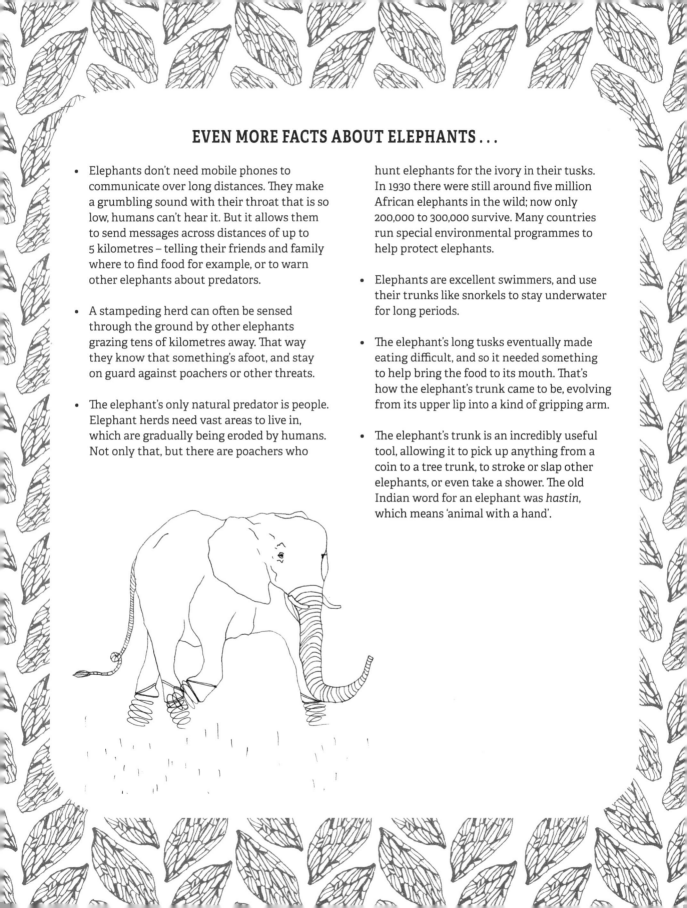

6 SPOOKFISH HAVE SEE-THROUGH HEADS

The bottom of the ocean is pitch-black, and home to a host of super-strange fish. One example is the **barreleye**, also sometimes called the 'spookfish'. Its Latin name is *Macropinna microstoma*.

The body of the barreleye fish is dark brown, but its eyes sit inside a transparent dome on its head. The eyes can turn in any direction, but usually point straight upwards, searching for prey. On the front of its face the fish has two large nostrils that look a lot like eyes, with a small mouth underneath. The eyes themselves are on top of the fish's head, allowing it to track its prey and avoid enemies. The tubular shape of the eyes is what gives the fish its name – the barreleye. It uses its fins to hover very gently in the water, so it goes unnoticed by other fish.

The barreleye is usually less than 15 centimetres long, and can live in ocean waters up to 2,500 metres deep. Because so few creatures live so far down, barreleyes need their wits about them in order to catch any food. Sometimes they steal food from jellyfish-like creatures called siphonophores (part of the *Cnidaria* family), which means 'tube-bearing' animals. They trap tiny jellyfish and shellfish in shallower seas, then dive down to gobble them up – that is, of course, unless a waiting barreleye can wrestle the catch out of their tentacles.

BONUS SEE-THROUGH FACTS

See-through animals also exist on land and in the air:

A type of frog called a glass frog often has a transparent belly. Its internal organs clearly show through, providing the perfect camouflage in its rainforest habitat.

The glasswing butterfly has transparent wings. Look it up – it looks like a stained-glass window!

One species of beetle, *Aspidimorpha miliaris*, has an orange body covered by a pair of transparent wings, like a see-through suit of armour.

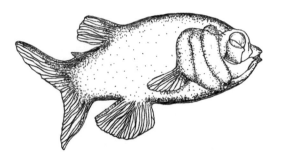

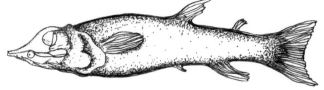

barreleye fish

7 LIONS REALLY ARE JUST BIG CATS

- **Lions** might look fierce, but they're really just as lazy as other cats. They sleep an incredible twenty hours a day, which means they are only active for four hours.

- Lions weigh between 120 and 250 kilograms, making them the largest of all the African big cats. Males are roughly 70 kilograms heavier than females.

- Male lions have a thick ring of hair around their necks, called a mane. It gives them a threatening look, but also protects their head and neck while fighting. The mane starts to grow at the age of about three – the bigger the mane, the stronger and more masculine the lion.

- Lions are very sociable creatures, and live in groups called prides. Each pride is made up of around fifteen lions including one adult male (called the alpha male), a few females (lionesses), and their young. The lionesses are usually sisters and daughters to one another; they all have equal status and get along extremely well.

- To win a group of females, male lions need to fight each other. The battles can get quite vicious, which is why male lions in the wild often don't survive beyond the age of ten. The older males are eventually ousted by younger, stronger lions.

- Pride males use their roar to warn other lions to keep away from their territory. It's very loud, and can be heard from up to 8 kilometres away.

- Aside from defending their pride, males don't do an awful lot. The lionesses go out hunting and bring the food back home with them. They hunt in packs, because it allows them to encircle and trap larger prey. Even though the alpha male doesn't take part in the hunt, he is still the first to eat!

- Lions usually eat antelope, warthogs and zebras, but will occasionally dare to attack a buffalo, gnu, hippopotamus, or even a young rhinoceros or elephant.

- Lions can reach speeds of up to 60 kilometres per hour, but only for 100 metres at a time. When on the hunt, they usually hide in the tall grass, silently stalking their prey. Once they are about 30 metres away, they launch into a sprint and try to strangle the poor victim by clamping down on its nose or windpipe with their teeth.

YAAAAWN!

8 MONARCH BUTTERFLIES ALL MAKE THE TRIP OF A LIFETIME

The journey of the **monarch butterfly** is one of the greatest marvels in nature. Each year, millions of these butterflies leave Canada, travelling across the USA to the mountains of central Mexico. Some of them fly distances of up to 8,000 kilometres.

Like all butterflies, the monarch starts life as a small caterpillar. It feeds on poisonous plants, and although it is immune to the poison, the caterpillar cannot digest it. The poison therefore remains inside the caterpillar's body, making it deadly to all kinds of natural predators such as birds, reptiles or rodents, who have learned to avoid it.

The caterpillar sheds its skin four times over the course of its life. The fifth time, it surrounds itself in a black cocoon, emerging some time later as a splendid butterfly with orange and black wings.

Two months after leaving their cocoons, the monarch butterflies come together to prepare for an almost magical journey. At the end of the summer, around a hundred million butterflies all fly south from Canada as one large group. They only stop along the way to gather water and nectar, or to shelter from extreme weather conditions. Although none of the butterflies have ever made the journey before, they all know exactly how to reach their destination without fail. How they do so is still a mystery to scientists.

People in Mexico are always extremely happy when the butterflies arrive. The population sees them as the souls of their departed loved ones returning to their homes. They even build little shrines offering fruit and flowers, where the monarch butterflies can eat and rest after their long journey.

The butterflies eat their fill, and in the late autumn hang in the trees in large clusters called roosts. By huddling close together, they conserve their body heat and use less energy. Now and again they will leave to find water or nectar, but they always return quickly to the roost.

The roosts can be seen all winter long, until spring comes again. Then the butterflies will carefully open their wings and separate from one another, flying off again for the north in large groups. Their first pitstop is Texas, where they make camp to breed.

After the females have laid three to four hundred eggs, the parent butterflies die. Then the new caterpillars hatch, and eventually turn into butterflies. This second generation continues the journey north, where they mate once more, and more new butterflies are born. The same thing happens with the third generation – it's rather like a relay race. The fourth generation arrives in Canada in the summer, when the entire cycle starts again.

9 THE COMMON SWIFT EATS 'ON THE FLY'

- The **common swift** might look a lot like a swallow, but they are actually two different species – they only look similar because they evolved under similar conditions (this phenomenon is called convergent evolution). The swift belongs to the family of *Apodidae*, which literally means without feet – that, too, is a little confusing. Swifts do have feet, they are just very small. Each foot has four toes with very sharp nails or talons that allow them to cling to the sides of walls or perch on roof edges.

- Swifts barely ever touch the ground. They were built to fly, and are among the world's best flyers! They reach speeds of up to 170 kilometres per hour, devouring hundreds of insects as they go. To drink, they skim the surfaces of pools or rivers, scooping up water in their beaks.

- To raise their young, swifts build nests in hollows and cracks in houses or other buildings. They catch pieces of thread, fluff and small plants while zipping through the air, and glue them together into a nest using their saliva. But if they can find an old sparrow or starling nest, they will just re-use that.

- Swifts always return to the same nest every year. If they ever find their nest has disappeared – if the building has been demolished, for example – they become quite distressed and sad.

- The parents hunt to feed their offspring, catching between 20,000 and 50,000 insects in the air every day. To be sure that their young have enough food, they will sometimes travel hundreds of kilometres.

YUM!

10 NEVER INVITE A 'COOKIECUTTER' TO TEA!

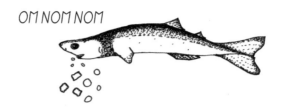

OM NOM NOM

Though the name sounds delicious, be careful if there's one in the area. This small species of shark carves perfectly round chunks of flesh out of its victims, as if cut out by a cookie-cutter. Their prey can include fish or humans, and occasionally even submarines! **Cookiecutter sharks** are found in the Atlantic and Indian oceans, and have specialized jaws whose lower teeth are much longer than their upper teeth.

In 1970, American submarines sustained so much damage from these sharks that they needed to dock for repairs. At first, the crews didn't realize that the culprits were cookiecutters. The hulls were so full of holes, the vessels were leaking oil and the crew thought they had been under enemy attack. Eventually, they discovered they had fallen prey to the cookiecutters!

11 GIRAFFES CAN LICK THEIR OWN EARS

- It's logical that big animals need lots of food. But the **giraffe's** skull, jaw and front teeth are actually too small for it to consume enough. Luckily, they have big lips and an enormous tongue, which together form a kind of extension to the mouth.

- Giraffe tongues can grow up to an amazing 50 centimetres long, allowing the long-necked beasts to scrape gunk out of their own ears. Of course, the tongue's main purpose is to rip leaves and twigs from trees for food. The tongue is incredibly hardy and tough, so it doesn't get hurt by the thorns on the giraffe's favourite meal – the leaves of the acacia tree.

- Next time you're at the zoo, take a look at the colour of the giraffe's tongue. It's blue! That's to protect it from the sun's ultraviolet rays. Giraffes like to leave their tongues hanging out of their mouths, and the blue colour acts like a kind of sunscreen.

YUMMY!

EVEN MORE GIRAFFE FACTS . . .

- At birth, giraffes are already 2 metres tall and can reach the dizzy heights of up to 5 metres in adulthood.

- The okapi is the giraffe's closest relative. Together they form the *Giraffidae* family.

- A giraffe's eyes are on the sides of its head, giving it an excellent view of its surroundings, far into the distance. Its long eyelashes aren't just for fluttering seductively at other giraffes – they also offer protection from dust and the thorns of trees. And just like people, giraffes can also wink!

- The giraffe's heart is small, but is still strong enough to pump blood all the way up its neck to its brain.

- Giraffes have the same number of neck bones as humans: seven. The giraffe's are much longer than ours, of course!

- Male giraffes use their necks to 'duel' with: they rub or smack their necks against each other, and the last giraffe to remain standing is the winner. Giraffes who win these 'neck wrestling' matches are more likely to find a mate.

- Giraffes can go for more than a month without water. And a good thing too, since they are most vulnerable when bending down to drink from a pool or river. To do so, they need to splay out their front legs almost to the ground – from that position, it's hard to make a fast getaway.

- Julius Caesar was the first person to bring a giraffe to Europe.

YUM!

12 THE WHALE SHARK IS THE WORLD'S BIGGEST FISH

We know what you're thinking – what about the **blue whale**? Well, read the heading carefully: the blue whale is a mammal, not a fish.

On average, **whale sharks** grow to be 9.7 metres long. The largest ever measured was 12.7 metres, although fishermen and divers claim to have seen specimens up to 18 metres long.

They live in all of the world's oceans. It's difficult to estimate exactly how many there are, but scientists believe there are still tens of thousands in the wild.

Compared to other sharks, whale sharks are slow swimmers at around 5 kilometres per hour.

They move their entire bodies when coursing through the water, not just their tails like most other sharks.

Whale sharks can live to be a hundred, but they don't produce young until they are thirty or so. That, plus the fact that they are slow swimmers, is probably one of the reasons why they are an endangered species.

Despite their size, whale sharks are not especially dangerous. They won't attack humans, but their enormous tail can still pack an enormous punch, so watch out just in case!

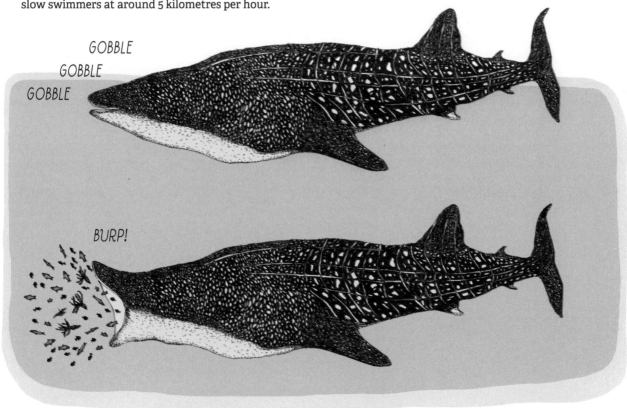

While swimming along, the whale shark holds its mouth open to collect food, which can include plankton, krill (tiny ocean shrimp), small fish and squid. When it closes its mouth, the water is filtered through its gills: the water returns to the ocean, but the food stays trapped inside. The whale shark can filter thousands of litres of water per day like this.

Orcas aside, whale sharks have few natural predators. Only humans hunt them: their flesh is used in fish dishes, and the fins for soup. The liver contains a substance useful in shipbuilding, and the skin also fetches a high price.

13 FISH CAN SOMETIMES BE FOUND IN TREES

Imagine you're sitting in one of your favourite trees, when suddenly a fish appears beside you! You've just found a **climbing perch**, also known as a **labyrinth fish**.

- Labyrinth fish have adapted to live in waters with low oxygen levels. To survive, they evolved a special organ called the labyrinth organ, located on the top of the head between the eyes. The fish suck in air from the surface of the water and force it through the labyrinth organ, extracting oxygen. They also use the air they inhale to build protective 'bubble nests' in the water, where they lay their eggs.

- But do they really climb trees? Researchers have occasionally found labyrinth fish in the treetops, and they just assumed that the fish climbed up there themselves.

- In 1927, one clever scientist figured out that the fish hadn't climbed the trees under their own steam. Because they swim just below the water's surface, they are often snapped up by birds, which sometimes deposit them in the treetops as a snack for later. Because the fish can survive out of water for days, it looked like they had climbed up there themselves.

- Labyrinth fish can travel across land from one pool to another. Usually these are group migrations, involving large numbers of fish looking for fresher waters together.

climbing perch

ALLEY-OOP!

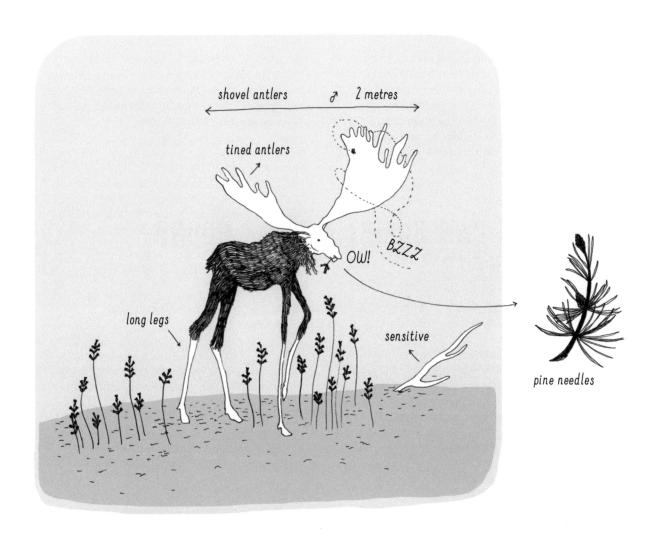

shovel antlers ♂ 2 metres

tined antlers

BZZZ

OW!

long legs

sensitive

pine needles

14 A MOOSE CAN FEEL A FLY LANDING ON ITS ANTLERS

Moose are the largest members of the deer family (or *Cervidae*), and they live in northern Europe, the United States and in Siberia. They even used to live in the UK, but disappeared between 3,000 and 4,000 years ago.

The males (or bulls) have large, broad antlers with small pegs sticking out – these are known as palmate or shovel antlers. Other antlers are

shaped more like branches and these are called tined antlers. Moose antlers can grow up to 2 metres wide!

The bulls shed their antlers once a year between December and March, and in April they grow back again. Moose antlers are incredibly sensitive: the moose can even feel when a fly has landed somewhere on them.

Moose don't just have big antlers – they also have strikingly long legs, which are useful for running through deep snow.

Moose have a very good sense of smell and hearing, but would benefit from contact lenses as they don't have very good eyesight.

Their favourite things to eat are the shoots and twigs from pine trees, the bark of poplars and willows, as well as other leaves, grasses and water plants. In the autumn, they sometimes snack on grains and seeds.

Moose love to swim, and feel most at home beside a lake or river. Only in the wintertime do they go off in search of drier places to live. In the summer they are solitary roamers, but come together to form small herds in winter.

To mate, a bull will spend a few days in the company of a female (a cow), but will quickly leave her alone again afterwards. Moose calves remain with their mothers almost until the following calf is born. When it is nearly time, the mother will chase her previous calf away, forcing it to learn to survive on its own four feet.

15 TRY GAMING WITH A PIG! (YOU MIGHT NOT WIN...)

After primates, whales, elephants and ravens, **pigs** are probably the most intelligent animals on earth.

- They use twenty different sounds to communicate with each other.

- They also use a complex system of body language to warn other pigs of danger, and to express their emotions.

- Pigs can be taught to answer to their names, and are very quick to learn new things.

- Mother pigs (sows) even sing to their piglets during feeding!

- Scientific research has shown that pigs can think ahead into the future, and understand what humans try to say to them.

- Some pigs can even play computer games, and understand that the joystick is used to make things move on the computer screen. After a little while they figure the game out, and do even better than chimpanzees!

In the wild, pigs are actually very clean creatures.

- They like bathing in mud, because mud offers protection against the sun, heat and parasites.

- To do their business, wild pigs will choose a special spot that is far away from their nest, to make sure everything stays nice and clean.

Maybe consider a pet pig instead of a dog?

16 WOMBAT POO IS SQUARE

With their stubby legs, round bodies and short tails, **wombats** are adorable creatures. They live in Australia, but nobody seems to know what they evolved from. Like koalas, they are marsupials of the *Diprotodontia* family.

Wombats are true herbivores, and eat grass, seeds, herbs, bark and roots. After being digested, the food leaves their body as cube-shaped droppings about 2 centimetres across.

The cubes of poo are often deposited on rocks or tree stumps. Their square shape means they won't fall off or roll away.

Wombats are nocturnal animals with poor eyesight. Their droppings are used to mark territory that has already been claimed by other animals. The droppings also let female wombats know that there are males nearby, who might be interested in a date.

WANNA GO OUT?

sniff sniff

yum!

17 SHEEP ARE SMARTER THAN YOU THINK

Admittedly, **sheep** do look a little dopey with their thick, woolly heads and fluffy bodies. Bleating also isn't the smartest-sounding noise in the world. But appearances can be deceiving!

Research by Cambridge University has shown that sheep are actually much smarter than we thought. They can remember the face of a friend for up to two years, they recognize each other by their noses, know which families plants belong to, and some breeds can even remember the path through a maze. In some tests, sheep even outperform monkeys!

To make sure sheep stay within a certain area, grilles are often laid that they cannot walk across. But many farmers will tell stories of sheep that roll across the grilles to the other side to escape – how clever is that?

Sheep do best at tests when they're not part of a flock; scientists think that's because a 'herd mentality' tends to dull the intellect a little.

Beta vulgaris

Taxus baccata

BORING (BUT YUMMY)

BERRY (BEWARE)

18 HUMMINGBIRDS CAN FLY BACKWARDS

Hummingbirds are found most commonly in South America.

- The smallest species of hummingbird is the **bee hummingbird**: it's only 5–6 centimetres tall and weighs less than 2 grams.

- The **giant hummingbird** is the largest member of the hummingbird family, at 20 grams and 22 centimetres. It lives mostly in the Andes.

- The wings of the hummingbird beat astonishingly fast – up to 80 times per second – which allows them to hover perfectly still in mid-air while they feed. Their fast flappers also let them fly straight up or straight down, like a helicopter.

- The hummingbird is the only bird that can fly backwards. But it's exhausting, so they don't do it very often.

- Hummingbirds have tiny hearts, but they beat up to 1,000 times a minute. So hummingbirds need to keep feeding all day long to obtain enough energy.

- To extract nectar from flowers, the hummingbird uses its long, pointy beak, rolling out its long tongue to get at the deep stores that even insects can't reach. Nectar from yellow and red-coloured flowers is the hummingbird's favourite.

19 HOW DO SHARKS MEDITATE? THE NOSE KNOWS

AND RELAX...

There are some species of **shark** that enter a trance-like state if you roll them on their back and stroke their noses. Scientists call the phenomenon 'tonic immobility', and it's a reflex that causes temporary paralysis and makes the animal appear dead. Nobody knows for sure how or why it works – probably there is some kind of physical reaction that disables the shark's voluntary muscles for a while. If left alone, the animal will usually wake up again after about 15 minutes.

But watch out! It doesn't work with all sharks. So the next time you meet a shark, be certain it's the right species before turning it over and giving it a nose-rub.

Other animals exhibit a behaviour called **thanatosis** – or playing dead – which looks similar but is not the same. Thanatosis is actually a voluntary instinctive response, and occurs in mammals, reptiles and insects. They usually use it to fool predators into thinking they are already dead; in the best-case scenario, the predator will loosen its grip for a moment, giving the prey a chance to escape.

Other fish use thanatosis to catch their prey, floating perfectly still in the water and tricking other fish into thinking they are already dead. When an unsuspecting fish gets close enough, they attack!

20 THE GIANT OCEANIC MANTA RAY IS 7 METRES WIDE

Giant manta rays are enormous fish, with a fin-span that can be up to 7 metres wide, measured from tip to tip. A single manta ray can weigh between 1,350 and 3,000 kilograms.

Manta rays are already 1.2 metres wide at birth, and the young fish come into the world fully developed.

Giant manta rays look like huge UFOs. Normally they drift elegantly through the water, but they can also rocket straight upwards by beating their powerful fins, sometimes catapulting themselves metres out of the water. Because their fins resemble wings, when they do this, it almost looks like they're flying!

The manta ray's body is dark on top and light on the bottom, making it hard for predators to spot. From the top they appear black against a dark background, and seen from below, their light-coloured underbelly blends in perfectly with the ocean's surface.

Mantas feed on plankton and small fish by sucking in and filtering the water as they swim.

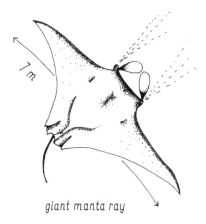

giant manta ray

21 SOME FISH HAVE TEETHING PROBLEMS

- **Viperfish** look very creepy. They have bluish-black bodies, and their enormous jaws are full of long, transparent, needle-like teeth that stick out everywhere. Their teeth are so big, in fact, they don't even fit inside the fish's mouth, and they are also covered in tiny barbs to prevent any prey from escaping once caught. Viperfish use their teeth to catch other fish swimming in deep, dark waters. They might not win a beauty contest, but they certainly aren't the only deep-sea fish with a terrifying appearance.

- **Piranhas**, native to the Amazon rainforest in Brazil, are usually timid but can be very aggressive. They have even been known to attack humans with their razor-sharp teeth, but only if they are really hungry.

- Then there's the **electric eel**, another charming creature. They can grow up to 2.5 metres long and emit a 600-volt electric shock, enough to knock a human unconscious and drown them.

- **Sharks** have had a bad reputation for eating humans. But did you know that sharks don't really eat human meat at all? Great white sharks, tiger sharks and bull sharks sometmes bite people, but not because they're hungry. Most likely, it's because the person was in the shark's way.

GOT A TOOTHPICK?

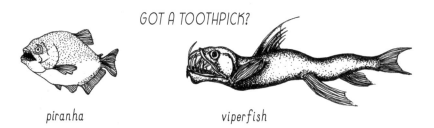

piranha   *viperfish*

22 PANDAS DO A HANDSTAND TO PEE

Pandas are not born fighters. They try to avoid their rivals as much as possible, and leave scent signals to mark territories that have already been claimed.

They also use these signals to communicate, rubbing their heads and bodies against trees to let other pandas know whether they are male or female, and how old they are. They are the only bears with scent glands that can release a smell lasting up to three months. They also leave droppings in strategic locations, to warn other pandas to stay out of their territory.

Male pandas have one very strange habit: they balance on their front paws and lean against a tree – like a handstand – and try to pee against the tree as high as they can. Passing females can then identify the male that has peed the highest, and choose him as a mate. That male is considered the winner, and can mate with the female without having to fight the other pandas.

The mating, incidentally, has to occur during a very short period of time. The females are only fertile for a few days a year, so the chances of a baby panda are extremely small. That's why pandas have been on the endangered species list for a very long time. In China, fewer than two thousand pandas are left in the wild.

BONUS PANDA FACTS

Newborn pandas are super-tiny, about as long as a pencil. At birth they weigh between 100 and 160 grams, and are carried in their mother's paws. Only after 9 to 10 months do baby pandas become a little more independent.

Pandas need to eat for around twelve hours a day. During that time, they devour up to 40 kilos of bamboo.

Pandas have six digits on their front paws – the sixth one is used to hold onto bamboo stalks, and is in roughly the same place as your thumb.

MALE, AGE 7, SEEKS FEMALE PARTNER

SPOT THE DIFFERENCE

3114545   2652181

23 NO TWO ZEBRAS ARE ALIKE

- **Zebras** are striking creatures with their dazzling black-and-white stripes, but did you know that each zebra has its own unique pattern? No two zebras in the world are exactly the same.

- The reason why zebras have stripes is still something of a mystery. It's not really camouflage, since the grass on the savannah isn't black or white. Scientists think that the pattern might serve to confuse lions, the zebra's main predator. Lions are colour blind, and the pattern of stripes produces an optical illusion that dances around and confuses them. Other scientists think that the stripes might deter flies and other insects, or that the zebras use the patterns to recognize one another.

- People used to think that zebras were white with black stripes, because their bellies are white. But research has shown that the opposite is true: zebras are actually black, with a pattern of white stripes.

- Funnily enough, despite being black-and-white themselves, zebras can probably see colours just fine. They also have reasonable night vision, excellent hearing and can swivel their ears to pick up sounds from all directions. Their senses of smell and taste are not as good, however.

- A group of zebras is often called a harem, and is made up of a single male with a few females and their young. Males that don't yet have mates all live in a group of bachelors together.

- Zebras only sleep if there are other zebras in the vicinity who can sound the alarm if there's any danger. Instead of lying down, they remain standing so they can run away quickly if need be.

- It's impossible to tame zebras: they are natural prey animals, and become panicked and run away at the slightest sign of danger.

24 THE EYES OF THE GIANT SQUID ARE... GIGANTIC

Remember when Little Red Riding Hood said: 'Oh grandmother, what big eyes you have!' And the wolf replied: 'All the better to see you with'? Bigger eyes do indeed make it easier to see.

- **Nocturnal** animals are active at night, and so their **eyes** are extremely large relative to their bodies, making it easier for them to catch tasty flies or juicy worms in the dark. Each eye is often as big as the animal's entire brain!

27 cm

I SPY WITH MY GINORMOUS EYE...

- **Humans** are not like that. Human eyes are much smaller than human brains.

- The animal with the biggest eyes on the planet is the **giant squid**. Its eyes have a diameter of 27 centimetres – that's eleven times wider than a human eye, and about the size of a beach ball! Giant squid need such enormous eyes to look around the murky darkness of the deep sea.

- Of course, giant squid don't just have giant eyes. Scientists estimate that the species can grow up to 12–14 metres long, making it the largest invertebrate on earth.

- Despite its menacing size, the giant squid isn't a big hunter. They eat relatively little, and don't have much energy to spend on hunting. Its eyes are probably most useful for spotting predators, giving it plenty of time to escape. Sharks and sperm whales are particularly partial to a squid meal!

25 MOSQUITOES LOVE SWEAT

Have you ever noticed that **mosquitoes** bite some people more than others?

- That's because some people smell better to mosquitoes. People breathe out carbon dioxide, which attracts mosquitoes in general.

- Mosquitoes probably also like the smell of sweat and other body odours, and can detect your personal smell from 30 metres away – sometimes even from 70 metres!

- All members of the *Nematocera* family (which includes gnats, black flies and midges) have a long, tube-like mouth called a proboscis, but most species don't bite humans. Only members of the mosquito family go out at night in search of blood.

YUM, SWEAT!

- Only the female mosquitoes bite: they need nutrients from the blood to allow their eggs to grow. Male mosquitoes stick to nectar from flowers. But they are both equally capable of keeping you awake at night with their annoying buzz!

- These tiny pests can sometimes be incredibly dangerous to humans. Consider the **malaria mosquito**, which causes over half a million deaths each year. It is also mosquitoes that spread the Zika virus, which causes birth abnormalities.

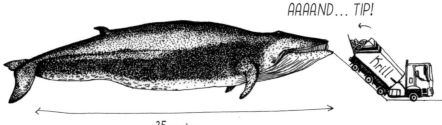

AAAAND... TIP!

25 metres

26 BLUE WHALES EAT A TRUCKLOAD OF SHRIMP EACH DAY

In the wintertime, a **blue whale** eats 3.5 tonnes of krill (tiny shrimp) per day. That's equivalent to the weight of about three cars, or one large lorry.

They eat less during the summer, when they roam the warmer waters near the equator.

It's not surprising that they need so much food – they are the largest animals on earth. Blue whales are mammals, and belong to the order called **baleen whales**. They weigh around 150 tonnes and are on average about 25 metres long.

They travel thousands of kilometres in search of food, from the poles to the equator.

Blue whales dive down every 100 metres or so, then rise back up again with their jaws wide open. Their mouths have a filter-feeding system inside called a baleen, which traps small creatures while allowing the water to escape.

The blue whale's only natural predators are human beings, who hunt it for its meat and fat. By 1966, only 1% of the original blue whale population remained. Since that time, hunting blue whales has been illegal. Scientists estimate that there are around 25,000 blue whales left in the wild.

BONUS WHALE FACTS

Female blue whales are larger than the males. The average male is 25 metres long, while the average female reaches 27 metres.

The largest blue whale ever measured was 33.85 metres long.

The heaviest blue whale ever found weighed 190 tonnes – that's heavier than a Boeing 747!

The tongue of a blue whale is as big as an elephant, and weighs roughly 2 tonnes.

On average, blue whales swim at about 22 kilometres per hour, but could easily reach 40 or 50 kilometres per hour.

Blue whales sing! They have the loudest voices in the animal kingdom, making sounds up to 188 decibels (to give you an idea, a jet engine roars at about 120 decibels). Their singing is carried along by the water, and is what allows them to talk to other whales. Blue whales can also hum at very low pitches, which they probably do to get a better idea of their surroundings, since blue whales can't see very well.

27 GETTING (A) LONG WITH SNAKES

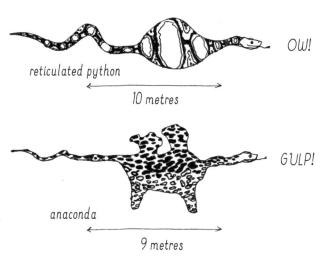

reticulated python

OW!

10 metres

anaconda

GULP!

9 metres

At a whopping 10 metres, the **reticulated python** is the world's longest snake. The name reticulated means 'net-like', which describes the complex pattern on the snake's skin. They live in Asia and generally seek out watery places, where they lie in wait for unsuspecting animals that come to drink. Reticulated pythons aren't venomous, but instead kill their prey by strangling them to death (snakes that do this are called constrictors). Although they usually target birds or small mammals, they have been known to attack people too – but not very often, thankfully. Reticulated pythons need about a week to digest their food.

The world's second-longest snake is the **anaconda**, which can grow up to nine metres long. Also called the water boa, it lives in the northern rainforests of South America, and like the python, feeds on birds, reptiles and small mammals. They are also constrictors, and will even dare to attack a crocodile or deer on occasion.

Other large snakes include the **rock python** (7.5 metres), the **tiger python** (5.7 metres), the **king cobra** (5.7 metres), the **bushmaster** (4.6 metres), the **boa constrictor** (4.3 metres), the **indigo snake** or **cribo** (2.6 metres), the **diamond rattlesnake** (2.5 metres) and the **eastern brown snake** (2.4 metres). Smaller snake species are usually venomous; the larger ones tend to be constrictors.

28 JELLY CAN BE DEADLY

The venom from a **box jellyfish** is a hundred times stronger than cobra venom, making the box jellyfish the most poisonous animal on earth.

A box jellyfish looks like a box with tentacles. Each side of the box has six eyes (except the top and bottom). It uses its 24 eyes to scour the ocean for prey, which it kills using its long tentacles. Box jellyfish can have up to sixty tentacles, which grow up to 3 metres long. Each one has up to five thousand harpoon-like stinging cells (called cnidocytes) that excrete a powerful venom causing intense pain, and even death. An anti-venom is now available, but the scars of a box jellyfish sting often never go away.

There's no need to be afraid of meeting a box jellyfish in the waters of Europe – they only live in the oceans surrounding Australia, south-east Asia and New Zealand. There are nineteen different species of box jellyfish.

BLOB
BLOB
BLOB

29 THE GOLIATH BIRDEATER SPIDER WEIGHS AS MUCH AS TWO APPLES

Find two small apples and hold them in your hand for a moment – that's the weight of the **Goliath birdeater spider**, the largest heavyweight among all spiders.

They are 28 centimetres wide, measured from the tip of one leg to the tip of the opposite leg (this distance is called the leg span). That means they're approximately the size of a large dinner plate.

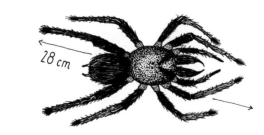

Goliath birdeater spider

Thankfully there isn't much chance of running into one anywhere in Europe. They live in South America, where they feed on insects, rodents, bats, snakes, lizards and – occasionally – small birds.

When hungry, it drops on top of its prey and sprays venom from its *chelicera*, fang-like structures that are 2 centimetres long and hidden inside its hairy upper jaw.

The Goliath birdeater spider may be huge, but it is not the world's biggest spider by legspan. That honour goes to the **giant huntsman spider** from Laos, which measures 30 cm from tip to tip. However, the giant huntsman has a smaller body, which is only 5 centimetres long.

VERSUS

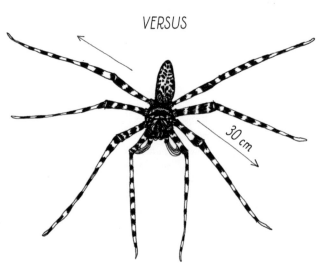

giant huntsman spider

30 SMALL SPIDERS HAVE BRAINS IN THEIR FEET

Researchers from the Smithsonian Tropical Research Institute in Panama once investigated nine different spider species, from rainforest mammoths to minuscule spiders no larger than a pinhead.

They discovered that very tiny spiders have brains not only in their bodies, but also in their feet. Small spiders still need to spin webs to catch their prey, which means they need just as much brain-power as their larger cousins. There's just no room for them in their tiny bodies.

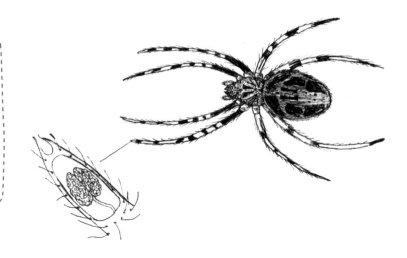

31 INSECTS CAN BE IMMENSE

An isolated island in New Zealand is home to the **giant weta,** a kind of enormous cricket. The weta weighs 70 grams (about as much as three small mice) and is about the same size as the hand of an adult human. The reason the insect is so large is because it evolved on a secluded island where it had no natural predators, a phenomenon known as **island gigantism**.

The weta has lived on the island for over a hundred million years, and remained unchanged all that time. It is therefore a primitive animal, and has earned a reputation as the 'dinosaur of the insect world'. Wetas like to feed on the roots and stalks of plants.

More immense insects can be found in other parts of the world.

- The **Titan beetle**, or *Titanus giganteus*, certainly lives up to its name. Titan is another word for a giant, and *giganteus* means gigantic. This colossal character is a species of longhorn beetle from the South American rainforest, and can reach sizes of up to 16.5 centimetres – roughly the size of a rat. It is so strong, in fact, that it can snap a pencil in half between its jaws.

- **Chan's megastick** is without a doubt the world's longest insect. It's a stick insect from the island of Borneo, and is around 57 centimetres long with outstretched legs.

- Measured by wingspan, the **atlas moth** is the world's largest insect. This nocturnal creature is about 30 centimetres wide from wingtip to wingtip!

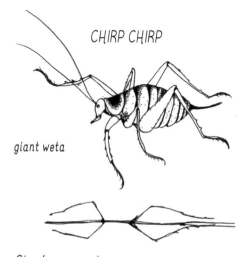

CHIRP CHIRP

giant weta

Chan's megastick

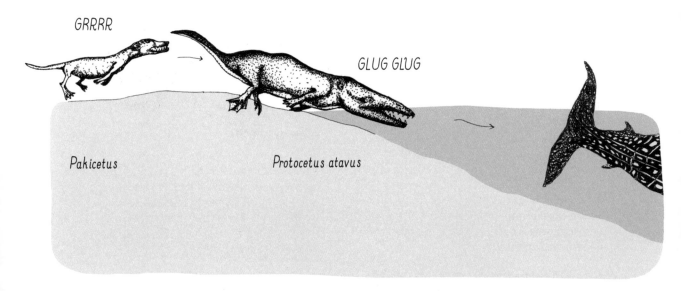

GRRRR

Pakicetus

GLUG GLUG

Protocetus atavus

32 WHALES USED TO LIVE ON LAND

If you're a clever-clogs, you'll already know that **whales** aren't fish, but **mammals**. That means they give birth to live young instead of laying eggs like most fish.

But did you know that the ancestors of whales and other sea mammals – such as porpoises and dolphins – used to be land-dwelling creatures?

- That's why they need to come to the surface to breathe, and why they have bones in their fins. Their spines also move when they swim – like an animal that runs – unlike fish, whose spines remain fully horizontal when swimming.

- Whales are actually closely related to the hippopotamus, but the hippo never chose to return to the water for good.

- The predecessor of the whale was called **Pakicetus** and wandered the earth about 50 million years ago. Pakicetus was no bigger than a Great Dane, and could run at terrific speeds. It hunted the fish in lakes and rivers, which is why it became such a good swimmer.

- Several million years later (things on earth take time!) the Pakicetus gave rise to ***Protocetus atavus*** (a name meaning 'first whale'), the direct ancestor of dolphins and whales. It became gradually more at home in the water, and eventually evolved into an aquatic animal. It also increased in size, becoming the colossal creature that we know today.

BONUS WHALE FACT

Dolphins and whales swim long distances, which is extremely tiring. A nap would be ideal of course, but falling asleep completely would be too dangerous, and they still need to resurface regularly to breathe. So whales and dolphins have developed the ability to 'power down' one half of their brain at a time, while leaving the other half awake. Whales and dolphins can therefore literally be half asleep, and always sleep with one eye open.

33 PAPA SEAHORSE IS HAVING A BABY!

Although a **seahorse** is a type of fish, it is very different from most of its aquatic cousins.

- A seahorse has a uniquely-shaped head. Its long snout makes it look a bit like a horse's head, which is where the animal gets its name.

- Seahorses have even more special features. Instead of scales, they have bony plates arranged in rings around their body. These form a hard exoskeleton, which is awkward to eat and discourages other predators from trying to make a meal of them.

- When they swim, seahorses propel themselves forward by rippling their dorsal fin on their back; they use their pectoral or front fins to help them steer.

- Seahorses come in all sorts of colours, from bright blue to vivid yellow. But most types are a shade of greenish-brown, so they don't stand out among the seaweed, sea grasses or corals.

- They use their curly tails to grab hold of plants, and bob up and down with the ocean currents.

- While some species are barely 2 centimetres long, seahorses can grow up to 30 centimetres in size.

- Seahorses don't just have a striking appearance – their reproductive habits are also unique in the animal kingdom. It all begins with a stunning courtship display, when both seahorses can change colour and the female seahorses compete for the males' attention.

- When a couple have chosen each other, the female deposits egg cells into the male's belly, which contains a special brood pouch. The male fertilizes the eggs and carries them around until they hatch. In the meantime, the female starts producing more eggs.

- Although there are various species of fish fathers who care for their young, seahorses are the only species where the male actually becomes pregnant!

HEY, FANCY A DANCE?

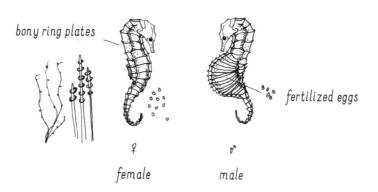

bony ring plates

fertilized eggs

♀
female

♂
male

34 SOME BEES STING EACH OTHER

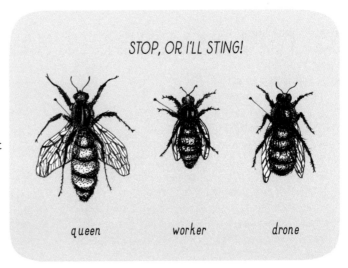

STOP, OR I'LL STING!

queen   worker   drone

There are over twenty thousand different **bee** species on earth.

- In most species, the female has a sting that she can use to protect her colony from all kinds of enemies. These include bears and humans, who sometimes come to steal the bees' tasty honey.

- The honeybees will attack the worker bees of any other colony who attempt to infiltrate the hive, killing them with their sting. Unfortunately, the stinging bees also usually die in the process: the sting detaches and remains in the body of the other bee, leaving a gaping wound that causes the first bee to die.

- One peculiar habit of the queen is that she only stings other queens. It goes like this: once a queen bee is born, she will scour the beehive for cells containing other developing queens, which she kills off one by one. Only she herself remains alive.

- The queen is the ruler of the colony, and is the only one capable of laying eggs to produce new bees. Actually, that's all she does her entire life, while the worker bees feed her plenty of **royal jelly**, a special food intended only for the queen. The male bees, or **drones**, mate with the queen and fertilize her eggs during what is called a nuptial flight. Other than that, the males don't do much. The female worker bees are by far the busiest in the beehive.

35 BOBBY REALLY WAS MAN'S BEST FRIEND

John Gray was a night-watchman for the Edinburgh police in Scotland. He had a dog called Bobby, who followed him wherever he went.

John died in 1858, and was buried at Greyfriars Kirkyard in the centre of Edinburgh. Bobby was left alone, as John himself had no wife or children.

Bobby was devastated, and missed his master terribly. So he stood guard by his grave every day; at one o'clock on the dot he would visit a local café to eat a bowl of dry dog food, and then return to lie on John's grave again.

Bobby kept the same routine for fourteen years, never missing a single day. In 1872, Bobby himself died. The residents of Edinburgh were so touched by Bobby's loyalty, they buried him in the same graveyard as his master John. They even erected a statue in his honour, so you can even go visit him yourself in Greyfriars!

In 2005, a movie was made all about him called *The Adventures of Greyfriars Bobby*.

BOBBY

36 RATS AND DOLPHINS CAN DETECT LAND MINES

Cambodia was a war-torn country for a very long time, and there are still lots of land mines hidden under the ground. Land mines are extremely dangerous – they explode when people step on them. Since 1979, 20,000 people have lost their lives by stepping on land mines.

SQUEAK!

BEEP

BEEP   BEEP

- Using a metal detector, it can easily take a person five days to find a single land mine, and there is still a risk that it might explode. That's why **rats** are now being trained to detect them – they learn what the explosives smell like, and run off in search of them. Rats can usually find a mine within eleven minutes. But don't worry, the rats aren't risking their lives: because they are so light, they can easily scamper across a mine without setting it off.

- Rats can't find mines underwater, but that's where **dolphins** come in. Using their inbuilt sonar, they probe the seas and warn people of any underwater mines, so they can be defused.

They're real animal heroes!

37 BIRDS OF A FEATHER FLOCK TOGETHER... USUALLY

Do you know that card game where you can put the different halves of animals together to create non-existent, fantastical creatures? Well, sometimes it actually happens for real – if the mother and father are from closely-related species, they can produce offspring. These offspring are called hybrids.

The phenomenon rarely occurs naturally in the wild. Hybrids are usually produced as part of special breeding programmes or in zoos.

- A cross between a dolphin and a false killer whale is called a **wholphin**.

- A **shoat** is a pairing between a male sheep (a ram) and a female goat (a doe).

- To make a **zeedonk** you need a zebra and a donkey, and a **zorse** is a cross between a zebra and a horse.

- The new animal names can sometimes sound really funny. A male polar bear and a female grizzly bear together produce a **pizzly bear**; if a male goat mates with a female sheep, the result is a **geep**.

- If a llama mates with a dromedary camel, they produce a **cama**. This pairing is only possible through artificial insemination, since dromedaries are much bigger and heavier than llamas. Camas are large animals, and produce very soft wool.

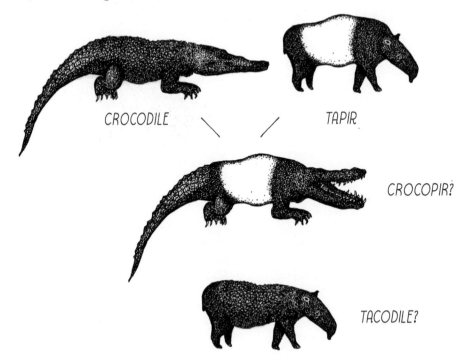

CROCODILE   TAPIR

CROCOPIR?

TACODILE?

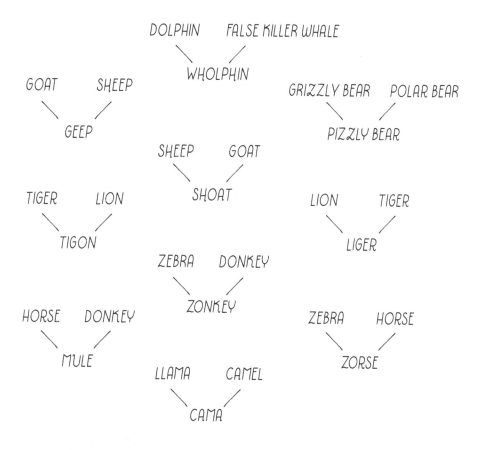

- The **wolfdog** needs no explanation!

- Crossing a stallion (a male horse) with a female donkey (a jenny) makes a **hinny**. If the parents are the other way around (a mare with a jack) the offspring is called a **mule**.

- A very special case is the **liger**, or the offspring of a lion and a tigress. Ligers grow to be enormous. That's because male lions carry the genes that code for growth, while lionesses provide the genes to stop it. Because tigresses don't carry the same genes, the ligers have only their father's growth genes and just keep growing and growing! One very famous liger is named Hercules: he's 4 metres long, weighs 410 kilograms and is officially the world's largest living cat.

- **Tigons** are the product of a lioness and a male tiger. They don't grow as big as ligers.

- An **ashera cat** is a combination of three animals. First you need to cross an ordinary domestic cat with a Bengal cat. Breeding the result with an African serval – a large wild cat – will produce an ashera. They look like huge housecats, and grow to around a metre long. They are among the world's rarest and most exotic cats, fetching prices up to $22,000.

38 PENGUINS HAVE KNEES!

Penguins might look a little comical as they waddle awkwardly over the ice. That's because they are forced to stand upright on their entire foot – other walking birds walk on tiptoe, giving them a more elegant gait.

Once in the water, however, the penguin's body transforms into a perfectly streamlined rocket. They shoot around like lightning as they gather krill (tiny shrimp) and avoid the deadly jaws of predators, such as orcas and sealions.

Despite appearances, penguins actually do have knees. Just look at a penguin's skeleton and you'll be surprised by its long legs with bendable joints near the bottom. They are hidden deep within the thick folds of its feathery coat, which hangs down as a necessary protection against the cold.

In addition to being cute, the penguin's waddling walk is also economical, as it uses less energy.

BONUS PENGUIN FACTS

Penguins' stomachs are very low down in their bodies, hanging somewhere between their invisible knees. So they need a very long **oesophagus** to carry their food all the way down.

Penguins have no teeth and swallow fish whole, straight into their bellies, where they are digested. Sometimes penguins also swallow stones, to help grind things up.

Penguins and polar bears are not natural enemies. Penguins live in Antarctica (the South Pole), while polar bears live in the Arctic (the North Pole). So they never meet!

READY

STEADY

GO!

WHOOSH!

39 WANT TO UNDERSTAND YOUR CAT? LOOK AT ITS TAIL!

Although **cats** sometimes meow, it's hard to know what they really mean when they do. It's far more useful to look at the shape of their tails – that will tell you a lot more.

- If the cat's tail is pointing straight up with flat hair, it's happily saying hello. Say hello back!

- Mother cats point their tails upward to let their kittens know they should follow her.

- Cats also greet each other this way, rubbing up against each other with their tails in the air.

- Sometimes they even hook their tails around each other. That means 'Hey, I'm your friend, no need to be afraid of me.'

- If your cat wraps its tail around your legs, that definitely means it wants to be friends with you. Perhaps it wants some attention... or maybe just some food.

- Look at the tip of the cat's tail – is it a little wonky? That might mean it's unsure of the situation, and is on guard.

- If the tip is waving back and forth, you need to be careful – the cat probably feels insecure, and may start scratching or biting.

- Also look at the cat's fur: if the tail is pointing upwards with its hair raised, the cat feels threatened and may become aggressive or attack. The hair and tail rise up to make the cat look bigger than it actually is.

- A stiff, horizontal tail waving back and forth means the cat might attack at any moment. Cats do the same when stalking their prey and are ready to pounce, and their whole body tenses up, from their ears to the tip of their tail.

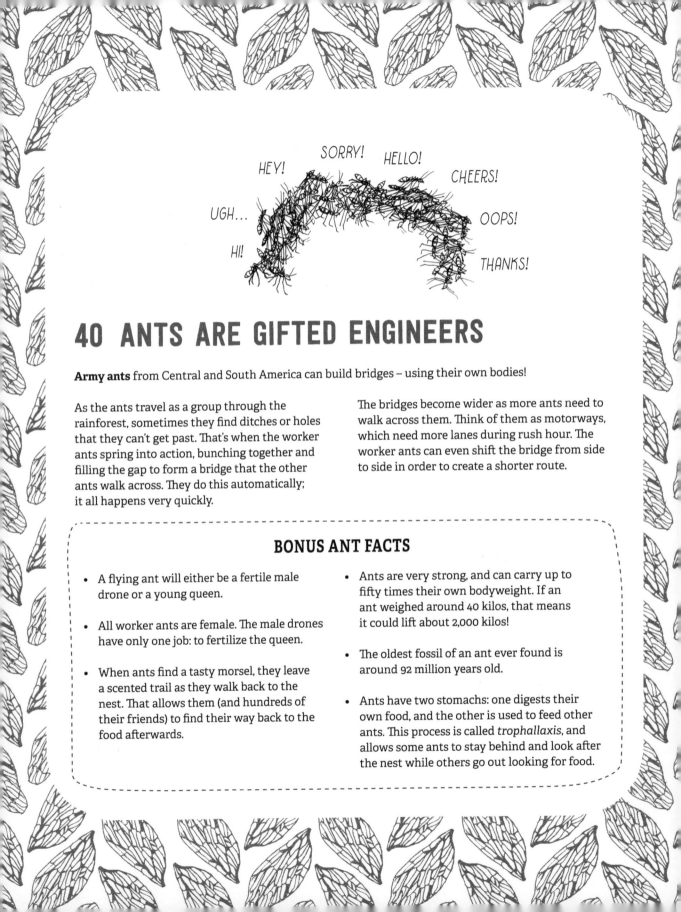

40 ANTS ARE GIFTED ENGINEERS

Army ants from Central and South America can build bridges – using their own bodies!

As the ants travel as a group through the rainforest, sometimes they find ditches or holes that they can't get past. That's when the worker ants spring into action, bunching together and filling the gap to form a bridge that the other ants walk across. They do this automatically; it all happens very quickly.

The bridges become wider as more ants need to walk across them. Think of them as motorways, which need more lanes during rush hour. The worker ants can even shift the bridge from side to side in order to create a shorter route.

BONUS ANT FACTS

- A flying ant will either be a fertile male drone or a young queen.

- All worker ants are female. The male drones have only one job: to fertilize the queen.

- When ants find a tasty morsel, they leave a scented trail as they walk back to the nest. That allows them (and hundreds of their friends) to find their way back to the food afterwards.

- Ants are very strong, and can carry up to fifty times their own bodyweight. If an ant weighed around 40 kilos, that means it could lift about 2,000 kilos!

- The oldest fossil of an ant ever found is around 92 million years old.

- Ants have two stomachs: one digests their own food, and the other is used to feed other ants. This process is called *trophallaxis*, and allows some ants to stay behind and look after the nest while others go out looking for food.

41 EARTHWORMS SHARE TOILETS

One day, scientists in Colombia and Venezuela discovered huge piles of mud and dirt. On closer inspection, they turned out to be made of **earthworm** droppings. Although the worms live mostly underground, they always come to the surface to do their business in the same place. Because all earthworms use the same toilet, a large pile eventually appears.

Some mounds are only 30 centimetres wide, while others can measure up to 2 metres across. The larger ones are probably made up of several closely-spaced toilets that have clumped together.

However, we've no idea if there are earthworm toilet attendants, who keep everything spick and span!

ALL DONE?

YEP...

2

THE INCREDIBLE HUMAN BODY

42 HUMANS CAN SWEAT UP TO EIGHT LITRES PER DAY

The **human body** produces between 100 millilitres and 8 litres of sweat every 24 hours. Of course, sweat production depends on what you're doing, and what the weather is like.

You'll sweat more when jogging or playing sports than when sitting in front of the television, for example. And if the temperature is high enough, you'll perspire without doing anything at all.

Sweating does a useful job: it helps to maintain your body temperature. Your body cools down naturally as the moisture from the sweat evaporates.

Your body has sweat glands all over, but most are concentrated in your hands, feet and armpits. That's where you lose the most fluid.

If you've ever licked your arm during really hot weather, you will have noticed that your sweat isn't just made of water – it also contains salt.

SWEATY SPOTS

armpit stains

sweaty palms

stinky feet

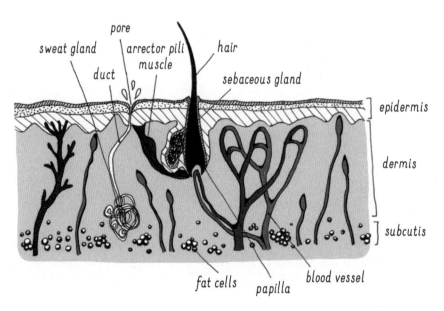

THE SKIN

But did you know that sweat also contains antiseptic substances? These are called **orthocresol** and **paracresol**. Unfortunately, paracresol also has a scent which attracts female mosquitoes!

Children's sweat hardly smells at all. That's because children only perspire through their eccrine sweat glands, which prevent the body from overheating. During puberty, however, the apocrine glands are activated, which excrete an oil-like substance. As soon as it meets the bacteria on the skin, it starts to smell – this is what is known as 'body odour'. This type of sweat is produced constantly in very small quantities throughout the day, not just when you're hot.

Most people use deodorant to mask the unpleasant smell of body odour. Of course, that will only work for so long. That's why it's important to bathe and wash your clothes regularly.

43 WATCH OUT: LAUGHTER IS CONTAGIOUS!

Would you rather spend time with a grumpy person, or somebody who laughs a lot? Most people would choose option two – one reason is because when we see people laugh, we tend to start laughing ourselves.

- Activating your 'laughter muscles' triggers a reaction in the brain. Brains like laughter, and as a reward for the sensation, yours will release a substance that makes you even happier.

It can even act as a painkiller! These substances are called **endorphins**, and belong to a type of messaging system in the body called **hormones**. Even fake laughter can trigger the production of endorphins.

- Your brain goes crazy for endorphins, and might even get a little addicted to laughter to get as many endorphin shots as possible.

- So laughter really is a medicine of sorts. Laughing regularly will stop you getting sick as often and helps you to deal with stressful situations. So ask somebody for a friendly tickle, and giggle your way to good health!

44 BABIES HAVE MORE BONES THAN ADULTS

The average adult **skeleton** consists of around 206 bones, which all help you do things like stand upright and move around. The muscles that allow motion are connected to these bones. The skeleton also provides protection for delicate internal organs, such as the heart, brain and lungs.

Babies have around three hundred bones – nearly a hundred more than a fully-grown adult. That's because certain bones fuse together to become one as we get older. And for good reason: the bones in a baby's skull (the cranial plates) all remain separate, to allow the baby to be born more easily. A newborn's head needs to be squished together a little so it can pass through the birth canal.

ADULT BONES

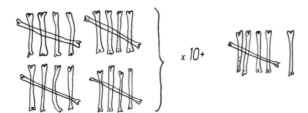

x 10+

BABY BONES

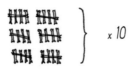

} x 10

EXTRA BONE FACT

The tiniest bone in the human body is the **stapes** or 'stirrup', one of the hearing bones inside your inner ear. It's only 2 millimetres long! The longest and strongest bone is the thighbone or **femur**, which runs from your hip to your knee.

| whole body 55% | blood cells 10% | bone cells 20% | brain cells 70% | skin cells 80% | lung cells 90% |

PERCENTAGES OF WATER IN THE BODY

45 YOUR BODY IS MOSTLY WATER

- **Water** is the most common **molecule** (see Fact 220) in the human body. Babies are roughly 75% water, but the amount decreases as we get older. An adult body is only 55–60% water.

- Most of the water is contained in the body's cells, and the amount varies from organ to organ. Lung cells are about 90% water, skin cells are about 80%, and brain cells only 70%. Bones, on the other hand, are 20% water, and our teeth only 10%.

- 40% of all the water in our bodies is located outside the cells. Ten per cent is in our blood – hardly surprising, since blood is a liquid. The rest is held in the spaces in between the various cells.

- If there's so much water in your body, it must do an important job, right? It certainly does! Water is one of the building blocks of cells, and ensures that all kinds of substances are dissolved and transported across the body.

- It also acts as a kind of lubricant between your organs so they don't wear out by rubbing against each other. Whenever you sweat or urinate, water helps eliminate waste products that are harmful to the body.

- Humans can't survive long without water. Exactly how long depends on the ambient temperature, and whether you've had anything to eat. In hot weather and without any food, you would die of dehydration within a few hours. In the best-case scenario, you might last 2–3 days.

- Interestingly, it is possible to die from drinking too much water – an overdose will dilute too many of the body's vital substances, resulting in 'water poisoning'. Thankfully it's not a very common condition.

46 HUMAN EARS NEVER STOP GROWING

But there's no need to be scared – you won't be lumbering about with elephant ears by the time you're sixty. However, it is true that our **ears** continue to grow throughout our lifetimes.

- Between the ages of thirty and seventy, human ears can increase in size by 8–10 millimetres. They grow especially in men aged 65 and over – probably because that's when skin becomes less elastic, and starts to stretch and sag.

- Ears also become broader, and start to sit differently on the sides of your face. The skin behind the ears becomes thinner as you get older, pulling the ear flap closer to the head.

Perhaps Little Red Riding Hood was right when she said 'But Grandma, what big ears you have…'

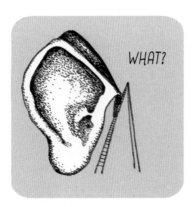

WHAT?

OWWW!

47 DON'T CUT YOUR FINGER ON THIS PAGE
(IT'LL HURT!)

There's a good reason why. Your **fingertips** are full of sensitive **nerve endings**, which are there to help you explore the world around you and perform precise, delicate tasks. The nerve endings even help prevent dangerous behaviour, like pressing your fingers against a red-hot surface.

But your sensitive fingertips are only half of the problem – the other half is the paper. Although paper edges look crisp and thin, in reality they are anything but. A paper cut can be compared to a slice from an extremely fine but very blunt knife, which causes your skin to rip and fray. Paper cuts are also usually quite deep, reaching all the way to the nerves themselves.

Paper cuts need proper care – pages are often covered in bacteria, which will happily make a home in your fingertips. Your finger may become infected, which will make it hurt even more!

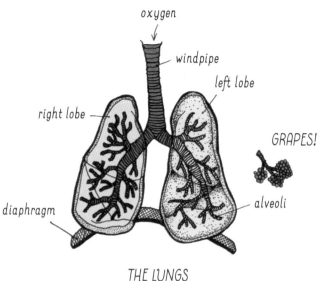

oxygen

windpipe

left lobe

right lobe

GRAPES!

diaphragm

alveoli

THE LUNGS

48 YOU INHALE ABOUT 10,000 LITRES OF AIR EACH DAY

The average adult takes about 12–18 breaths per minute. That means that during a 24-hour period, about 10,000 litres of air will pass through our lungs.

- **Oxygen** is the most important gas that we need to survive, and makes up about one-fifth of the air around us. Oxygen flows into the lungs and is absorbed into the blood through the walls of the alveoli, or air sacs. Oxygen bonds with haemoglobin, a substance contained in the red blood cells, which then deliver the oxygen to all cells in the body. This oxygen is what allows for the combustion of food in the body, producing the energy you need.

- Humans cannot survive without oxygen. If your brain is deprived of it for half a minute, you will lose consciousness; after several minutes, irreparable brain damage is caused. Any longer than that and you will die. Any other tissues* that are starved of oxygen will die off as well: this is what happens when people suffer a heart attack.

- Thankfully you don't need to think about your breathing, it all happens automatically. Of course, everybody's played the game to see who can hold their breath the longest. We can control our breathing to hold it in – when we do, our **cerebellum** (the 'little brain') takes over to tell us when we need to start breathing again. That's why it's impossible to die from holding your own breath.

* Tissues are groups of identical cells that are attached together. Some examples include muscle tissue, connective tissue and nerve tissue. Organs are made up of different types of tissue.

49 PEOPLE ARE TALLER IN THE MORNINGS THAN THE EVENINGS

Believe it or not, you're about a centimetre taller in the morning when you get up than when you go to bed at night. Why is that?

- Your **spine** or backbone is made up of circular bones called **vertebrae**: there are seven in your neck (the cervical vertebrae), twelve in your upper back (thoracic vertebrae) and five in your lower back (lumbar vertebrae). The vertebrae are cushioned and separated from each other by flexible discs.

- The discs act like shock absorbers, protecting the vertebrae from strong impacts and making sure the bones don't scrape against each other.

- In the mornings, the discs are thick and full of water. But as soon as you stand up, gravity sets in and the discs become compressed. Some of the water is squeezed out so they get thinner, making you a tiny bit shorter. Over the course of the day, the discs can lose up to one-tenth of their thickness.

- When you lie down to sleep at night, the discs refill themselves with fluids and water, plumping up once more. This is just one way in which your body repairs itself during sleep, so you can be fighting fit again the next day!

BONUS FACT

This is why elderly people get shorter as they get older. The discs between the vertebrae start to dry out and don't recover as quickly. Senior citizens can shrink by up to 4–6 centimetres!

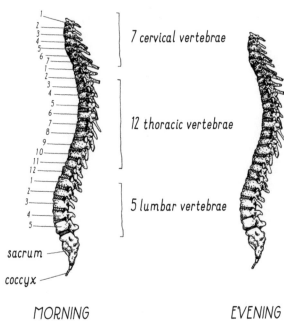

7 cervical vertebrae

12 thoracic vertebrae

5 lumbar vertebrae

sacrum

coccyx

MORNING   EVENING

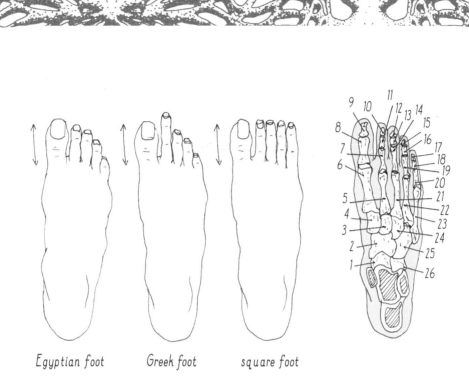

Egyptian foot   *Greek foot*   *square foot*

50 ONE-QUARTER OF YOUR BONES ARE IN YOUR FEET

- The human **skeleton** is made up of 206 bones. There are twenty-six in each foot, making fifty-two in total. That's over one-quarter of all your bones!

- The human foot is a true marvel of engineering. In addition to its 26 bones, the foot also contains 33 joints, more than 100 muscles, tendons and ligaments (the connective tissue that surrounds the joints), and 250,000 sweat glands.

- Take a look at your toes. If your big toe is the longest one, you have what is called an 'Egyptian foot'. 60% of people fall into this category. If your second toe is longer, you have what is called a 'Greek foot' or 'Morton's toe', which occurs in about ten per cent of the population. If your big toe and second toe are equally long, you have a 'square foot'.

BONUS FOOT FACT

Humans are the only mammals that always walk on two legs. That frees up our hands, allowing us to do all kinds of other useful things!

artery   vein   capillary

51 ARTERIES, VEINS AND CAPILLARIES

- If all the **blood vessels** inside an adult were laid end-to-end, it would make a tube 100,000 kilometres long, or two-and-a-half times the circumference of the earth. That's quite a long way!

WHEE!

- Humans have three types of blood vessels: **arteries**, **veins** and **capillaries**. Arteries are the ones that transport oxygen and other nutrients to cells in the body, while veins carry away the carbon dioxide and other waste products.

- The heart pumps blood around your body through the arteries, which lead to the body's tissues. The body's largest artery is called the aorta, which is 3 centimetres across at its widest point. After it leaves the heart, it runs down along the spinal column towards the stomach. When the body is at rest, the aorta transports about five litres of blood per minute.

- The arteries gradually divide into smaller and smaller tubes. By the time they reach the body's tissues, they are thinner than a hair and only just wide enough for a red blood cell to pass through. These tiny blood vessels are called capillaries, and have walls that are so thin, substances can pass from the vessels into the tissues and back again.

capillary cluster

52 YOUR EARS HELP YOU TO BALANCE

Your **ears** are what you hear with; they are organs that developed specifically to allow the detection of sound waves.

- The outer ear consists of the auricle or 'pinna', (the part made of wrinkly skin that we can see) and the ear canal, or passage leading inside the ear. The purpose of the auricle is to capture and channel as much sound as possible into the ear canal.

- The middle ear consists of three bones that convey the vibrations to the inner ear, or 'cochlea', which is named after the Latin for 'snail shell' because it is in the shape of a spiral.

- The cochlea contains the sensory cells that communicate the vibrations to the auditory nerves, which carry the signals to the brain.

But your ears also give you a sense of balance!

- The inner ear has three small tubes with minuscule hairs growing inside them, called the semicircular canals. These are full of fluid, and the hairs wave back and forth inside as the fluid moves around, a bit like seaweed swaying in the ocean currents. The hairs let your brain know what it is you are doing: perhaps jumping on a trampoline, or sitting on the sofa reading a book. If you're sitting still, the fluid in your inner ear will be still as well, so the little hairs won't move and your brain knows you are at rest. But if you put your book down and suddenly start spinning around like crazy, the fluid in the canals will start to swish around and the hairs will tell your brain that you're turning in circles. If they didn't, you'd lose your balance and topple over straight away. Your ability to remain upright depends on the little hairs in the semicircular canals – they are what help you keep your balance.

- If you suddenly stop after spinning for a while, you'll get dizzy and feel like you're still whirling around even though you're standing still. That's because the fluid takes some time to come to rest. Although your eyes can see that you've stopped whizzing around, for a few moments the hairs are still communicating the wrong signal to your brain. These mixed messages are what cause the dizzy feeling.

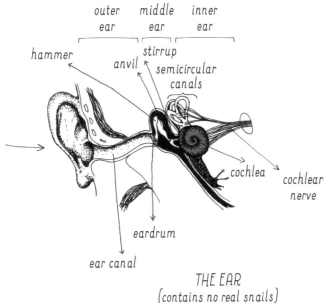

outer ear   middle ear   inner ear

hammer
anvil   stirrup
semicircular canals

cochlea

cochlear nerve

eardrum

ear canal

THE EAR
(contains no real snails)

WOO HOO!

53 YOUR TONGUE IS UNIQUE

You probably already know that everybody has a unique set of fingerprints. Detective shows are always full of investigators taking fingerprints to identify criminals.

But did you know that you also have a unique 'tongueprint'? No two people's **tongues** are exactly alike. Your taste buds, along with the shape, size and pattern of grooves on your tongue are yours and yours alone.

Because your tongue is so well-protected inside your mouth, it may be an even better way to identify people than fingerprints.

> **BONUS FACT**
>
> Your tongue has muscles on both the inside and the outside that you can use to move it around in all directions. Eight muscles in total are needed to manipulate and change the shape of the tongue.

Some airports now ask you to look into a camera that scans your iris, the ring of muscle that gives your eye its colour. Like your fingerprint and your tongueprint, your iris is also unique.

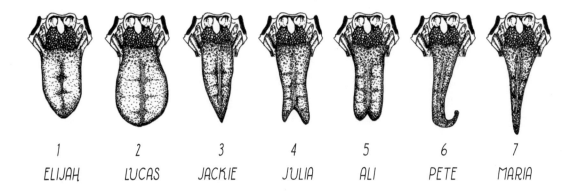

| 1 | 2 | 3 | 4 | 5 | 6 | 7 |
| ELIJAH | LUCAS | JACKIE | JULIA | ALI | PETE | MARIA |

54 ALL BLUE-EYED PEOPLE HAVE A SHARED ANCESTOR

- According to Danish researchers, all people with **blue eyes** descended from a single ancestor, who lived between 6,000 and 10,000 years ago in the region near the Black Sea.

- Professor Hans Eiberg tested eight hundred blue-eyed people from all over the world: these included regions such as Scandinavia and Turkey, but also Jordan and other countries where blue eyes are fairly uncommon.

- Your eye colour is genetic, or 'hereditary,' which means you inherit it from your parents. A gene is a tiny piece of DNA (short for deoxyribonucleic acid) that contains instructions for manufacturing a part of your body. We inherit half of our genes from each of our parents.

- Almost all of the blue-eyed test subjects had a small mutation on the gene for determining eye colour.

- The default eye colour in humans is brown, because of a brown pigment (like a kind of dye) inside the tissues called 'melanin'. Blue-eyed people have a genetic mutation that stops the production of melanin in the eye – that's why everybody with blue eyes must have a common ancestor, since they all have the 'glitch' in precisely the same place.

- So if you and one of your friends both have blue eyes, you now know that both of you also share the same far-distant grandmother or grandfather!

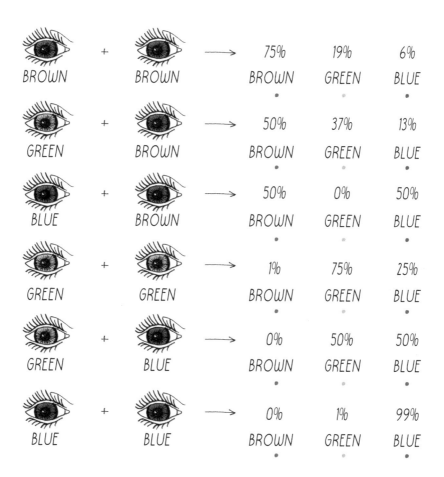

			BROWN	GREEN	BLUE
BROWN	+ BROWN	→	75%	19%	6%
GREEN	+ BROWN	→	50%	37%	13%
BLUE	+ BROWN	→	50%	0%	50%
GREEN	+ GREEN	→	1%	75%	25%
GREEN	+ BLUE	→	0%	50%	50%
BLUE	+ BLUE	→	0%	1%	99%

55 IT'S IMPOSSIBLE TO TICKLE YOURSELF

TICKLE TICKLE!

Try this now, before reading any further. Glide a feather across the sole of your foot, or tickle yourself all over… nothing. This is because your **brain** is one step ahead of you!

- Your brain is always working incredibly hard. Not only does it process whatever it is that you are doing right now (reading, for example), but it is also doing its best to predict what is about to happen to you.

- When babies are born, they are unable to walk. After some months they try taking a few careful steps at a time, but always fall down flat on their bottoms. Eventually their brains figure out exactly what they need to do to walk properly, and after that they no longer need to think at all about which foot to use when. They just decide where they want to go, and the brain does the rest. The same goes for cycling or anything else we do automatically.

- But what happens when you hit a bump in the road and stumble? The brain leaps into action:

it knows that something has broken the usual pattern, and tries to correct it. If you do trip over, your brain will make you stretch out your arms to break your fall (you might also break your arm, but that's life).

- So your brain already knows what's about to happen if you try to tickle yourself. It knows that you're about to raise your arm, bend your fingers and dig them into your sides. There's no surprise and it all feels completely normal.

- If somebody else tickles you, your brain is unprepared. It doesn't know exactly when or where the tickling will happen, which makes it feel completely different. So if you like being tickled, you'll need to rely on some good friends to do it for you.

56 WITHOUT A LIVER, YOU CAN'T LIVE

*THE SKIN
4 kg*

The **liver** is the body's second-heaviest* organ, weighing about 1.5 kilograms in a healthy adult.

Your liver does five hundred different jobs, and can be compared to a factory where all different types of chemicals are produced. Your liver is located beside the **stomach** on the right-hand side of your body, and is a very special organ. Without a liver, we can't live.

* The **skin** is the body's heaviest organ. An average person's skin weighs approximately 4 kilograms.

The liver's main job is to manufacture bile or 'gall', a liquid that is stored in the **gall bladder**. Whenever you eat hot chips or other fatty snacks, the bile helps to digest the grease and oils.

Your liver also maintains a supply of sugar, stored in the form of **glycogen**. Whenever you need energy, glycogen can be reconverted into sugar (glucose) to help you do things like play football or go for a run.

Every day, toxic substances are produced and absorbed by your body. You might take medicine, eat food dyes or drink alcohol – these are all substances that the body doesn't want hanging around. The liver acts like a kind of filter, cleansing the body of substances it doesn't need.

If a part of the liver is removed (due to illness, for example), after some time it may grow back into a complete organ again.

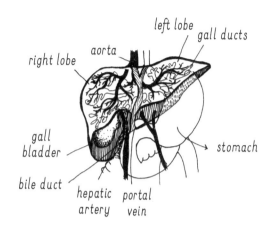

THE LIVER
approx. 1.5 kg

57 IT HELPS TO HAVE A GOOD CRY

Has this ever happened to you? Sometimes you just need a good cry, and afterwards you feel a sense of relief, like a weight has been lifted from your shoulders.

- There was once a professor who wanted to know why. So he collected tears from people who cried from cutting onions, and from others who had cried tears of sadness or frustration. He found that tears of 'emotion' contained different substances than tears produced by physical irritation, and suggested that crying might be the body's way of ridding itself of certain chemicals that make us unhappy.

- Not all scientists are convinced by this professor's conclusion, and suggest another theory: that we cry in order to show other people that we are unhappy. When we see somebody crying, our hearts go out to them and we want to help them. So crying could be a way of seeking comfort and attention.

- But what about people who cry tears of happiness? Just look at the athletes who win medals at the Olympics. Scientists are still not exactly sure how it all works.

Solving the mystery of why we cry will probably take plenty more blood, sweat and – of course – tears.

58 YOUR SKIN COVERS AN AREA OF 2 SQUARE METRES

Your **skin** is the largest organ in your body and accounts for about 15% of your body weight. It also contains around 300 millions skin cells. If you could peel it all off, it would cover an area of about 2 square metres.

Skin protects your bones, muscles and internal organs. It's a pretty amazing organ that stretches enough so that we can jump, crawl and fall over but is still strong enough to withstand scrapes, cuts and minor burns. Scientists are still amazed at the way in which skin is able to repair itself. Skin that is severely damaged can form a scar. This can look slightly different from the rest of your skin as it often doesn't contain hair and sweat glands.

What's more, skin is your first line of defence against the outside world. It's waterproof and protects you from extremes of temperature. For example, sweating is one way in which your body regulates your temperature. Another way it stays cool is because of the blood vessels below the skin. When you're hot, these dilate, or get wider, which helps your body keep cool. When you feel cold, those blood vessels narrow, which decreases the amount of heat your body loses, so your body stays warm.

The outer layer of your skin is called the epidermis. The thickest parts are found on the palms of your hands and on the soles of your feet. The skin on your eyelids is the thinnest part of your skin. The layer below the dermis is called the subcutis. This layer stores fat and contains all your blood vessels, hair roots and nerves.

Did you know you have something in common with snakes? Like a snake, we also shed our skin. In fact, every minute, your skin actually sheds more than 30,000 dead cells. That adds up to around 4 kilograms a year! So the next time you're cleaning your room, remember that over 50% of the dust is dead skin cells. Yuck!

59 YOUR EYES BLINK ABOUT 14,500 TIMES A DAY

It's something you hardly notice, but you do it all the time: **blinking**.

- On average, humans blink between 10 and 15 times per minute. That's about 900 times per hour. If you're awake for sixteen hours a day, the blinks start to rack up fairly quickly. Over the course of one day, you'll blink between 14,500 and 15,000 times.

- Of course there are reasons why we blink. Blinking helps to keep the eyeballs moist, and protects them against dust and dirt.

- At some times we blink more often than others – like when we're nervous, for example. People who are in love blink more to show their interest in the other person.

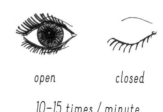

open   closed

10–15 times / minute

- Important people (like presidents) try to blink as little as possible when giving speeches or talking to other VIPs, to give the impression that they are confident and self-assured.

BONUS BLINKING FACTS

Fish have no eyelids, so they can't blink at all. The only exception is sharks, which do have eyelids.

We close our eyes automatically whenever we sneeze. It's possible to learn to sneeze with open eyes, but it's very difficult. Give it a try!

Close your left eye, and try to glance over your left shoulder. Now try the same with your right eye and right shoulder. See why it doesn't work? That's right – your nose is in the way!

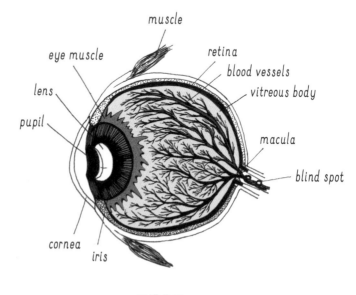

THE EYE

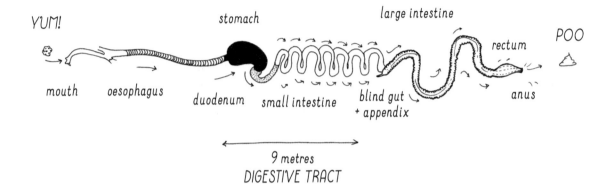

YUM!

stomach

large intestine

POO

rectum

mouth   oesophagus

duodenum   small intestine

blind gut
+ appendix

anus

9 metres
DIGESTIVE TRACT

60 YOUR DIGESTIVE TRACT IS ABOUT 9 METRES LONG

Imagine a tube about 9 metres long that all your food has to pass through. That's your **digestive tract**, which runs from your mouth to your anus (the small hole in your bottom where your poo comes out).

- The longest continuous section of the digestive tract is the **small intestine**, which is approximately 6.5 metres long and is all rolled up inside your belly.

- Say you're enjoying a delicious biscuit with your tea. First you bite off a piece with your teeth, and your molars start grinding it up into a pulp. The pulp mixes with saliva (spit), which contains some digestive juices that start to break down the nutrients in the biscuit.

- When you swallow, the biscuit pulp then travels via the **oesophagus** to the **stomach**, which contracts and continues to grind down the mixture. Your stomach contains acids, which kill any bacteria that may have hitched a ride on the biscuit pieces. The acids also help to digest proteins in the food.

- After the stomach, the food moves on to the **duodenum** where the acidity of the mixture is neutralized. Then everything passes through the small intestine, which is a trip that takes several hours. As many nutrients as possible are extracted by the small intestine and taken up into the bloodstream, which transports them all over the body to be used.

- The **large intestine** only extracts water from the digestive mixture. Whatever is left then collects in the final section of the intestine called the **rectum**. Eventually, everything that could not be digested is squeezed out through your anus as stools (that's just a special word for poo).

Each meal you eat takes about 24 hours to be fully digested.

61 SPERM CELLS CAN SWIM AT 20 CENTIMETRES PER HOUR

That might not seem very fast, but considering how big (or rather: how small) **sperm cells** are, they would easily qualify for the Olympics. And that's no surprise, because the competition is fierce. Each sperm cell races against two hundred million other sperm cells to reach the womb, and all of them want to fertilize the single **egg** that will eventually grow into a baby.

Very few sperm cells actually reach the egg. Only several hundred make it through the womb to the fallopian tubes, and the ones that do still need to find a ripe egg cell that is ready to be fertilized. If a single sperm cell succeeds, then a baby will start to grow from the combination of the sperm and the egg.

BONUS FACTS

Girls are born with an incredible number of egg cells: approximately one million. Around 10,000 egg cells die off every year, leaving about 400,000 by the time the girl reaches puberty.

Sperm cells can only survive for a maximum of five days inside a woman's body, although fertilizing an egg is probably only possible during the first three days. That means that eggs can be fertilized by sperm that have already been inside a woman's body for several days.

Sperm cells were discovered in 1677, by a Dutch scientist named Antoni van Leeuwenhoek. He examined his own sperm using a microscope that he had built, and was astounded at the number of moving cells he saw through the lens!

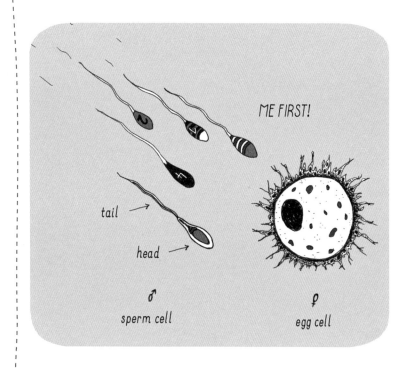

ME FIRST!

tail

head

♂
sperm cell

♀
egg cell

62 YOU HAVE BODY PARTS YOU DON'T USE

The human body is a miracle, and every cell inside it has a unique function. Still, there are parts of our body that we can easily live without – they are remnants of our distant past that haven't yet disappeared completely.

- **Wisdom teeth** were used by our ancestors to chew up tough pieces of meat or plants. The extra teeth were useful to grind things up very finely, but nowadays we can boil and bake food to make it easier to chew, or cut it up into small pieces with a knife and fork. So our wisdom teeth are no longer needed (in other words, they are 'obsolete'). All they do now is cause toothache!

- We all have a pink-coloured membrane in the corner of our eye: that's a vestige (like a leftover) of a third eyelid that is still present in many animals. It was once used to protect our eyes against bright lights or strong winds. But now we can use sunglasses, goggles or other clothing to protect our eyes, and we don't spend as much time in rough weather. So we can manage just fine with two eyelids now.

- Our evolutionary ancestors once needed to be able to move their ears around to detect precisely where sounds came from – a useful ability for detecting prey, or sensing where a predator was lurking. But humans don't have to do that anymore, and the muscles

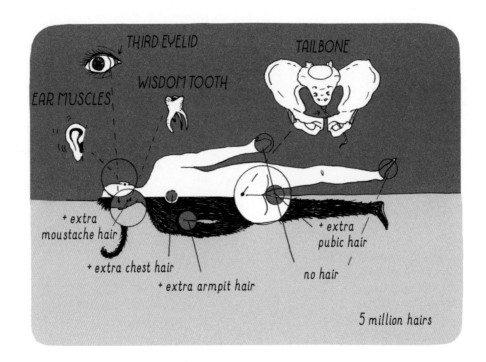

THIRD EYELID

TAILBONE

WISDOM TOOTH

EAR MUSCLES

+ extra moustache hair

+ extra chest hair

+ extra armpit hair

+ extra pubic hair

no hair

5 million hairs

in our ears have become superfluous (that means 'no longer necessary'). Many people's ear muscles have disappeared completely, but some can still wiggle their ears a bit. Can you?

- At the base of your spine is a bone called the **coccyx**, a tiny tailbone that serves no purpose to humans anymore. Our distant ancestors had long tails that were used to help them balance. You might think it's a pity that we humans have lost our tails. Whatever the case, our coccyx isn't much use to us these days.

- At the start of your large intestine, there is a pouch hanging to the side called the 'blind gut'. Attached to it is the **appendix**: a small, worm-shaped organ that our ancestors probably needed to digest plant matter. In modern humans, it mostly just causes trouble when it gets infected. If that happens, you need to get to hospital quickly for an operation to have your appendix removed.

63 HOW MANY HAIRS DOES A HUMAN HAVE? ABOUT FIVE MILLION!

- Approximately 100,000 **hairs** grow on top of your head – the rest are spread across your entire body. That means humans are just as hairy as dogs or cats. The only places on our bodies where hair doesn't grow are the palms of our hands and the soles of our feet.

- Of course, our body hair looks different to the hair of other mammals. Most of our hairs are thin and downy, and spread out thinly across our bodies. Only our heads, armpits and genitals have more hair than the other parts of our body.

- Although men go bald more often than women, they still have around 25,000 more hairs than women do – that's due to the hairs on their arms and legs. Many men also grow hair on their chest and back. And don't forget beards and moustaches, of course!

- Babies still inside their mother's belly are covered in a layer of downy fuzz called lanugo. It looks like a woolly fur coat, and scientists still don't really know what it's for.

Shortly before birth (or sometimes afterwards), all this extra hair falls out, leaving only a thin layer on your arms and legs.

- The hairs on your head and your eyebrows and eyelashes are already in place before you're born, and don't fall out at birth. When you hit puberty, more hair will start growing in your armpits and around your genitals. This is also the time when boys start growing chest and facial hair.

BONUS HAIR FACTS

The number of hairs on your head depends on your hair colour. Redheads have about 85,000 hairs on average; people with black or brown hair have approximately 100,000, and blonds have the most – roughly 140,000 hairs!

64 WHO'S THE TALLEST?

Researchers measured the height of 18.6 million people from two hundred different countries, all born between 1896 and 1996.

- At an average height of 182.5 centimetres, Dutch men came out as the tallest men in the world. Other places with very tall people included Belgium, Estonia, Latvia and Denmark.

- The world's tallest women were from Latvia, the Netherlands, Estonia and the Czech Republic.

- The world's shortest men hail from East Timor, Yemen and Laos, with an average height of 160 centimetres. Women from Guatemala are the shortest, at only 149.4 centimetres.

- The scientists also tried to figure out why there were so many height differences between people of different nationalities. The reason is partly genetic – tall parents tend to have taller children. But genes aren't the most important factor. Malnutrition or diseases can also stop people from growing.

- Scientists have also noticed that taller people tend to get sick less often, and they live longer. Exactly why is still a mystery.

HELLO DOWN THERE!

182.5 cm

65 ONE IN FIVE CHILDREN SLEEPWALK

Ever woken up beside your parents on the sofa, with no idea how you got there? If so, there's a good chance you've been sleepwalking. There is a fancy word for people who walk in their sleep: they are called **somnambulists**.

feeling sleep-pee?

- One-fifth of children aged 5–12 are sleepwalkers. They talk, shout and wander about in their sleep, but they can also do more complicated things – even fry an egg.

- Sleepwalking occurs during deep sleep, when our brainwaves are very slow (these are called delta waves). Something else is going on at the same time, however: the brain also produces faster alpha waves, and it's the combination of both types that causes sleepwalking. The alpha waves allow you to perform all kinds of different activities, but the delta waves mean you won't remember them if you do.

- Sleepwalking usually stops at around puberty. After that, less than 3% of the population continues to sleepwalk.

- Funnily enough, sleepwalking can cause real problems in adults. Some sleepwalkers try things like climbing the curtains, and everything comes crashing down around them. Others go in search of a different place to sleep, and end up in bed with somebody else!

66 IT'S NORMAL TO 'FALL' ASLEEP

You've probably experienced it: you're all tucked up in bed and just about to drift off, when suddenly you feel like you've fallen into a deep hole and jolt awake with a start. Don't worry, this is a very normal phenomenon that happens to most people at some time in their lives.

- The plummeting sensation as you 'fall' asleep has a scientific name. Called **myoclonus** or a 'hypnic jerk', it refers to a group of muscles that suddenly pull together involuntarily. It's a bit like the hiccups, which is a form of myoclonus of the diaphragm. When falling asleep, it's like your whole body experiences a hiccup.

- Actually, your **brain** is the culprit. A few moments before falling asleep, your body relaxes entirely. The brain can sense what's going on, but perceives the situation as dangerous and sends out an emergency signal to your muscles. The signal says something like 'Help! Something's gone wrong and your muscles aren't working properly anymore.' The muscles respond with a sudden spasm and you feel like you're falling over, which jolts you awake again.

- People who sleep on their backs experience myoclonus more frequently than people who sleep on their side. Sleeping on your side keeps more of your muscles tensed, so the brain is less alarmed when you drift off.

myoclonus

ZZZZ

OUCH!

THE BRAIN

...OR DO THEY?

67 YOUR HAIR AND NAILS DON'T KEEP GROWING AFTER YOU DIE

For a long time, people thought that people's **hair** and **nails** kept growing after they died. But that's a myth.

- Your hair and fingernails need **glucose** to grow. Glucose is also known as 'blood sugar', and can only be produced while your heart is still beating.

- Living people's nails grow at a rate of roughly one-tenth of a millimetre per day. New nail cells are produced at the base of the nail, and they push the old ones forward. The cells at the tips of your nails are dead already – that's why it doesn't hurt when you cut them. If no new cells are produced, the nails can no longer grow.

- The same applies to your hair. As long as you are alive, your hair grows at a rate of roughly one centimetre per month. When you die, your hair stops growing.

- So why did people think otherwise? The reason is dehydration: when blood stops circulating, the body dries out and shrinks a little, making your hair and nails seem longer. In reality, the extra 'length' is less than half a millimetre.

68 HUMANS HAVE BEEN BRUSHING THEIR TEETH FOR THOUSANDS OF YEARS

Do your parents ever nag you to **brush** your teeth? Well, take heart: parents have been doing the same to their children for thousands of years.

the first toothbrushes

- A long time ago, humans brushed their teeth by rubbing ash, ground-up eggshells or salt across them with their fingers. It's not clear whether this actually helped to keep them clean.

- Around the year 3,000 BCE, the Babylonians and Egyptians broke twigs off trees that were thought to have healing benefits. Chewing on the end for a while would create a small brush that they used to clean their teeth.

- The first proper toothbrush was invented by the Chinese. They used a piece of animal bone or bamboo as a shaft, to which they attached bristles made of pig's hair. Because of their length and thickness, pig hairs were considered the most suitable for teeth-cleaning purposes.

3

SPORT IS GOOD FOR YOU (MOST OF THE TIME)

69 FORMULA 1 DRIVERS ARE SUPER-FIT

It all looks so easy: put on an awesome suit and a cool helmet, get behind the wheel of a racing car and drive round and round the course at lightning speeds. Surely you don't need to be fit for that – the car does all the work for you, right?

Well, think again! **Formula 1** drivers are incredibly fit sportspeople, and motor racing is one of the most physically demanding sports there is.

- During a race, the heartbeat of a driver can rise up to 200 beats per minute. That's way higher than footballers or runners, who reach rates of up to 150 or 160 beats per minute. Motor racing is physically very tiring, but the elevated heart rate is also due to the superhuman levels of concentration required by drivers – they are literally on the edge of their seat the whole time. Suddenly braking or executing a risky manoeuvre can cause the driver's heart rate to soar even higher.

- To cope with the enormous pressure, Formula 1 drivers train for 4–5 hours a day. They go to the gym, run or cycle, and even do strength training.

- Drivers' neck muscles are under particularly severe strain. When braking through a corner they experience forces up to four or five times higher than gravity. To the driver, it feels like their head suddenly becomes 4–5 times heavier than normal. They need powerful

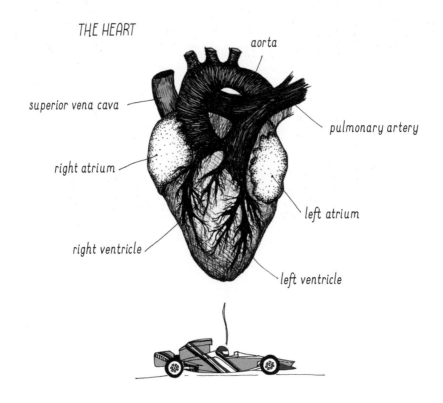

THE HEART

aorta

superior vena cava

pulmonary artery

right atrium

left atrium

right ventricle

left ventricle

back and neck muscles to literally 'keep a level head'! Some drivers even practise wearing a 10-kilogram helmet during their training.

- Keeping the wheel steady requires strong arms, and the driver's legs need enough power to apply the brakes at incredibly high speeds.

- Of course, drivers also need to stay focused throughout the race – losing concentration, even for a split-second, can be fatal. That's why racing drivers also need very strong minds.

70 GET INTO KORFBALL – THE ONLY MIXED BALL SPORT (ALMOST)!

Korfball is a bit like netball, and is one of the few group sports where men and women play together on the same team. It originated in the Netherlands, and each korfball team is made up of four men and four women. The other players stay on the bench and rotate during the match. If there aren't enough men, a woman can put on a special shirt and substitute for a male player. But not vice versa: according to the rules of korfball, men are physically stronger than women and may never number more than four.

Korfball is played mostly in the Netherlands and Belgium. Hardly surprising, since the game was invented by Dutch teacher Nico Broekhuysen in 1902. He had seen people playing a game in Sweden called ringboll, and invented his own version that would later come to be known as korfball. Like netball, the aim of the game is to put the ball through your opponent's ring on the top of a pole.

There are a few other ball sports that men and women can play together: there's mixed doubles in tennis, table tennis or badminton, as well as equestrian sports (with horses) that allow men and women to compete against each other. And of course, men and women form couples in ballroom dancing.

71 EDDIE EAGAN WON GOLD AT BOTH THE WINTER AND SUMMER OLYMPICS

Eddie Eagan was born in 1897 in Denver, USA. Although he came from a poor family, he still managed to study law at two of the world's top universities: Oxford and Harvard.

In 1920, the Summer Olympics were held in Antwerp in Belgium, where Eddie Eagan won gold as a light heavyweight boxer. Over a decade later, in 1932, he travelled to the Winter Olympics at Lake Placid, New York, where he was a member of the four-man bobsleigh team that won a gold medal. To this day, Eddie Eagan is the only person ever to have won gold at both the winter and summer Olympic games.

However, plenty of athletes have competed in both sets of Olympic games.

- Jacob Tullin Thams was a Norwegian who won gold for ski jumping and silver for sailing.

- Christa Luding-Rothenburger from Germany won gold for 500-metre speedskating, and a silver medal for track cycling.

Property of Eddie Eagan

- Clara Hughes from Canada is another athlete to have won medals for both cycling and skating.

- Lastly, Lauryn Williams won silver for the USA in both sprinting and bobsleigh.

72 ARCHITECTURE, LITERATURE, MUSIC, PAINTING AND SCULPTURE USED TO BE OLYMPIC EVENTS

- Pierre de Frédy, Baron de Coubertin (or Pierre de Coubertin for short) was a Frenchman who, in 1896, laid the foundations for the **Olympic Games** as we know them today.

- Alongside athletic and sports events, the Baron also insisted that 'artistic competitions' be held, in which the various artists took their inspiration from sport. So from the 1912 to the 1948 Olympics, medals were up for grabs in architecture, literature, music, painting and even sculpture.

- The Baron's rules might have been the only way that he could take part in the games himself. In 1912, for example, he won gold for his poem called *Ode to Sport*. To ensure a fair contest, he submitted his entries under fake names: Georges Hohrod and M. Eschbach.

73 THE OLDEST MARATHON RUNNER WAS 100 YEARS OLD

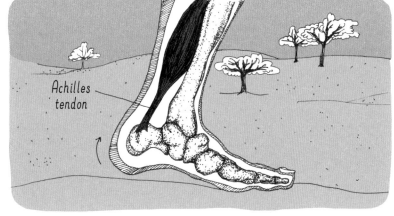

Achilles tendon

- Fauja Singth is the oldest person to ever take part in a **marathon**. At the age of 100, he ran the 2011 Toronto Waterfront Marathon and completed it in a time of 8 hours and 11 minutes.

- The Boston Marathon in the United States is the world's oldest annual marathon. It began on 19 April 1897, and was inspired by the success of the marathon competition at the 1896 Olympics. It is one of the world's most respected road racing events.

- Abebe Bikila was an Ethiopian marathon runner who was a back-to-back Olympic marathon champion. He was the first African Olympic gold medalist, winning his first gold medal at the 1960 Summer Olympics in Rome while running barefoot.

- It seems ridiculous, but women once weren't allowed to take part in marathons because it was thought to be too dangerous for them! It wasn't until 1984 that the first women's Olympic marathon took place, with US runner Joan Benoit Samuelson winning the race in a time of 2 hours, 24 minutes and 52 seconds. It's now widely believed that women are actually better suited, both physically and mentally, to running long distances than men are.

- Your foot contains 26 bones, 33 joints, more than 100 ligaments, tendons and muscles, and a network of nerves and blood vessels. All of these have to work together when we run!

- The most common runners' injuries include runner's knee, shin splints and Achilles tendinitis. Ouch!

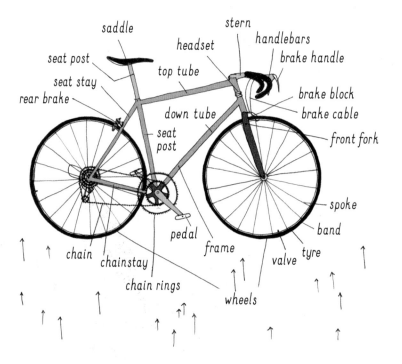

saddle · stern · headset · handlebars · brake handle · seat post · top tube · seat stay · rear brake · down tube · brake block · brake cable · seat post · front fork · spoke · band · pedal · frame · valve · tyre · chain · chainstay · wheels · chain rings

74 THE WORLD'S LIGHTEST RACING BIKE WEIGHS LESS THAN A NEWBORN BABY

- The world's lightest **racing bike** weighs only 2.7 kilograms. It can easily be lifted with one hand, and feels lighter than a small bag of potatoes.

- To make it, German Gunter Mai built a bicycle frame that weighed only 642.5 grams. The bicycle's fork (the two prongs on either side of the front wheel) weighs only 185.9 grams. Mai worked on his design until it weighed only 2.8 kilos, then sold it to an American bicycle manufacturer who made special wheels weighing only 583 grams. That made the bike even lighter, but certainly not cheaper: all in all, the bicycle's construction cost $45,000.

- Bicycles that are too light aren't allowed to be used in official races. According to the International Cycling Union (the UCI), competition bicycles must not be any lighter than 6.8 kilograms.

75 FOOTBALL WAS INVENTED IN CHINA

It wasn't the English or the French but the Chinese who invented the world's most popular ball sport. Over two thousand years before **football** spread throughout Europe, Chinese soldiers were playing a game called 'tsu-cho', which literally means 'kick-ball'. A leather ball was filled with feathers or fur, and two teams tried to score points by kicking it through a goal. Use of the hands was not allowed. The game became extremely popular later during the Song dynasty, which lasted from 960–1279 CE.

AAH!

a game of tsu-cho

Professional football as we know it today started in 1863 in England. In its early years, football was a much rougher game than it is now: stamping on an opponent's foot was usually allowed, even when they didn't have the ball. If the keeper was in possession of the ball, you could even try to ram him into the goal yourself to score.

76 YO-YO CHAMPIONSHIPS ARE A THING!

Yo-yos are heaps of fun to play with, and you might even know a few tricks yourself. But if you want to go pro, you could sign up for the World Yo-yo Championships!

- The competition consists of two parts. First there are several compulsory tricks you need to perform. After that, there's a freestyle section when you can show off your individual and artistic talents. Points are awarded by a panel of judges, and whoever scores the highest wins. Music is allowed when freestyling, and competitors are even allowed to dance or jump around!

- To get to the world championships, you first need to make it through the national championships, although not every country has its own. Japan is home to a lot of great yo-yoers: Shinji Saito has won the world title no fewer than 13 times.

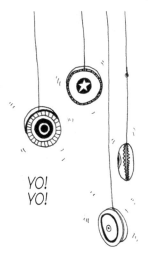

YO! YO!

77 SUMO WRESTLERS EAT EIGHT HUGE BOWLS OF RICE A DAY

Sumo wrestlers need a lot of discipline, and a huge appetite! They have to eat mountains of food to help them grow into true champions.

- Sumo wrestlers skip breakfast and start every day with a five-hour training session, because it's impossible to tackle your opponent on a full stomach. That means they are ravenous by lunchtime, so a chef makes sure there is always plenty to eat.

- Konishiki, a world-famous sumo champion, said that he could easily eat ten bowls of chanko-nabe (see below), eight enormous bowls of rice, a hundred and thirty pieces of sushi and twenty-five pieces of meat. And he still always had room for dessert!

- Chanko, or chanko-nabe, is a high-protein meal made of steamed meat, chicken, fish or tofu, with plenty of vegetables on the side. It's actually quite a healthy dish, but sumo wrestlers eat it by the bucketload and wash it down with plenty of beer. After lunch they take a nap to conserve their energy, then eat a similar meal in the evening. In total they eat around 4,000–5,000 calories a day, which is more than double the requirements of an average adult man.

- Sumo wrestlers weigh between 150 and 270 kilograms. Much of their bodyweight is muscle, but they also have lots of fat around their hips and waist – that makes it harder for them to be toppled by an opponent. Fat also helps to cushion the impact if they fall down.

- Because there are no weight classes in sumo championships, competitors do all they can to put on as much weight as possible, and gain an advantage over their opponents.

- A sumo wrestler's life is tough. It takes about ten years to put on enough weight and complete the training necessary to start fighting. A group of sumo wrestlers will live together in a 'stable', which is the name given to a professional sumo academy. The students must follow a strict routine of sleep, training and meals. Because the sumo life demands so much discipline, the Japanese people have a great deal of respect for their wrestlers. They are treated like real heroes!

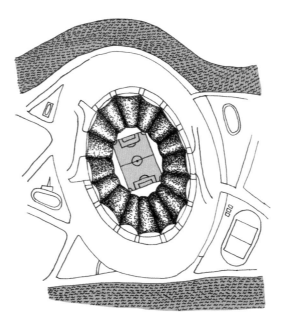

1st of May Stadium, Pyongyang

78 THE WORLD'S LARGEST FOOTBALL STADIUM IS IN NORTH KOREA

- The 1st of May Stadium in Pyongyang, the capital of North Korea, seats around 150,000 spectators. The stadium is shaped like a huge magnolia blossom, and sometimes hosts football matches or athletics events. But it's mostly used to hold enormous military parades or gymnastics and dance events in praise of the country's leader, involving 100,000 people or more.

- Europe's largest football stadium is Camp Nou in Barcelona, Spain, where 99,354 spectators can watch FC Barcelona play. Camp Nou is probably one of the best-known stadiums in the world.

- But the biggest stadiums aren't always the most impressive. Take Eidi stadium in the Pharaoh Islands, for example: an open-air football field located right next to the sea. Try not to kick the ball out of bounds – someone will need to get wet to get it back!

- The same goes for the Marina Bay stadium in Singapore, which floats on the waters of the harbour itself. The stadium has seating for up to 27,000 spectators, and looks very futuristic.

79 OLYMPIC GOLD MEDALS DON'T CONTAIN MUCH GOLD

1–2% gold
100% glory

So you've done your best, trained for years, and finally made it first over the finish line: Congratulations! The **gold medal** is yours! But while a medal is amazing and everything, don't think you can save it for a rainy day to pay for your shopping or your bills. Only a tiny portion of the medal (1–2%) is actually made of gold – the rest is silver, and some even contain a bit of bronze. Of course, it's all about the glory the medal represents, not the material it's made of.

BONUS MEDAL FACT

The United States is the country that has won the most Olympic gold medals so far, with 1,127. Great Britain is in fourth place with 274; Australia and Canada are 14th and 16th with 152 and 137 gold medals respectively.

- The most successful Olympian of all time is Michael Phelps from the USA. He won a whopping twenty-three Olympic gold medals for swimming between 2004 and 2016, earning him the nickname of 'The Baltimore Bullet'.

- Those next on the list have nine gold medals each: gymnast Larisa Latnyina, athlete Paavo Nurmi, swimmer Mark Spitz and athlete Carl Lewis.

- The most successful Olympians from Great Britain are Chris Hoy and Jason Kenny, both cyclists who have won six gold and one silver medal each.

80 MICHAEL PHELPS WAS BUILT TO SWIM

With twenty-three gold medals to his name, American swimmer Michael Phelps is the most successful Olympian of all time.

Of course he owes much of his success to his dedication, discipline and many hours of training each day. But he also has the shape of his body to thank for his ability to swim so fast.

OFF WE GO!

- First of all, Michael Phelps has very large hands and feet. His feet are a size 13.5, putting him far above the average.

- He also has a very narrow waist and long arms: the length of his outstretched arms (measured from the tip of one index finger to the other) is 8 centimetres longer than his height, which is extremely uncommon. The ratio between these two measurements is called the 'ape index'. Phelps's long arms help pull him through the water faster.

- The distance from his hips to his ribs is also 10 centimetres longer than normal.

- Because he can stretch his joints further than most people, his legs have a wider range of motion, which also helps him with certain strokes in the pool.

- Besides his physical form, Michael Phelps also has an advantage in the way his body digests food (this is called 'metabolism'). He can eat stupendous amounts of food and convert it rapidly into energy. His favourite restaurant is Pete's Bar & Grill in his home town of Baltimore. For breakfast he easily wolfs down two or three sandwiches laden with eggs, cheese, lettuce, tomato and mayonnaise, followed by a five-egg omelette with more cheese, five slices of toast, a double serving of sausages, a bowl of porridge, three pieces of French toast, and three chocolate pancakes just to fill in the gaps. On an average day Phelps consumes 10,000-12,000 calories, which is five or six times what the average person eats. Still, he doesn't have an ounce of fat on his body – he is 193 centimetres tall and weighs 90 kilos, which is quite a normal bodyweight.

81 THE LONGEST EVER TENNIS MATCH LASTED OVER ELEVEN HOURS

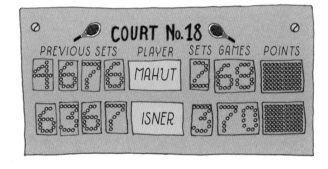

In June 2010, John Isner and Nicolas Mahut faced each other in the **tennis** championships at Wimbledon. The match began on 22 June and lasted eleven hours and five minutes. They played 183 games in total.

The match wasn't just exhausting for the players – even the scoreboard gave up after a while. Once the score had reached 47–47, the board stopped working and broke down. The programmers later explained that the board had not been designed to count any higher than 47, so it malfunctioned. Isner eventually won against Mahut, with a score of 70–68.

When the two players faced each other at Wimbledon the following year, they managed to finish the match in only two hours and three minutes. Isner once again emerged victorious, and told the journalists afterwards that he was happy things didn't go on as long as they did the first time!

82 THE WORLD'S SHORTEST BASKETBALL PLAYER WAS ONLY 1.6 METRES TALL

Have you always wanted to play **basketball**, but didn't think you were tall enough? Well, take heart! Professional basketballer Muggsy Bogues was only 1.6 metres tall, and weighed 62 kilos.

- Tyrone Curtis 'Muggsy' Bogues was born in Baltimore in 1965. He played basketball all through high school, and again later at university. He became so good, in fact, he was drafted by the Washington Bullets in 1987.

- Funnily enough, he played on the same team as one of the tallest basketballers ever: Manute Bol, who measured a massive 2.31 metres. At that time, Muggsy and Manute were actually the shortest and tallest players in the NBA, with a height difference of 71 centimetres.

- Muggsy Bogues wasn't the only basketball player who never reached 1.7 metres. Earl Boykins was only 1.65 metres, and Mel Hirsch measured 1.68 metres.

- Of course, the courts have always been full of extremely tall players. The record for the tallest player is shared by Romanian Gheorge Muresan and Sudanese Manute Bol (mentioned above), both of whom were 2.31 metres tall.

- The average height for professional basketball players is just over 2 metres, which is already pretty tall!

- Some height stats for the die-hard basketball fans:
  LeBron James: 2.03 metres
  Michael Jordan: 1.98 metres
  Magic Johnson: 2.06 metres

PASS! I'M OPEN!

Muggsy Bogues

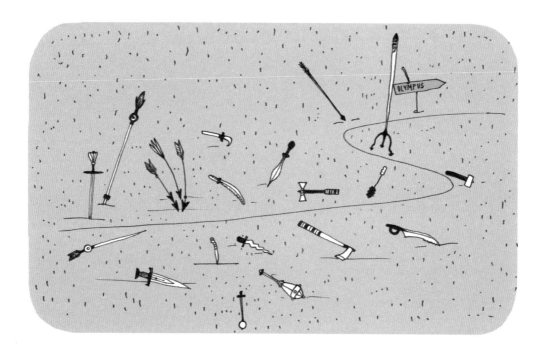

83 NO WARS ARE ALLOWED DURING THE OLYMPICS

In ancient Greece, the Olympics were always accompanied by a period of *ekecheiria*, or 'armistice', a time when weapons were laid down and war was forbidden. This was necessary because the Greek city-states were always fighting with each other, and halting the wars allowed the athletes to travel to Olympus and compete in the Games unimpeded.

In 1993, the United Nations revived the notion of an armistice during the Olympic Games, and issued a Resolution calling all nations to lay down arms starting seven days before the Games until seven days afterwards.

Unfortunately, nobody has ever paid any attention to the UN's Resolution. Over the last twenty-six years, not a single conflict has been put on hold for the sake of the Olympics.

84 THE OLDEST PERSON TO WIN AN OLYMPIC MEDAL WAS 72

- In 1920, the Summer Olympics were held in Antwerp in Belgium, and twenty-nine countries took part. Germany and Austria weren't invited, since the First World War had only just ended. And because Russia was in the middle of a civil war, no Russian athletes took part.

keeping the flame alive!

- During the 1920 Games, an athlete took the Olympic oath for the first time. Belgian fencer Victor Boin promised that all athletes would abide by the rules, and would not take any drugs or engage in other forms of 'doping'. Since then, the oath has been read at every Olympic Games by a different athlete.

- In 1928, the Netherlands hosted the Olympics in Amsterdam. It was the first time the Olympic flame was lit not by an athlete, but by an employee of the gas company!

- Fun fact: Swedish athlete Oscar Gomer Swahn won a silver medal for shooting during the Antwerp Olympics. He was aged 72 at the time, and still holds the record as the world's oldest Olympic medal winner.

I'm so tired!

OSCAR

- Sports history buffs may know that Tarzan himself won two gold medals for swimming at the 1928 Summer Olympics. Or rather: the medals were won by Johnny Weissmuller, who sixteen years later would go on to play Tarzan in twelve Hollywood movies.

85 EDDY MERCKX NEVER WON AN OLYMPIC MEDAL (BUT HIS SON AND GRANDSON DID)

Cycling fans may well have heard of Eddy Merckx, a world-famous Belgian cyclist who has won virtually every biking race in existence:

- Tour de France (five times)
- Milan-San Remo (seven times)
- Tour of Flanders (twice)
- Paris-Roubaix (three times)
- Amstel Gold Race (twice)

- Liège-Bastenaken-Liège (five times)
- Tour of Italy (five times)
- Tour of Spain (once)
- UCI Road World Championship (three times)

He left an amazing legacy that has gone unmatched ever since. But there's one thing missing on his list of achievements: an Olympic medal.

That's where Eddy's son and grandson come in. Axel Merckx won a bronze medal at the 2004 Summer Olympics, when he came third in the Olympic road cycling event.

His grandson Luca even won gold, but not as a cyclist and not for Belgium. Eddy Merckx's daughter Sabrina married an Argentinian, and their son Luca plays for Argentina's national hockey team.

Eddy   Luca   Axel

The Argentinian team won gold at the 2016 Rio Olympics by beating the Belgian Red Lions in the final. The question is: which team was Eddy supporting that night?

86 CYCLISTS SHAVE THEIR LEGS

If ever you've watched a cycling race, you've probably noticed how incredibly smooth all the racers' legs are. That's not just because cyclists are vain and don't want to look like Bigfoot on a bike – smooth legs also serve a practical purpose.

First of all, smooth legs are easier to massage. Professional cyclists get lots of massages in order to keep their muscles relaxed and flexible. Smooth skin is easier for masseurs to work with and causes less pain for the cyclist; it also requires less oil, and there's less chance a hair follicle will become infected.

Secondly, it's very common for cyclists to take a tumble during a race, leaving nasty wounds that need immediate attention. Treatment is much easier without any hair in the way, and ripping off a sticking plaster hurts way less too!

The idea that smooth legs are more aerodynamic and increase speed is a myth. Shaved legs are more of a tradition, or a 'code' among cyclists – everybody does it, and you won't be taken seriously if you turn up to a race with hairy legs.

TO SHAVE . . .
OR NOT TO SHAVE?

But some famous cyclists do occasionally flout the shaving regulations. The Slovak cyclist Peter Sagan sometimes refuses to shave his legs, for example, and has still won plenty of races. He's even been world champion twice!

87 ALL GOLFERS HAVE A 'HANDICAP'

The word 'handicap' means something quite different in the game of **golf**.

GOLF

In golf, a player's handicap is an indication of how well they play. The lower the handicap, the better the golfer.

A golf handicap is the number of strokes a player usually needs to complete 18 holes above the course par. That's a complicated sentence, so let's explain: a 'hole' is literally just that – a hole in the ground – and the aim of golf is to hit the ball into the hole. Each course is made up of several holes, usually 9 or 18, and players try to get the ball into all the holes in as few hits (or 'strokes') as possible. Players who can get the ball from the starting point (the 'tee') into the hole in a single stroke score a 'hole in one'.

The 'par' of a hole is the number of strokes needed by the average golfer to complete it. It is determined in advance, and every hole has a par of 3, 4 or 5. All pars added together form the par for the course.

Here's where the handicap comes in. Imagine you're playing an 18-hole course with par 72. If you need about 92 strokes to complete it, that means your handicap for that course is 20. If you take 112 strokes, your handicap will be 40.

Each player's score starts from their own handicap, which is what allows players of differing ability to compete against one another. Each player tries to play below their handicap – that means a player with a handicap of 30 can still beat a player whose handicap is 20, even though the second player is actually better.

Different rules apply in professional golf tournaments.

HOLE IN ONE!
YEAH!

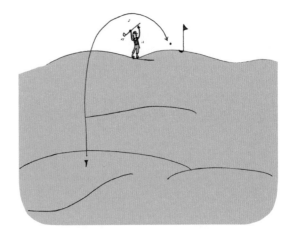

88 A MARATHON IS OFFICIALLY 42.195 KILOMETRES LONG

Bit of a strange number, don't you think? Why not just pick 42, or 43 kilometres?
To understand why, we need to take a look at the history of the **marathon**.

- The origins of the marathon lie way back in 490 BCE, when a soldier named Pheidippides ran from the city of Marathon to Athens to report the victory of the Athenian army over the Persians. Alas, no sooner had the messenger delivered his report than he dropped dead, probably from sunstroke.

- It would be 1896 before a proper marathon was run as part of the Olympic Games. The distance run was 25 miles, or roughly 40 kilometres.

- When London hosted the Olympics in 1908, the Queen wanted the starting shot to be fired on the grounds of Windsor Castle, and for the race to finish before the royal box at White City Stadium in West London. The distance was exactly 42.195 kilometres, which became fixed from then on as the distance for any official marathon.

- The world record for men currently stands at 2 hours, 1 minute and 39 seconds, a time achieved by Kenyan athlete Eliud Kipchoge in Berlin in 2018.

- The fastest time for a woman is 2 hours, 14 minutes and 4 seconds, run by Kenyan athlete Brigid Kosgei.

(Or rather: these were the best times when this book was written. The records may have been broken by now!)

4

(IN)FAMOUS FACES

89 REINHOLD MESSNER WAS THE FIRST TO CLIMB THE WORLD'S FOURTEEN TALLEST MOUNTAINS

Reinhold Messner was born in Italy on 17 September 1944. He grew up in Villnöss, a village in South Tyrol in northern Italy, and could always see the Alps from his window. It was a breathtaking sight, and it wasn't long before he decided to strap on his backpack and go out climbing. He was only five years old when his father took him out to conquer his first mountaintop.

When he was thirteen, Reinhold started getting serious. He and his younger brother Günther climbed all the local peaks, and by the time they were adults, they were among the best mountain climbers in Europe.

In 1970, Reinhold and his brother climbed the Himalayan mountain Nanga Parbat for the first time. Sadly, there was an accident on the way down and Günther lost his life; Reinhold lost seven toes to frostbite. In 2010, a film was made about the brothers' climb, named after the mountain itself: *Nanga Parbat*.

In 1978, Reinhold Messner was the first to ever climb Mount Everest without taking additional oxygen. The air at that altitude is very thin and makes breathing difficult, which is why most climbers take extra canisters of oxygen with them.

In 1986 he became the first person to reach every point on Earth that is 8,000 metres above sea level – these fourteen mountain peaks are collectively called the 'eight-thousanders.'

Messner has written dozens of books about his experiences. Right now, he is busy with his work on the Messner Mountain Museum, a project that he founded himself.

90 ARCHIMEDES MADE A GROUND-BREAKING DISCOVERY IN THE BATH

The Greek **Archimedes** lived a very long time ago, from 287–212 BCE, and yet he is still remembered today. Why did he leave such a lasting legacy? Well, Archimedes was one of the most important scientists ever to have lived, and discovered several natural laws that are still applied in mathematics and physics today.

- Archimedes' Principle is one of the most fundamental laws of physics. The king once asked Archimedes to determine whether his crown was made of pure gold or not. But there was one condition that made it a difficult task: Archimedes was not allowed to damage the crown in any way.

- One day, when Archimedes was stepping into the bath, he saw the water rise and suddenly realized that he could measure the volume of his body using the water that spilled over the edge. According to legend, he leapt out of the bath and ran naked down the street, crying 'Eureka!' (which means 'I've found it!').

- He knew how much gold weighed, as well as the weights of other metals. By comparing the volume of the crown to its weight, he could work out its density and hence whether it was made of pure gold or not.*

- Archimedes also invented plenty of other things, such as a planetarium for studying the movements of heavenly bodies, and a compound pulley system (or 'block and tackle') that could be used to move extremely heavy objects. The compound pulley remains in use to this day.

- Archimedes also built war machines (such as catapults) when the city where he lived was besieged by the Romans.

- In 212 BCE, the Romans occupied the city of Syracuse, where Archimedes lived at the time. One day the scholar was busy studying three circles he had drawn in the sand. A Roman soldier was stupid enough to wander through the sand-circles, which made Archimedes lose his temper. The soldier killed him, despite the general's orders not to harm the old man.

EUREKA!

BONUS ARCHIMEDES FACT

Many of Archimedes' discoveries are still used in mathematics classrooms today, such as integral calculus, or the Axiom of Archimedes. So it's quite possible that Archimedes has given you a headache or two over the years...

* Spoiler alert: it wasn't.

91 THE FIRST WOMAN IN SPACE WAS RUSSIAN

On 16 June 1963, **Valentina Vladimirovna Tereshkova** travelled into space as a cosmonaut on the Vostok 6. 'Cosmonaut' is the Russian word for astronaut.

- Valentina was born on 6 March 1937. When she finished her schooling, she went to work in a textiles factory. But she wanted to achieve more in life, so she studied engineering and went parachuting in her spare time.

- When she heard the government was looking for cosmonauts, she (and four hundred other applicants) signed up, hoping one day to travel into space.

- Valentina's dream became a reality, and in June 1963 she boarded the Vostok 6. She orbited the earth 48 times in total, remaining in space for three days before returning to earth. Her people were so proud that her picture was put on a postage stamp.

- For nineteen years, Valentina Tereshkova would remain the only woman who had ever been to space. The second woman to travel to space – Svetlana Savitskaya, also a Russian – would not do so until 1982.

- After her return, Valentina studied at the Russian Air Force Engineering Academy and became an aeronautical engineer.

- In 2013, Valentina Tereshkova put herself forward as a candidate to fly to Mars, even though she knew she would never return from the journey. And in 2014 she carried the Olympic flag at the Winter Olympics in Russia.

Valentina Tereshkova

92 LEONARDO DA VINCI DREW A HELICOPTER LONG BEFORE IT WAS INVENTED

You've probably heard of the **Mona Lisa**, the portrait of a beautiful woman with a mysterious smile. It is probably one of the most famous paintings in the world, and it was painted by **Leonardo da Vinci**.

- Leonardo was born on 15 April 1452, near the Italian town of Vinci. He was the son of a civil law notary, but his father wasn't married to his mother. Leonardo lived with his mother until he was five, and then moved in with his father, where he received a good education.

- The young Leonardo was apprenticed to the sculptor and painter Andrea del Verrocchio, who lived in nearby Florence.

- Leonardo received his first independent art assignment at the age of twenty-six, and when he was thirty, he moved to Milan to work for a rich family as a painter, engineer, sculptor and architect. He painted many portraits there, but the only one that remains is the famous Mona Lisa. Leonardo frequently left works unfinished, and destroyed the ones he didn't like. That's why of Leonardo's many paintings, only seventeen have survived.

- Leonardo also jotted down thousands of ideas in a collection of notebooks. He studied human anatomy, geological problems, gravity and ways to achieve flight. The subjects covered in the notebooks switch quickly and without warning; sometimes he even wrote about multiple topics on a single page.

- He also added fantastical sketches of all manner of marvellous things – including the concepts of a bicycle, a helicopter, a parachute and an aeroplane – long before any of them were actually invented. In order to draw humans better from the outside, he studied their insides and became a master of anatomy.

- Leonardo da Vinci died in 1519. He was, without a doubt, one of the greatest geniuses the world has ever known.

93 CHARLIE CHAPLIN SUPPOSEDLY LOST A CHARLIE CHAPLIN LOOKALIKE CONTEST

Everyone's heard of **Charlie Chaplin**, the American comic actor with the bowler hat and walking cane. In the 1920s, his movies were incredibly popular, and competitions were even held to see who could do the best impersonation of him. Entrants were judged not only on their appearance, but also on their waddling walk, their body language and their facial expressions.

The story goes that Charlie Chaplin wanted to give it a go himself. So one time, for a laugh, he signed up for a lookalike contest in San Francisco. The judges weren't impressed with his performance, and he came seventh. Charlie's brother was also in the contest, and took third place. But although this is a funny story, we still don't know for sure whether it's true.

94 ADRIEN DE GERLACHE WAS THE FIRST TO SPEND WINTER AT THE SOUTH POLE

Adrien de Gerlache was born on 2 August 1866 in Hasselt in Belgium, and went to school in Brussels. During his studies at the maritime academy (a seafaring school), he spent time on large ships bound for Montevideo in Uruguay and New York in the United States. That was also when he heard of Antarctica for the first time, the unexplored region at the South Pole.

After graduation, Adrien got a job on the ferry between Ostend and Dover. But his real dream was to sail to Antarctica. He couldn't find anyone to sponsor the journey, so he decided to launch his own expedition to the South Pole on board a ship called the *Belgica*.

His journey was the first ever scientific expedition to Antarctica. The *Belgica* sailed through the ice for two months, but eventually the ship became hemmed in by the freezing waters, leaving the crew no choice but to spend winter at the South Pole. De Gerlache used the time to conduct lots of research.

De Gerlache would go on to make many other expeditions, to places including Greenland and Spitsbergen (an island to the north of Norway).

BONUS SOUTH POLE FACTS

Because of Adrien de Gerlache's expedition, many places in Antarctica are named after places in Belgium. You can visit Antwerp Island, Brabant Island, the Solvay Mountains or the Gerlache Strait.

Adrien de Gerlache

LAND AHOY!

BELGICA

🏅 Antwerp Island   🏅 Solvay Mountains   🏅 Gerlache Strait   🏅 Brabant Island

Washington   Jefferson   Teddy   Lincoln

MOUNT PLUSH-MORE

95 THE TEDDY BEAR IS NAMED AFTER AN AMERICAN PRESIDENT

Theodore Roosevelt was President of the United States from 1901 to 1909. He was very popular and beloved by the people, who gave him the pet name of 'Teddy' Roosevelt.

Roosevelt enjoyed hunting. One day while out hunting with a group of friends, everybody had managed to shoot a bear except for the president. The rangers thought it was a pity, and when one of them encountered an old, sick bear in the woods, he tied the poor creature to a tree so the president could come and shoot it for himself.

Theodore Roosevelt refused, saying it would be cowardly to shoot down a defenceless creature like that. The tale spread quickly, and the Americans were taken by their president's noble gesture.

That was also the time when the first toy bears were being mass-produced in factories. The Americans dubbed them 'teddy bears' after their beloved president, and the name has stuck ever since.

96 CAPTAIN JAMES COOK WAS ON A SECRET MISSION

In August 1768, **Captain James Cook** set sail from Plymouth, England on the ship HMS *Endeavour*. He was on a research expedition, along with nearly one hundred crew members and scientists. His primary goal was to collect information on the planet Venus, as scientists wanted to know how the planet moved past the sun. To do so, Cook needed to sail to the island of Tahiti, where Venus could best be observed.

Cook had an envelope in his pocket, which he wasn't allowed to open until he was finished observing Venus. The letter contained a secret mission: he was to try to discover a new continent. The scientists were convinced that there was an enormous piece of land in the southern hemisphere that had not yet been discovered.

After the Venus mission, Cook left Tahiti and sailed south to complete his mission. On 6 October the HMS *Endeavour* arrived in New Zealand – could this be the new land they were looking for? Cook wasn't convinced, but mapped the islands anyway. He then travelled on to Australia, where his crew collected samples from hundreds of unknown plant species.

Three years later the HMS *Endeavour* returned to England, and Cook was forced to confess that he had failed to discover the new continent. Now we know the reason why: it simply didn't exist.

97 CHRISTOPHER COLUMBUS MADE A HUGE MISTAKE

As you probably know, **Christopher Columbus** was an explorer. In 1492 the Spanish queen asked him to go in search of a new sailing route to China and Japan via the west. Columbus set off with three ships, and after a long time at sea eventually spotted the coastline of a country.

according to Columbus

He was convinced he had discovered the western route to Asia, and so he called the people he met there 'Indians', since he believed them to be the inhabitants of India. Fortunately, Columbus' error was eventually set right.

Amerigo Vespucci was another explorer in the same period. In around 1500 he too sailed out west on the orders of the Spanish queen. Although he knew he hadn't landed in Asia, he knew that he was in a land that didn't yet have a European name. So he gave it his own name, which it still bears today: America.

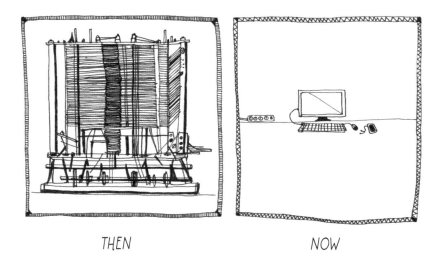

THEN   NOW

98 COMPUTER PROGRAMMING WAS INVENTED BY A WOMAN

Ada Lovelace was hardly one month old when her parents separated; her father was the famous poet Lord Byron, and her mother was a noble lady from the English aristocracy.

Ada's mother was especially strict on her daughter. She was afraid that Ada might want to become a poet like her father, so she made her study mathematics and science. Luckily Ada was an excellent student.

When she was nineteen, she met mathematician and inventor Charles Babbage, who was working on what he called an 'analytical engine'. Ada was impressed by the idea, and instantly saw possibilities that Babbage himself had not yet envisaged. According to Lovelace, the machine would be able to compose music, do drawings and solve all kinds of scientific problems. What's more, it would be able to use an algorithm to calculate Bernoulli numbers.*

She devised a plan, including an outline of the language that would be used to operate the machine. Her design is now regarded as the world's first ever computer program, even though it was written before the first computer was created. Ada simply imagined how computers would eventually need to work, in a time when they did not yet exist.

In 1979, the American Ministry of Defense named a new programming language 'Ada' in honour of this very special mathematician.

8 digits = 1 byte
1 digit = 1 bit
1 byte = 8 bits

*Bernoulli numbers are rational numbers that occur regularly in number theory. Ask your maths teacher to explain them to you sometime!

99 MARIE CURIE DIDN'T WIN A NOBEL PRIZE – SHE WON TWO!

Marie Skłodowska was born in Poland, and was the youngest of five children. Her mother died when she was very young, and her father had difficulty making ends meet.

Marie was a model student and got excellent grades at school. Unfortunately, her family didn't have enough money to send her to university, so Marie worked as a teacher and governess (a cross between a private tutor and a babysitter) and tried to attend classes whenever she could.

She made a deal with her sister Bronia: Marie agreed to help pay for Bronia's medical degree in Paris, on the condition that Bronia would do the same for Marie afterwards.

In 1891, when Marie was 24, she went to France to study mathematics, physics and chemistry at Sorbonne University in Paris. The Sorbonne is one of the best universities in France, and Marie passed with flying colours.

She then married Pierre Curie, a scientist who was busy experimenting with magnetism. Marie worked in his lab and conducted research on many different types of radiation, having been inspired by Wilhelm Röntgen, the inventor of the X-ray. Marie and her husband discovered two new substances that emit radiation. They named them polonium – after Marie's country of birth – and radium, after the name they had given to the substances' special property: radioactivity.

In 1903, Pierre and Marie were jointly awarded the Nobel Prize for Physics for their ground-breaking work on radiation. Marie Curie was the first woman ever to receive this accolade. In 1911 she received a second Nobel Prize, this time for chemistry. In 1935, Marie Curie's daughter, Irène Joliot-Curie, also won a joint Nobel Prize for Chemistry along with her husband Frédéric.

BONUS NOBEL PRIZE FACTS

Only three other people have ever won two Nobel Prizes. **Linus Pauling** won Nobel Prizes for Chemistry and Peace; **John Bardeen** won two for Physics; and **Frederick Sanger** won two for Chemistry.

100 YURI GAGARIN WAS THE FIRST MAN IN SPACE

Yuri Gagarin was a Russian fighter jet pilot, whose biggest dream was to explore space in a rocket. His ambition became a reality on 12 April 1961, when he was allowed on board the Vostok 1 to make a space flight. Nobody had ever done it before, and he had no idea if he would ever return to earth.

Yuri was all alone in the rocket, strapped firmly into his seat. He had an emergency supply of food with him, enough to survive for ten days. The cosmonaut eventually remained in space for 108 minutes. His re-entry almost ended in disaster, when the landing capsule came free of the rocket with a powerful jolt. Yuri was ejected from the capsule 7 kilometres above the surface, after which he drifted down to earth on a parachute.

On that day Yuri became an international hero, and began travelling around the world to talk about his journey through space. Sadly, he died at the age of 34, in a plane crash.

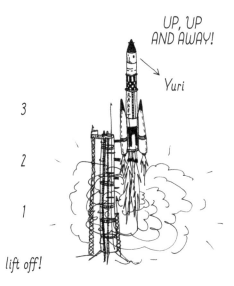

UP, UP AND AWAY!

Yuri

3

2

1

lift off!

BONUS SPACE FACTS

Eight years after Yuri Gagarin's historic journey, the USA successfully sent a crew of three men to the moon in a rocket. Two of them actually walked on the moon: their names were **Neil Armstrong** and **Buzz Aldrin**.

Buzz

Neil

The first human walked on the moon on 21 July 1969.

The rocket that first took humans to the moon was called **Apollo 11**.

The journey to the moon took four days. The crew was away from home for just over eight days.

The third crew member – **Michael Collins** – never actually walked on the moon. He stayed in the spaceship, while his comrades Buzz and Neil explored the moon's surface in the lunar module.

The footprints made by the first 'moonwalkers' are still visible on the moon's surface, as there is no wind or rain to blow or wash them away.

101 ÖTZI THE ICEMAN HAD 61 TATTOOS

On 19 September 1991, Erika and Helmut Simon were hiking through the Öztaler Alps in the Austrian region of Tyrol, and got the shock of their lives when they discovered a body in the ice. When special excavation teams freed the body from its icy tomb, it turned out it had been frozen solid for a very long time – more than five thousand years! The find was the oldest mummy ever discovered in Europe, and because it had been lying in a kind of deep-freeze, it was extremely well-preserved. The man was nicknamed **Ötzi the Iceman**, and taught scientists a lot about ancient humans.

- When Ötzi was alive, he was roughly 160 centimetres tall and weighed about 50 kilos. Researchers estimate that he was about 45 years old when he died, which was quite old for humans at that time.

- Humans clearly had no dentists in those days, because Ötzi's teeth were in very poor condition.

- Ötzi's body had no fewer than 61 tattoos. But they weren't love hearts, his sweethearts' names or the logos of his favourite football clubs. Those kinds of tattoos didn't exist yet – Ötzi's tattoos are simple lines and crosses drawn on his back, wrists, knees and feet. Exactly why he had these tattoos is a mystery yet to be unravelled by historians.

- The iceman was dressed in the pelts (skins) of various animals: he had a hood made from the fur of a brown bear, a deerskin quiver and a jacket made of goatskin and sheepskin.

- Researchers also tried to figure out how Ötzi died. The iceman had an arrow fragment embedded in his shoulder, and a deep cut above his eye. He was probably being attacked and ran up the glacier to escape, which is where they found him thousands of years later.

1.60 m

YETI OR ÖTZI?

102 HAYDN'S GRAVE CONTAINS TWO SKULLS

Joseph Haydn was an Austrian composer. He was born in 1732 and died in 1809. Along with Wolfgang Amadeus Mozart and Ludwig van Beethoven, he is one of the greatest composers ever to have lived. Among musicians he is known affectionately as 'Papa Haydn' and 'the father of the symphony'.

Haydn died on 31 May 1809, after a long illness. Because Austria was at war, there was no way to give him a grand funeral, so he was buried in an ordinary grave. Unfortunately Haydn wasn't able to rest in peace, as two graverobbers stole his skull in order to figure out where Haydn's genius had come from (they thought the size and shape of his skull had something to do with his intellectual and musical gifts). The man who had originally dug the grave was bribed to detach Haydn's head from his body.

After some time, the skull became the property of one of Haydn's friends, Joseph Carl Rosenbaum, who held onto it for a while. But that's not the end of the story. When the war was over, Prince Nikolaus Esterházy II wanted to give the composer the funeral he deserved. So the body was exhumed (that means 'dug up'), and Nikolaus saw that the skull was missing. He went to see Rosenbaum, who quickly hid the skull beneath his wife's mattress. When the prince gave him money to return the skull, Rosenbaum simply got hold of another man's skull, and gave that to the prince instead. So at the funeral, a stranger's skull was laid in the new grave with Haydn's body.

The real skull eventually made its way to the Friends of Music Society in Vienna, where it was occasionally put on display during parties and celebrations. There is a rumour that Johannes Brahms enjoyed composing music with Haydn's skull sitting on the table in front of him.

Haydn's skull and body were finally reunited in the new marble tomb that was built for him in 1954. But the fake skull that had lain there all those years was allowed to stay, so after having 'lost his head' for so long, Haydn now has two to make up for it. Maybe it's true – two heads *are* better than one.

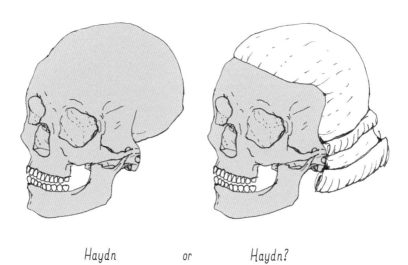

Haydn   or   Haydn?

103 ROALD DAHL WAS ONCE A SPY

Everybody knows **Roald Dahl** as the author of marvellous children's books such as *Charlie and the Chocolate Factory*, *Matilda*, *The BFG*, and many others. That's what made him famous, and it's how he will always be remembered. But Roald Dahl wasn't always a writer...

Trouble with Gremlins?

- During the Second World War he worked as a spy for a little while, gathering information on the Americans for the British Secret Service. He was sent to the British Embassy in Washington, where it was his job to find out whether the Americans were planning to get involved in the war. That was also where he became friends with Ian Fleming, who was also a spy and a writer. Fleming was the creator of James Bond.

- Roald Dahl was also a fighter pilot in the British air force for a while. Alas, he was seriously injured when his plane crashed, and he even went blind for some time.

- Roald Dahl wrote his first children's book in 1943. It was called *The Gremlins*, and was inspired by his time in the air force – whenever pilots had unexplained engine trouble, they said it was caused by 'gremlins' in the engine.

BONUS DAHL FACTS

Roald Dahl had a real hatred of beards. Just read his book *The Twits* and you'll see!

The grave of Roald Dahl contains several of his most treasured possessions: a bottle of fine wine, some pencils, chocolate, a power saw and a snooker cue.

Roald Dahl did his writing in a small hut that stood in his garden.

104 MOZART WAS A *WUNDERKIND*

Wolfgang Amadeus Mozart was born in 1756 in Austria, and is one of the most famous composers of all time. Composers are people who think of music, and then write it down so that other musicians can play it.

- Mozart's father Leopold knew that his son was a *Wunderkind* (which is the German word for a 'child prodigy', or a young genius) and arranged to have Mozart perform for the emperor of Austria.

- Later, Mozart also visited the kings of France and England. They were all big fans of his music.

- Mozart wrote his first major opera when he was only fourteen. It was called *Mitidrate*, and was first performed in the Teatro Regio Ducal in Milan, Italy. Over his life, Mozart wrote astonishing amounts of music and was extremely popular for a very long time.

- Despite his success, Mozart had lots of debts at the end of his life. Although he was earning plenty of money, he also led a life of luxury with lots of servants, expensive clothes and fancy furniture. He also gambled quite a lot on cards and billiards. He died young, leaving his wife with virtually nothing to survive on.

Mini Mozart

A CREEPY FEELING...

Mozart wrote a Requiem – a sung mass for the dead – which is one of the most beautiful pieces he ever composed. When writing it, he had the feeling he was composing his own funeral mass. His hunch was right, and he died very soon afterwards.

105 FRANZ LISZT SENT DOG HAIR TO HIS FANS

Franz Liszt didn't just write amazing music: he was also an incredible virtuoso pianist. He was born in Hungary in 1811, but lived most of his life in Vienna. In 1859 he was raised to the nobility by Emperor Francis Joseph I, after which he was allowed to use the name Franz Ritter (= knight) von Liszt.

Liszt had magnificent long hair, and his admirers often asked him to send him a lock or two. Originally Liszt did send locks of his own hair, but after a while he couldn't keep up with the demand without shaving himself bald. The story goes that he bought himself a long-haired dog, so that instead of sending his own hair to his fans, he could just clip some off the dog!

Long-haired Liszt

HA HA

HO HO

HA HA

Florence Foster Jenkins

106 IF YOU'RE RICH, NOBODY WILL COMPLAIN ABOUT YOUR SINGING

It's quite possible that your singing sounds a bit like a cat yowling. If so, don't worry – it doesn't mean you can't become a famous singer!

Florence Foster Jenkins was a terrible singer. She couldn't hold a steady note, and her voice sounded dreadful. But she herself seemed not to notice, and it was her dream to become an opera singer. Her father had heard his daughter's singing and was against the whole plan, so he forbade Florence from taking singing lessons. She was so angry that she ran away from home.

When her parents died, Florence inherited a fortune which she used to found the Verdi Club for Women. The society gave money to musicians and artists to enable them to perform. Florence herself started making appearances as a soprano, and always sang the most challenging works by the great composers. Sometimes she even sang music that she had written herself, and never doubted its beauty for a moment. Florence liked to wear elaborate costumes covered in sequins and feathers, and often changed dresses for each new song.

Florence only ever invited her friends and admirers to her performances – all others were turned away at the door. Nobody ever told Florence how out of tune her singing was. Whenever it became unbearable, the audience simply started applauding and whistling loudly.

Many people asked Florence when she would finally give a performance that was open to the general public. Eventually she gave in to the pressure, and in 1944 she gave a recital in the most prestigious venue in New York: Carnegie Hall. The concert sold out in record time.

Sadly, terrible reviews appeared in the papers the next day. Florence was devastated when she read them. Five days later she had a heart attack, and she died less than a month afterwards. It's possible that she literally died of a 'broken heart'.

In 2016 her life story was turned into a film called *Florence Foster Jenkins*, with the lead role played by world-famous actor Meryl Streep.

107 HENRY WALTER BATES DISCOVERED THAT SOME ANIMALS ARE TRICKSTERS

Henry Walter Bates was a British naturalist and explorer. In 1848 he travelled to the Amazon rainforest, where he mostly studied butterflies.

- Many butterflies are brightly-coloured, which serves as a warning to birds and other animals who see butterflies as a tasty treat. In nature, bright colours are a code for 'Watch out, I'm poisonous to eat!'

- But Bates noticed that there were pretenders among them – animals that looked poisonous, but were actually harmless. In the animal world this is called 'mimicry', and is what happens when animals behave like other animals to save their own skin.

- Animals don't just mimic colours: some poisonous moths emit warnings by making certain noises. Bats – who are very partial to eating moths – hear the sounds made by the poisonous moths and keep away. Once the edible moth species figured that out, they began copying the same sounds, so the bats would leave them alone too.

camouflage

DON'T MIND ME

BONUS FACT

Animals don't just pretend to be dangerous: some animals do the reverse, and adopt a disguise in order to seem harmless. Then, as soon as they get close enough to their prey, they bare their jaws and attack!

For example: some kinds of spiders look like ants. Spiders have two more legs than insects (eight instead of six), and don't have antennae like ants do. So the ant-spider raises two of its legs above its head so they look like antennae. That gets it past the guards outside the ants' nest, so it can feed on all the juicy ants inside.

mimicry

DON'T EAT ME

108 AMELIA EARHART WAS THE FIRST WOMAN TO FLY ACROSS THE ATLANTIC

WHEE!

NR-965Y

Amelia Earhart

- **Amelia Earhart** was born on 24 July 1897 in the United States. She was always getting into mischief, and could often be found climbing trees or chasing rats with a gun.

- In 1920 she took her first ride on a plane as a passenger, and from that moment on, she had only one dream: to become a pilot herself. She took flying lessons, and used her own savings to buy an aeroplane.

- In May 1932 she took off from Newfoundland in Canada to make a journey across the ocean. Amelia knew it would be dangerous, as she would need to fly non-stop for fifteen hours through extreme weather conditions. Her fuel tank started leaking halfway; flames burst out of the engine, and the wings got covered with ice. But Amelia refused to give up. She succeeded in crossing the Atlantic Ocean, and landed safely in a field in Ireland.

- Amelia was a real daredevil. In 1937 she tried to fly around the world with Fred Noonan, but when they attempted to land on an island in the Pacific, things went wrong. The plane lost contact with the air base so it was unable to land, and then suddenly it just disappeared. Nobody knows what happened. Did they attempt an emergency landing at sea? Did they crash on a deserted island somewhere? It remains a mystery to this day. But whatever happened, Amelia Earhart was a very brave woman, that much is certain.

109 SALVADOR DALÍ WAS DESPERATE TO BECOME FAMOUS

- Just look at a photograph of the Spanish artist **Salvador Dalí**, and you'll see straightaway what a character he was. Beneath his nose grew an enormous moustache, whose pointed tips curled majestically all the way up to his eyes. Dalí enjoyed wearing outlandish jackets and capes, and liked to stand out from the crowd. Lots of people thought he was crazy. He once said: 'The only difference between me and a

madman is that I am not mad'. It's no surprise that people thought he was a bit of an oddball.

- Dalí's paintings were very strange. At first they seem to be paintings of ordinary objects, but when they're put together they form a bizarre dream world. This style of painting is called 'surrealism'.

- Dalí also invented crazy objects that were practically useless, but fun to look at. Two of his most famous designs were a telephone with a lobster stuck to it, and a sofa shaped like a pair of lips.

- One of Dalí's most famous paintings is called *The Persistence of Memory*, and depicts a bunch of melting clocks. He occasionally gave his paintings funny names, like *Eggs on a Plate without a Plate*.

- Dalí also made very strange films. In them, all sorts of creepy things happen that make the viewer feel uneasy. Some audiences really hated them, and would start throwing things at the screen during showings.

- Salvador Dalí died in 1989, and is buried in a crypt under the Dalí Theatre and Museum in Figueras, Spain. The works of Dalí can be seen in museums all over the world.

THE ONLY DIFFERENCE BETWEEN ME AND A MADMAN IS THAT I AM NOT MAD

110 BARBIE WAS A REAL GIRL

Mr and Mrs Handler from the United States owned a toy factory called 'Mattel'. At home, Mrs Handler noticed that her daughter Barbara's favourite thing to do was play dress-ups with her cardboard dolls. She made long dresses and hats for them, and could entertain herself for hours. In 1959, Mrs Handler decided to create a plastic doll that looked just like a real woman, with an enormous wardrobe to match. She named the doll '**Barbie**', which was what she always called her daughter, Barbara.

Barbie was a real innovation, because until that time the only dolls you could buy were big dolls that looked like newborn babies.

I'M ALIVE!

Other toymakers were originally sceptical about the new doll, but Barbie became a huge success in virtually no time.

Two years later Barbie got a new friend: Ken, who was named after Mrs Handler's son Kenneth.

Barbie and Ken toys have since become best-sellers all over the world.

BONUS BARBIE FACTS

Barbie's official birthday is 9 March 1959.

The first ever Barbie wore a black-and-white striped bathing suit, and had a ponytail.

111 MOCKINGBIRDS AND FINCHES HELPED DARWIN CREATE THE THEORY OF EVOLUTION

Charles Darwin is a famous scientist who lived from 1809 to 1882. He is called the 'father of evolution', because of his theory that all animals (including humans) slowly change and adapt to survive in their surroundings. Those that adapt the best are the ones that survive, and that's how humans and animals evolved over the millennia into what they are now.

From 1831 to 1836, Charles Darwin went travelling on a ship called the *Beagle*, which docked in South America, Africa, Australia and several islands in the Pacific and Indian oceans. Whenever he went ashore, Darwin looked closely at the animals, plants, fossils and different layers of soil he found there.

He saw mockingbirds on one of the islands, but also noticed mockingbirds on another island a little further away. Although they were all mockingbirds, there were clear differences between the two species, and they were strictly separated between the two islands. Darwin was intrigued. He continued his research by studying finches, and discovered that bird species aren't always exactly the same, and can vary according to their specific habitat.

His observations led him to formulate the theory of evolution, which is still studied today as one of the basic principles of biology.

He wrote a book on it called *On the Origin of Species by Means of Natural Selection*, which became a best-seller.

Not everybody believed (or believes) Darwin's theory. In his day he met with fierce opposition, and some Christian people in particular see the theory of evolution as an attack on the creation story from the Bible.

SPOT THE DIFFERENCE?

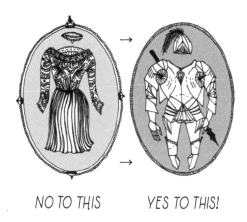

NO TO THIS   *YES TO THIS!*

112 JOAN OF ARC WAS A TOMBOY (AND SHE WAS BURNED AT THE STAKE)

During the Hundred Years' War, England tried to conquer France. One day a French farmer's daughter, **Joan of Arc**, paid a visit to the future French king. She told Charles VII that she had had a vision, in which God told her she would be the one to drive away the English. God would also ensure that Charles became king.

Joan cut her hair, put on a white suit of armour, and drove the English out of Orleans. She also secured several other victories, and Charles was eventually crowned king of France.

Sadly, Joan was captured by Burgundian troops and ransomed to the English, who put her to trial on charges of heresy. The judge sentenced Joan to death, and when she was only nineteen she was burned at the stake in Rouen. Her remains were thrown into the river Seine, to prevent anybody from building a monument in her honour.

Charles VII eventually chased the English out of France, putting an end to the Hundred Years' War. Joan's trial was reopened, and although she was already dead, her verdict was changed to 'not guilty'.

BONUS FACT

The Hundred Years' War actually lasted for 116 years – from 1337 until 1453 – and consisted of several separate wars alternating with periods of peace. Most of the war was fought in France.

113 IT'S HARD TO MAKE MONEY FROM ART UNTIL YOU'RE DEAD

A painter's life can be hard. Often their work is not appreciated during their lifetime, and they earn hardly enough money to survive. But later, sometimes even a hundred years after they die, people can start paying enormous sums for their works. **Paul Gauguin** was one such example: in 2015, an anonymous buyer paid $300 million for his painting titled *Nafea faa ipoipo?* ('When will you marry?'), which Gauguin painted on the island of Tahiti where he went to live after a difficult life in France. The painting is very colourful, and depicts two women kneeling in a landscape.

Dutch painter **Vincent van Gogh** was also down-and-out during his lifetime. He was often ill, and suffered from depression. He eventually committed suicide.

Like Gauguin's work, Van Gogh's paintings didn't become popular or well-known until after his death. Of his nine hundred paintings, only one was ever sold during his lifetime, and that was to the sister of one of his friends. How things have changed! Van Gogh's portrait of the doctor who took care of him during his final years is now one of the most expensive artworks ever sold,

by Paul Gauguin?

fetching $82.5 million in 1990. It was purchased by a Japanese businessman.

Paul Gauguin and Vincent van Gogh knew each other. Paul even lived with Vincent for a while, in the Yellow House in Arles. The two friends ended up in a fight because they both fell in love with the same woman – the landlady of a local inn. Gauguin then moved to Tahiti where he painted his best-known works. Van Gogh's illnesses continued to worsen, but during that time he painted masterpieces that would eventually make him world-famous.

114 NEMO IS PICASSO'S COUSIN

Remember the movie *Finding Nemo*? Then you probably know that Nemo was a clownfish. But the clownfish have many different family members, including one called the 'Picasso clownfish', which gets its name from the unusual patterns on its scales.

- **Pablo Picasso** was born in 1881 in Spain, but he spent much of his time in France. He worked as an artist, sculptor and potter. Some believe that Picasso was the greatest painter of the twentieth century.

- As a child, Pablo Picasso liked drawing outlandish, fantastical pictures. When he was nineteen, he often travelled to Paris to paint.

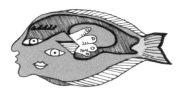

A PICASSO CLOWNFISH?

- Pablo continued to experiment, making paintings that consisted of many different blocks, each depicting one part of a single object. This style is known as 'cubism', a form of abstract art where it's often hard to recognize the object that's being painted.

- As well as painting, Picasso also enjoyed sculpture, and made artworks using things he found on the street. He once made a bull's head using the saddle and handlebars from an old bicycle.

- His most famous painting is called *Guernica* and is absolutely gigantic. The canvas is 8 metres long, and depicts Picasso's strong feelings about war.

- Pablo Picasso died aged 91, and continued to produce art until his dying day.

- Pablo became extremely depressed when a friend of his died, and it showed in his artwork. He began painting sad figures, often in shades of blue – this time in his life is known as his 'blue period'. When he met a lovely lady not long afterwards and fell in love, he dropped the blue and started painting in pink instead. This period is called his 'pink period', and his favourite subjects were circus performers.

115 JULIUS CAESAR HAD A COMB-OVER

Julius Caesar is often depicted wearing a laurel wreath, an honour that was supposed to be reserved for the winners of the Olympic Games. It was presented for the first time at the games held in the year 6 BCE in honour of the sun god, Apollo, who was always pictured wearing a wreath made of laurel leaves (also called bay leaves). The doctors of the day believed that laurel leaves had healing properties.

Julius Caesar liked wearing a laurel wreath, mostly because he was almost completely bald – a fact that really annoyed him because he cared a lot about his appearance. He used to comb his few remaining hairs forwards to hide his baldness as much as possible, a hairstyle known these days as a 'comb-over'.

Cleopatra, who was Caesar's girlfriend for a while, is said to have massaged his scalp using a special balm of her own making that contained the ashes

of mice, bear fat, horses' teeth and the spinal cord of a deer. Perhaps Cleopatra was pulling her boyfriend's leg. Whatever the case, the balm didn't work, and his head remained as bald as could be.

CLEO, WHERE'S THAT SHAMPOO?

116 ALEXANDER THE GREAT SOLVED A 'KNOTTY' PROBLEM

- Prince **Alexander the Great** was born in Macedonia in the year 356 BCE. When he turned 20, his father was assassinated and he came to the throne.

- Alexander went to battle straightaway. First he conquered the Persian Empire, then moved on to Egypt and Asia. His armies reached as far as India, but they eventually got homesick and decided they'd done enough conquering for a while.

- Alexander the Great didn't kill his enemies: he let them live instead, on the condition that they remained loyal to him forever. His dream was to unify the Greeks and Persians (modern-day Iranians) into a single people. That's why he married three Persian women.

- Alexander founded dozens of cities, some of which he named after himself. The Egyptian city of Alexandria is probably the most famous example.

- Alexander was a decisive leader. One day he attacked the city of Gordium, where the inhabitants told him the legend of King Gordius' chariot. The chariot had been fastened with a Gordian knot, and it was said that whoever could untie it was destined to become the ruler of Asia. Alexander didn't waste any time: he took his sword and cut through the knot in a single blow. The expression 'to cut the Gordian knot' is sometimes still used today, for people who are able to make important decisions quickly.

- Alexander the Great died when he was only 32. Nobody knows exactly why – perhaps he fell ill, or he may have died from battle injuries. Dying young was quite common in those days. In any case, Alexander certainly achieved a lot during his short life!

OVERHAND KNOT   REEF KNOT   FIGURE-EIGHT KNOT

Alexander the Great was never tied up in knots

117 POCAHONTAS IS BURIED IN GREAT BRITAIN

Pocahontas's grave is located in St George's cemetery in Gravesend, England. She died in 1617, when she was only 22.

Pocahontas was born in the United States and was the daughter of the chief of the Powhatan people. The Powhatan lived in modern-day Virginia, where the English colonists landed in 1607.

The Powhatan and the colonists were not always on the best of terms. They were sometimes at war with each other, and it was during one of these battles that Pocahontas was kidnapped by the colonists. She married the Englishman John Rolfe, who had fallen in love with her. History doesn't tell us whether Pocahontas returned his love; the marriage was mainly intended to put an end to the conflict between the Powhatan and the colonists.

Pocahontas moved to England in 1616 with her husband and son. They went to live in Brentford, where Pocahontas unfortunately fell ill and died.

118 HARRY POTTER HAS BEEN TRANSLATED INTO 79 LANGUAGES

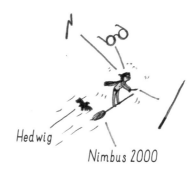

Hedwig

Nimbus 2000

Harry's fame went to his head

No fewer than 450 million copies of **Harry Potter** have been sold worldwide in over 79 languages, making the author J. K. Rowling the first ever to make so much money from selling books. Harry's adventures at Hogwarts made her not only one of the richest writers in the world, but also one of the richest women in Great Britain.

It wasn't just the books that brought home the bacon: the Harry Potter movies were also very lucrative. The film series took ten years to make, and the child characters were always played by the same actors. Daniel Radcliffe, who plays Harry Potter, was eleven years old when he starred in the first film, *Harry Potter and the Philosopher's Stone*. By the time the eighth and final film appeared in 2011, Radcliffe was already 21.

119 ANNE FRANK DIDN'T SEE THE SUN FOR TWO YEARS

You've probably heard of **Anne Frank**. She was a little girl who wrote a diary while hiding from the Nazi forces during the Second World War.

- In 1933, Hitler rose to power in Germany along with his political party, the National Socialists Party, known as the Nazis. Hitler hated Jewish people, and thought they should be eradicated.

- The Frank family no longer felt safe in Germany. So in 1933, the father Otto Frank moved to the Netherlands with his wife Edith to start his own company. But when Hitler declared war in 1940, not even Amsterdam was safe anymore. The Frank family tried to leave Europe for America or some other distant country, but all doors were closed to them.

- In 1942, the family had no choice but to go into hiding. They hid inside the secret attic of a large house on one of Amsterdam's canals – at Prinsengracht 263. The house stood behind Otto Frank's office, and had room for two families. A bookcase was put up as a secret door, to hide the staircase leading to the attic so that the German soldiers wouldn't know where the Jewish families were hiding. They received assistance from four of Otto Frank's employees: Miep Gies, Johannes Kleiman, Victor Kugler and Bep Voskuijl. They provided food, clothing, books and various other things. They also told the families what was going on in the city and the rest of the world.

- For over two years, the families stayed hidden in the secret attic without setting foot outside even once. Then one day, someone told the authorities where they were hiding.

- On 4 August 1944, Anne Frank and her family were transported to the concentration camp in Auschwitz. Otto Frank would eventually be the only member of the family to survive. It was never discovered who betrayed the Franks.

- Miep Gies and Bep Voskuijl were the ones who discovered Anne's diary. When Otto Frank returned to the Netherlands, they gave it back to him. Anne had written that it was her wish to publish the diary after the war. Her father decided to try to grant her wish, and the book is now compulsory reading in many schools all over the world.

- A film has also been made about the life of Anne Frank.

- If ever you visit Amsterdam, be sure to pay a visit to the house where the Frank family hid away for all those years. It has now been turned into the Anne Frank Museum.

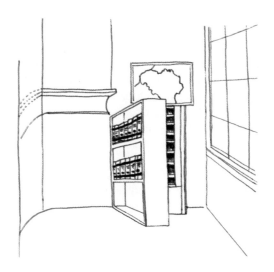

...and the wolf lived happily ever after.

120 FAIRY TALES USED TO BE HORROR STORIES

You probably know **fairy tales** like Cinderella and Snow White from the film versions made by Disney. But did you know that they were written down long ago by two German brothers, Jacob and Wilhelm Grimm? Jacob and Wilhelm were both linguists, who travelled around collecting old folk stories and legends by talking to anyone they could. They wrote the stories down in a book that they published in 1802, called *Children's and Household Tales*. Many of the stories are still well-known today: Little Red Riding Hood, Sleeping Beauty, Snow White, the Pied Piper of Hamelin, Rumpelstiltskin, the Frog Prince, and Hansel and Gretel are all in the collection.

The first volume was never really meant for children, as the stories were far too cruel and violent. The Grimm brothers' original purpose was to preserve the tales for future generations.

In the original version of Little Red Riding Hood, for example, the girl is eaten by the wolf and never comes back. And the evil witch from Snow White isn't banished from the kingdom, but instead is given a pair of iron shoes and forced to dance herself to death. Hansel and Gretel aren't locked up by a witch, but by the devil himself, who tries to kill them both.

These stories are of course much too scary for children. That's why the brothers began to change the stories themselves. As the years went on, they were adapted to suit children's ears.

Grimm's Fairy Tales (as they are more commonly known) have been translated into 160 languages. The brothers' grave can be visited at Old St Matthew's cemetery in Berlin, where they now lie buried alongside many other famous Germans.

AAARRR!

121 A PIRATE-HUNTER BECAME A PIRATE

You may never have heard of **Captain William Kidd**, but in his day he was quite famous – some might even say infamous.

William Kidd was born in 1645 in Scotland. Later in life he moved to the United States, where he married Sarah Bradley Cox Oort. Sarah was incredibly rich; Kidd became a merchant and the pair lived a life of luxury.

Kidd travelled to England regularly to do business. Some of the English nobility asked him if he might be willing to hunt French pirates in exchange for a handsome fee. Kidd was an adventurous sort, and gladly accepted the challenge. He bought a brand-new ship designed specially for hunting pirates called the *Adventure Galley*. But despite having more than thirty cannons on board, Kidd and his ship had little success bringing pirates to justice.

He ran up lots of debts that he couldn't repay, and eventually started attacking every non-English ship he came across, pirate or not. After some time, William Kidd stopped hunting pirates and actually became a pirate himself.

Kidd's situation went from bad to worse. He started fights with the crew, many of whom turned against him. Kidd returned to the United States, where he was imprisoned and deported to England to stand trial.

William Kidd was hanged on 23 May 1701. As a deterrent to other pirates, his body was put in an iron cage and suspended over the river Thames.

There is a legend that William Kidd left buried treasure somewhere. People sometimes even go out in search of it!

122 ANIMALS CAN ALSO SOAR TO FAME

This chapter was all about famous people, but did you know that there are lots of famous animals too?

BOW WOW... OW!

- **Laika** was a Russian street dog. In 1957, scientists gave her a spacesuit and put her in a rocket called Sputnik 2. Alas, Laika never returned home from her space mission. The Sputnik 2 had been designed to combust when re-entering the earth's atmosphere. According to scientists, however, Laika overheated while still in the space capsule and died several hours after the launch.

- The fate of **Lassie** was a much happier one, with a leading role in one of the most famous television shows ever. When trouble was near, Lassie the dog would always come to the rescue. Although Lassie's character was female, she was always played by different male dogs, all of whom were related to each other and looked almost the same. Lassie even got her own star on the Hollywood Walk of Fame!

- Because pigeons always know the way back to their roost (called a 'dovecote'), they were used to send messages during times of war. **Cher Ami** was an ordinary carrier pigeon, but was charged with delivering an extremely important message during World War One. Although Cher Ami was shot and injured by German troops, she still managed to take off again and delivered the message in record time, saving the lives of 194 trapped soldiers.

- Even animals of questionable intelligence can become world-famous. You might have heard of **Paul the Octopus**, whose job it was to predict the outcomes of the 2010 World Cup football matches for the German team. For each prediction, two tubs of food were placed in Paul's tank, each with the flag of a different team. The team on the tub that he went to first would supposedly win the match. Paul was put to the test seven times, and amazingly made seven correct predictions.

5

A JOURNEY THROUGH HISTORY

123 THE BLACK DEATH KILLED OVER 75 MILLION PEOPLE

From 1346 to 1352, Europe was ravaged by a deadly disease called **the plague**, also known as the **Black Death**. The plague originated in Asia, and spread to Europe by rats on board ships. Approximately 60% of Europeans died during the scourge of the plague.

The disease was caused by a type of bacteria called *Yersinia pestis*, which was spread by the fleas living on black rats. In those times, both rats and fleas could be found everywhere in the streets, and even inside people's homes.

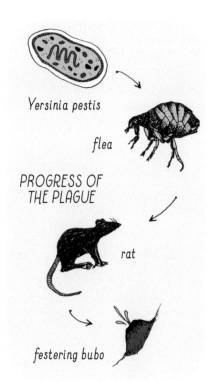

Yersinia pestis

flea

PROGRESS OF THE PLAGUE

rat

festering bubo

The people who fell ill developed large, black lumps called 'buboes' as large as eggs in their armpits and groin. The buboes oozed pus and blood, and after some time, black patches of dead skin started appearing (this is called 'gangrene'). Because the victims' skin turned black, the disease came to be known as the Black Death.

Back then, nobody knew where illnesses came from or what caused them. Jews, beggars and lepers were given the blame. It was true that Jews fell sick less often, which was seen as suspicious. People in the Middle Ages were convinced that they were poisoning the wells to kill the Christians, which of course wasn't true. The Jews were forced to live together in 'ghettos', or separate sections of the city, and because they followed lots of special rules (which they still do today), they were cleaner than the rest of the population. So the ghettos became small islands of hygiene.

Unfortunately, the connection between hygiene and illness had not yet been made. And because people believed the nasty stories about the Jews, violent attacks called 'pogroms' were organized. During a pogrom, Jews were burned alive and all of their possessions stolen from their homes. A large proportion of the Jewish population was killed this way.

The plague dealt a harsh blow to Europe, and it would be 1600 before the population once again reached fourteenth-century levels.

Canada
Australia
New Zealand
Jamaica
Barbados
The Bahamas
Grenada
Papua New Guinea
The Solomon Islands

Tuvalu
Saint Kitts and Nevis
Belize
Antigua and Barbuda
Saint Vincent and
the Grenadines
Saint Lucia
United Kingdom

QUEEN ELIZABETH II

124 QUEEN ELIZABETH IS THE RULER OF SIXTEEN COUNTRIES

Elizabeth Alexandra Mary, or **Elizabeth II** for short, is not just the Queen of the United Kingdom. In 1952 she also became the queen of Canada, Australia and New Zealand. Not only that, but she is also the queen of Jamaica, Barbados, the Bahamas, Grenada, Papua New Guinea, the Solomon Islands, Tuvalu, Saint Kitts and Nevis, Belize, Antigua and Barbuda, Saint Lucia, and Saint Vincent and the Grenadines. These last twelve are known as the Commonwealth Realms, and are all countries that have gained independence since Elizabeth became queen but are still part of the British Commonwealth (which includes Great Britain and most of the former British colonies).

Elizabeth II is currently the longest-reigning monarch in British history. She celebrated her ninetieth birthday in 2016, making her also the world's oldest living ruler. Still, she doesn't seem to have any plans for abdication (stepping down from the throne). In Great Britain, it is tradition that kings and queens continue to rule up until their death.

Elizabeth has four children. The eldest is Charles, who is the Prince of Wales and Elizabeth's heir. Next comes Charles's sister Anne, then two more brothers, Andrew and Edward.

125 ONE IN FIVE PEOPLE ARE CHINESE

China is home to 1.4 billion people. Although the country is not much bigger than the United States, it has four times as many inhabitants. So you can imagine just how busy it is on the streets of big Chinese cities!

The total global population is about 7.5 billion, which means that one-fifth of the humans on earth are Chinese. India is next at 1.3 billion, followed by the European Union (510 million), the United States (325 million) and Indonesia (265 million).

According to United Nations data, there will be around 10 billion people on the planet by 2050. Over half of those will live in Asia, and most of them will be in India.

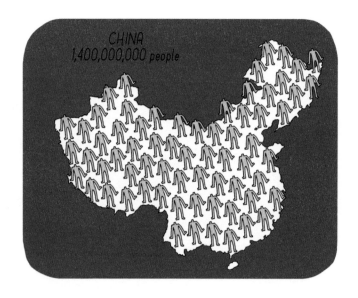

It is no surprise that Mandarin Chinese is the most widely-spoken language in the world, followed by Spanish, English, Hindi and Arabic.

126 THE WORLD'S OLDEST BANK IS IN SIENA, ITALY

- The Banca Monte dei Paschi di Siena is over five hundred years old. It was founded in 1472 in Siena, Italy, and is still exactly where it has stood for over 600 years.

- Some **banks** began as pawnshops, where people could borrow money in exchange for valuable objects, like an expensive piece of jewelry or art. In banking language, the deposited object was called a 'security' or 'collateral'. If people repaid their loan on time, they got their valuables back; if not, the object was sold and the money went to the pawnshop.

- In the north of Italy, banks emerged from a system using 'promissory notes', which enabled businesspeople to conduct trade across large distances without needing to carry large sums of money. The buyer would deposit cash with a money-changer, who issued a note stating the amount, the date, the location and the buyer's name. The note could then be given to a vendor in exchange for goods and services. After that, the vendor took the note to another money-changer, who issued cash to the value stated on the note. Money-changers were paid for their services and opened offices in large cities, so that anybody could take out a promissory note to conduct business.

- The Banca Monte dei Paschi di Siena is one such office. Its headquarters is still in the bank's original premises, in a beautiful building in Siena called the Palazzo Salimbeni.

Where money grows on trees?

Banca Monte dei Paschi di Siena

127 MOST ROMAN EMPERORS WERE CLEAN-SHAVEN

Perhaps you've already noticed that most statues of **Roman emperors** have very smooth cheeks? How do you suppose they managed it, in a time without electric shavers or modern razor blades?

The Romans were marvellous inventors, so it's no surprise that they had very sharp iron blades, capable of giving the cleanest of shaves. They looked like flick knives wrapped in wood or leather, so they could be safely transported in a pocket or bag. They had already discovered soap as well, so a Roman shave was probably not very different to the way men shave today.

It isn't known exactly why Roman rulers shaved off their facial hair. Perhaps it was just more comfortable, or they did it for hygiene reasons. They might have followed the example of the Greeks, who shaved to distinguish themselves from the 'barbarians,' or people who spoke no Latin or Greek. But it might also have been a question of fashion – large beards and imposing moustaches went in and out of style back then, just like they do today. By wearing their hair

a certain way, emperors could dictate what was 'in' and what was 'out'. Historians find this particularly useful, as they can use the images of men with and without facial hair depicted on vases and other objects to help them work out the date of some artworks.

But the Romans weren't the first humans to shave. Cave paintings in Europe, Africa and Australia also contain images of clean-shaven men. It's quite possible that they used sharp shards of flint to remove their hair – they may have suffered a nick or two, but nothing that prehistoric men couldn't handle.

A Roman razor

128 CESSPITS ARE FULL OF TREASURES

Have you heard of something called a **cesspit**? Nowadays, it's a deep hole where excrement (poo and wee) is collected. But in the Middle Ages, a cesspit was much more than that. People didn't just throw in the contents of their toilets – they also got rid of old clothing, kitchen utensils, broken crockery and all sorts of other objects.

Although cesspits used to be pretty disgusting, they are real gold mines for archaeologists. An archaeologist is someone who goes in search of artefacts (relics from the past) to try to work out how people lived during certain periods in history.

Cesspits were regularly emptied of excrement when they were full (it was used as fertilizer), but many objects simply remained at the bottom of the pit. This layer of 'historic garbage' is a treasure trove for archaeologists. They can use

it to find out whether people were rich or poor, what clothes they wore and what kinds of objects they used. For example, the cesspit of a doctor or apothecary (a medieval chemist or pharmacist) might contain the tools they used for certain procedures, or the bottles and jars they used for pills, creams and other ingredients. The various bones, seeds and peels found in cesspits also give scientists an idea of what people ate in the distant past.

This is why good archaeologists never turn their noses up at a well-used cesspit!

a fascinating archaeological find!

129 ROME'S LAST EMPEROR WAS A TEENAGER

Romulus Augustulus was the name of the last Roman emperor. He was born around 461 CE and was elected as emperor by the Roman army on 30 October 475. He was barely fourteen years old, and people referred to him affectionately as 'Augustulus', which is Latin for 'little emperor'.

DO YOU HAVE ANYTHING SMALLER?

Romulus Augustulus

In 476, the German mercenaries of the Western Roman Empire rose up in rebellion and threw emperor Augustulus off the throne – he had only just turned fifteen. Augustulus was no match for the troops of general Odoacer, and tried to escape. He was taken prisoner, but the general let him live. Many sources say it was because Augustulus was a particularly handsome boy.

The young emperor even received an allowance from Odoacer, and spent the rest of his life in a palace in Naples.

130 DID THE DINOSAURS STARVE TO DEATH?

Palaeontologists are scientists who study animals and plants that lived millions of years ago. So they know a lot about the time when the world was ruled by **dinosaurs**, and have various theories about how they all died out. One theory is that the dinosaurs died of starvation.

As you probably already know, many dinosaurs were very big and strong. A diplodocus, for example, could grow up to 25 metres long and weighed 12 tonnes. These gigantic animals needed lots of food in order to survive.

And that's where the problem was. Large animals that can't find food will die very quickly, no matter how big they are.

Sixty-six million years ago, the earth was hit by a huge meteorite. Meteorites are big lumps of space rock that survive the journey through the earth's atmosphere and hit the surface – they can start out as asteroids, or even small planets.

The impact of the meteorite filled the atmosphere with an enormous dust cloud, blocking out the sun's rays for many years. The plants stopped growing and died off, leaving nothing for the **herbivores** (plant-eaters) to eat. The **carnivores** (meat-eaters) ate the herbivores for a while, but once they were all gone, the carnivores went hungry too. So it didn't take long for all the large dinosaurs to become extinct.

However, smaller animals did manage to survive, by feeding on insects or maggots. They may have been pretty hungry much of the time, but they scraped through.

The smaller dinosaurs had a better chance of survival, especially if they could fly. The front legs of many dinosaurs may have slowly evolved into wings, allowing them to search for food across a wider area. Modern-day birds are all descended from the dinosaurs!

SQUAWK

Pterodactyl

Triceratops

GRRR

Brachiosaurus

Stegosaurus

Tyrannosaurus

131 THE FIRST GLADIATORS FOUGHT AT FUNERALS

Rome, 264 BCE. Several slaves have been gathered together and are forced to fight to the death, until only one remains standing. The battle is held during the funeral ceremony of a deceased senator, as a kind of memorial service.

Historians still don't know who came up with the idea of making slaves fight one another. What they do know is that during the first 150 years of the **gladiators**, battles were only held at funerals or other ceremonies and rituals. The bloody spectacles became so popular that the phenomenon quickly spread throughout the Roman Empire. They were not forbidden by the emperor until the year 404 CE.

All the modern movies about gladiators show well-built, muscular men with enormous six-packs. That probably isn't entirely accurate: gladiators most likely had solid rugby-player builds. By our standards, they might not have been very attractive, but Roman ladies fell head-over-heels for their rugged bodies covered in scars. Roman gladiators were true sports heroes: their pictures hung in the amphitheatre passageways, and some were even immortalized as statues.

Gladiators were sometimes sent into the arena to battle animals – lions, bears or even hippos. The gladiator Carpophorus was once said to have defeated twenty wild animals in a single day.

Occasionally, famous battles from Roman history were re-enacted. There are even several stories of the Colosseum in Rome being completely filled with water, to recreate battles at sea!

One of the best-known gladiators was **Spartacus**. He was a soldier, but was taken prisoner by the Romans who sold him as a slave to a gladiator school in Capua. But Spartacus was clever, and came up with a plan that would allow him and seventy other gladiators to escape. They took to the hills, hid on the slopes of Mount Vesuvius, and worked to free many other slaves. They eventually became so numerous that they formed an army, allowing Spartacus to launch attacks against the Roman legions. Spartacus escaped defeat for some time, but in 71 BCE he was finally beaten by an army of 50,000 men led by Marcus Licinius Crassus.

132 SOME MEDIEVAL KNIGHTS WERE WOMEN

Imagine a **knight** for a moment. Did you automatically picture a man? Wrong! Women and girls could also become knights. Whenever knights died, their obligations were passed on to their entire family. If a male knight had no sons, then his wife or daughter had to take up his knightly duties.

During peacetime, these responsibilities were fairly manageable. It was the knights' job to collect taxes for the king, repair bridges here and there, and keep the peace in the local district.

But in times of war, knights were charged with defending the country and serving their king. It is unlikely that female knights ever went that far – they probably let others do the fighting for them.

Order of the Hatchet

Medieval women were a hardy bunch and even had plenty of rights – they were allowed to manage their own businesses, for example. A female knight was originally called an *equitissa*, but new names emerged during the fourteenth century: a knight's wife was called a *chevaleresse*, and a female knight was a *chevaliere*.

There were even female knightly orders, such as the Order of the Hatchet (*Orden del Hacha*) in Catalonia, Spain. The women of the region had fought hard against the Moors, and they were gifted the order as a reward. There were also religious knightly orders, such as the Order of the Blessed Virgin Mary of Mercy (*Orden de la Merced*). The women in these orders did not go to war.

A few well-known female knights fought in battle:

- **Joanna of Flanders** led a unit of around three hundred mounted soldiers in the 14th century. She was described as a woman who 'brandished a sharp sword and fought with great courage'.

- **Isabella I of Castile** and her husband successfully drove the Moors out of the south of Spain in the 15th century.

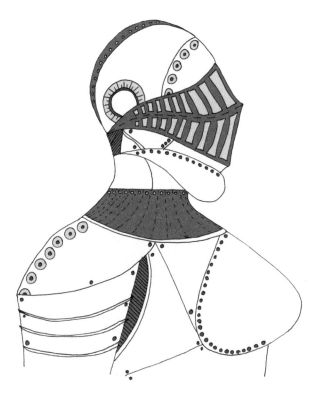

equitissa

133 THE FIRST BOOKS WERE MADE OF BAMBOO

The Chinese **writing** system was developed thousands of years ago. Originally it was used mainly to talk to the gods: priests would carve a question in the form of a drawing or a pictogram on a bone or a tortoiseshell, then throw it into a fire. As it heated up, cracks appeared in both the material and the drawings, which the priest interpreted as a message from the gods. The predictions were then written onto the bone or shell beside the cracks, and they can still be read by historians today.

Of course, bones and tortoiseshells don't really count as books. The very first books as we know them were made by joining bamboo strips together with string or rope and painting characters on them with a brush, producing a sheet that could be easily rolled up and transported. The characters told important stories that the Chinese wished to preserve, and the bamboo books were stored in temples.

Some of the books have survived, and contain the oldest known examples of any writing system that is still in use today. The Chinese language is said to have more than 100,000 different characters in total, although only 3,000 or so are used in everyday texts.

In the year 105 CE, Cai Lun – a Chinese official in the service of the emperor – made a thin material out of tree bark, hemp and silk that could be written on. He showed his invention to his ruler, who was so impressed that he gave Cai Lun a generous reward and a high status at court. From that time on, the Chinese wrote on paper instead of bamboo strips.

Printing was also invented in China, around the year 710 CE. They carved mirror images of the characters into little wooden blocks, brushed them with ink and then pressed them onto pieces of paper. That way, thousands of pages could be printed per day.

tortoiseshell picture book   bamboo book

launch of the
SS SULTANA

134 THESE PRISONERS OF WAR DIDN'T ENJOY FREEDOM FOR VERY LONG

- In the United States, a **civil war** raged between 1861 and 1865 between the Union and the Confederacy: the Union consisted of the northern states, and the Confederacy was made up of the southern states. Many prisoners of war were taken during the conflict.

- In April 1865, many of the Union prisoners of war were released, and returned home on board the SS *Sultana*. Even though the boat was only built for 376 passengers, over two thousand people were squeezed on board for the journey.

- Several days after embarking, there was a disaster on board. The boilers of the SS *Sultana* exploded and the ship caught fire. Most soldiers tried to escape the blaze by leaping overboard, but the water was ice-cold and many of the men drowned.

- That night, 1,196 men either burned to death or drowned. Afterwards it was discovered that the boiler was already broken before they left; the captain didn't have it repaired properly because he was in a hurry to set off and get paid. The captain was not among the survivors.

135 AT THE END OF THE FIRST WORLD WAR, MANY PEOPLE DIED – FROM THE FLU

The **First World War** was fought between 1914 and 1918, and took the lives of over seventeen million people. But during the final year, a strain of influenza broke out that made the catastrophe far worse. Over fifty million people died of the **Spanish flu**, and it is an astonishing fact that more soldiers were killed by the flu than by bombs or bullets.

Many people fell ill in the spring of 1918, but those cases were generally not serious. Then autumn came, and with it came a disease that was both deadly and far more contagious. It began as an ordinary cold with a fever, cough and sore throat, but soon afterwards patients developed a lung infection. Breathing became difficult, and people died very quickly after that.

Although the elderly and young children are usually most vulnerable to influenza, the victims of the Spanish flu were mainly aged from 20–40. That's because the disease was so common among soldiers: they were crammed into densely populated camps as they waited for boats to take them back home, allowing the illness to spread very quickly.

The Spanish flu spread across the globe. When that happens, the outbreak is called a 'pandemic', because it appears all over the world. Most of the pandemics in the 20th and 21st centuries have either been caused by an influenza virus or a coronavirus, such as the **Covid-19** outbreak that originated in China in 2019.

BONUS FLU FACTS

Different strains of the flu are sometimes named after the place where they originate. However, scientists are still unsure as to where this particular pandemic originated from.

Spain *was* the first country where newspapers reported the outbreak. This is why we still call this particular pandemic the Spanish flu, even though it didn't originate there.

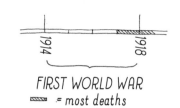

FIRST WORLD WAR
▨ = most deaths

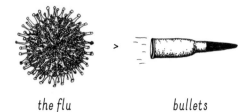

the flu   bullets

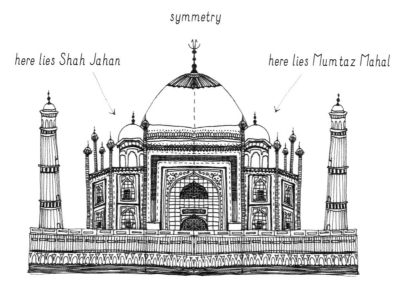

symmetry

here lies Shah Jahan

here lies Mumtaz Mahal

THE TAJ MAHAL

136 THE TAJ MAHAL IS A TOMB (AND A TRIBUTE TO LOVE)

- First and foremost, the **Taj Mahal** is an astonishingly beautiful building in India. Built entirely of white marble, it is completely symmetrical, which means the two sides match each other perfectly. If you were to fold the building down the centre, the two halves would fit onto each other exactly. The Taj Mahal is known as one of the seven 'new' wonders of the world.

- The Taj Mahal is actually a mausoleum, or a monumental tomb housing the mortal remains of a deceased person. It was built between 1632 and 1653 as the final resting place for the wife of **Shah Jahan**, then ruler of the Mughal Empire. Shah Jahan was devastated when his wife **Mumtaz Mahal** died while giving birth to their fourteenth child. That's why he built her a magnificent palace as her final resting place on earth.

- The Taj Mahal was built in the middle of a vast open landscape, so that no other nearby buildings could overshadow its splendour. In total 20,000 people worked on the Taj Mahal, and when Shah Jahan himself died, he was buried there too.

- Millions of tourists from all over the world visit this unique place every year.

137 A VOLCANO WIPED OUT POMPEII

- In the year 7 BCE, the Oscans built a village by the river Sarno. Life was good, although the leaders were constantly changing: the Etruscans, Samnites and Romans kept replacing each other as the rulers. During its Roman days especially, **Pompeii** grew into a large city with over 10,000 residents.

- Disaster struck for the first time in the year 62 CE, when Pompeii was destroyed by an earthquake. But the people rebuilt, and life went on as before. They didn't know that an even greater catastrophe was on the horizon.

- Mount Vesuvius had always stood peacefully beside the city, and the Pompeiians farmed vegetables and other crops on its slopes. They had no idea that Vesuvius was actually an active volcano, which could erupt at any moment. And that's exactly what happened on 24 August 79, when the mountain began rumbling and spewing out red-hot lava. Pompeii was covered in a thick layer of molten rock, ash and rubble. Most of the inhabitants had time to escape, but two thousand people were buried by the deluge of ash and debris. In a single day, Pompeii was wiped off the face of the earth.

- For a long time, few people remembered that the city had ever existed. It was rediscovered in the 16th century, but proper excavations didn't start until the 18th century. When the archaeologists started digging, they discovered an almost perfectly intact Roman city beneath the layers of debris. Many valuable artefacts were unearthed, and parts of the city are still being uncovered today. In recent years, however, most efforts and funding have concentrated on the preservation of the existing finds.

- There is a reason why the city remained intact: the residents of Pompeii were caught unawares by an enormous dust cloud. Those unable to escape were killed by the toxic gases and engulfed by the lava. Their bodies decomposed over the centuries, leaving behind cavities in the rock.

- Archaeologists filled the cavities with plaster, creating perfectly-shaped mannequins of the unfortunate people of Pompeii. These are now on display, and the images are beautiful but tragic: a mother desperately trying to protect her child, or people clinging together in fear...

- Around 60% of the city has now been excavated.

- Many tourists travel to Pompeii every year, to visit the ruins for themselves.

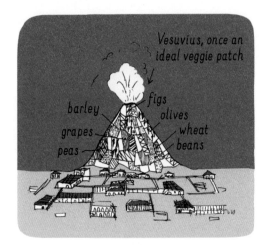

POMPEII
before 24 August 79 CE

curator aquarum

IT'S GOING SWIMMINGLY!

Roman aqueduct

138 THE ROMANS WERE EXCELLENT PLUMBERS

The **Romans** built an enormous empire, with Rome as its glorious centrepiece. But the city would never have reached its great size and influence without the gifted plumbers who helped to build it. They constructed gigantic **aqueducts** in the region to transport water to the fringes of the city, where it was then channelled to Rome's many luxurious homes, bathhouses, toilets and fountains through pipes made of wood, pottery or lead. An extensive sewer network transported the polluted water away again.

- In total, eleven aqueducts transported water from the surrounding countryside to Rome's city limits. They were built over a period of 500 years, under the supervision of 36 different emperors.

- Aqueducts were built throughout the Roman Empire. Usually they were underground, to prevent contamination by dead animals. The underground aqueducts also prevented enemies from shutting them off and depriving the cities of their water supply.

- The longest Roman aqueduct was a whopping 240 kilometres long.

- The person in charge of the aqueducts was called the *curator aquarum*. It was his job to ensure the structures were kept in working order, and that the water flowed to the right people – he was the 'chief plumber'. It was an important position: curators were appointed by the emperor, and were assigned large numbers of slaves to ensure enough manpower to inspect and maintain the aqueducts.

139 ROMAN EMPEROR CALIGULA MADE HIS HORSE AN ADVISER

Gaius Caesar Augustus Germanicus (or **Caligula** to his friends) was certainly no mister-nice-guy. He was emperor of Rome from 37 to 41 CE, and wasn't the most popular of rulers. Even historians at the time described him as a 'vengeful tyrant'.

Things started out well enough. When he first became emperor, Caligula managed to win the support of the wealthiest Romans: he promised them lower taxes, which made them happy. Caligula was also a huge fan of chariot races and gladiator battles. Under Caligula's reign, these sports became bloodier and more elaborate than ever before. The Romans liked that.

Then the emperor fell ill, and everything changed. After his recovery, Caligula revealed himself as a cruel tyrant, convinced that everyone was out to get him. He did away with both friends and enemies without wasting too many words. One day he invited King Ptolemy of Mauretania to Rome, had him assassinated during the visit and stole his kingdom.

Caligula often had people killed in order to claim their property and used their money to fuel his lavish lifestyle. The executions performed on his orders were always gruesome.

WHAT DO YOU THINK?   NEIGH!

Emperor Caligula   Consul Incitatus

He particularly liked torturing people to death – many historians believe he enjoyed the fact that people were so scared of him.

He was a lover of art, and arranged for important works to be brought to Rome. But instead of buying them, he simply gave the order to steal the statues and paintings from cities in Greece and Egypt.

Caligula often made strange decisions. Once, for example, he appointed his favourite horse Incitatus as an adviser, just to annoy the other members of the Roman government.

It should come as no surprise that Caligula ruled for only a short time. Four years after his coronation, he was murdered by a member of his own Praetorian Guard, an elite branch of the Roman army.

140 WHY ARE THERE 60 MINUTES IN AN HOUR?

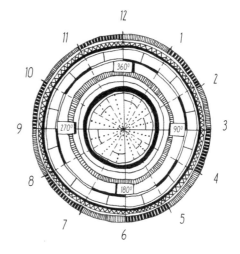

1 hour: 60 minutes
1 circle: 360 degrees

Have you ever wondered why there are 60 minutes in an hour? And why each minute has 60 seconds? It's all the Babylonians' fault.

In the early 18th century BCE, **Babylon** was ruled by king **Hammurabi**. Hammurabi tried to turn Babylon into a world centre for science. Babylonian scholars used a counting system based on groups of sixty, known as the 'sexagesimal' system. They decided that there should be 60 minutes in an hour, and also divided circles into 360 degrees. This system was later adopted by both the Greeks and the Romans.

But it was the Egyptians who decided that each day should have 24 hours: 12 hours of day and 12 hours of night. Each hour was equal to one-twelfth of the time between sunrise and sunset, and so the hours got longer and shorter with the seasons. Only on the dates of 20–21 March and 22–23 September (when day and night are the same length) were their hours exactly the same as ours are now. Years later, the clock was adjusted to make all hours the same length.

141 THE AZTECS AND THE MAYA USED CHOCOLATE AS MONEY

- Have you had chocolate coins wrapped in gold or silver foil? They're tasty but you couldn't use the coins to pay for anything. The **Maya** and the **Aztecs** did, however: these two ancient civilizations were mad about chocolate.

- To the Maya and Aztecs, cocoa beans were very valuable. They were ground into a powder, which could be used to pay for things.

- The Maya mixed cocoa powder with water to produce a frothy drink. It was quite bitter, and very different from the sweet hot chocolate that we enjoy today.

- The Aztecs made a tasty chocolate drink by adding vanilla, corn or chilli powder. They were convinced that a cup of chocolate gave enough energy to keep working all day, without needing any other sustenance. For this reason, cocoa powder was also thought to have healing properties and was used to help cure diseases.

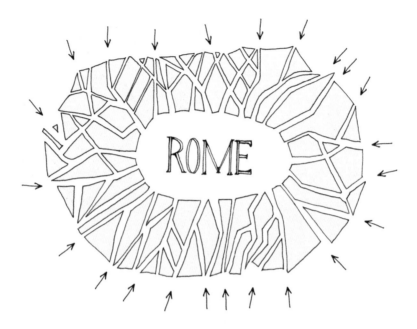

142 ALL ROADS REALLY DID LEAD TO ROME

The Romans once ruled over a very large part of the world. Their empire covered around 5 million square kilometres, and numbered around 85 million inhabitants. Rome was the centre of power, where the emperor lived.

Of course, it was important for the Romans to be able to travel to the places under their control. The sandy roads already in existence did not allow for very fast transport, so the Romans created an enormous network of paved roads leading through Africa, Europe and Asia.

Strictly speaking, the roads led *out of* Rome, not *to* Rome. The Romans ensured that the most important cities were connected to the capital via a road leading directly from their centre of power.

Many of the old Roman roads survived, and are sometimes referred to as 'military highways' as they were used mainly by the Roman armies.

If ever a revolt broke out somewhere in the vast Roman Empire, the highways allowed large groups of soldiers to be dispatched quickly. The military highways were straight roads, making them easy for the unwieldy Roman war wagons to navigate.

Historians believe that the Romans laid tens of thousands of kilometres' worth of paved roads, as well as hundreds of thousands of kilometres of sand roads. Some of these roads can still be driven on today!

BONUS FACT

The saying 'all roads lead to Rome' means there is more than one way of reaching your goal. It doesn't really matter how you get there – the outcome is the same.

143 ARE WE LIVING IN THE 'HUMAN ERA'?

The current period in the earth's history is referred to by some scientists as the Anthropocene age. *Anthropos* is Greek for 'human being', and some scientists believe we are now living in a time dominated by the influence of humankind.

Scientists have examined many layers of soil and ice, and conclude that in recent centuries, humans have had the greatest impact on the world's ecosystem. Atomic testing, pesticides and ash particles from the use of fossil fuels have changed the surface of the earth. Humans have also invented many new materials such as plastics and concrete, which have left their mark on the planet's ecology. One example of this is the 'plastic soup' in the oceans, and the small pieces of plastic that are now being found inside the stomachs of a wide variety of animals.

The term 'Anthropocene' was made popular by Paul Crutzen, a Dutch scientist who won the Nobel Prize for Chemistry. Not all scientists agree that humankind's impact on the earth is great enough to warrant the name, and many believe that in half a million years, humans' influence will be seen more as a 'significant event' rather than a new geological age.

The name 'Anthropocene' has been submitted for approval to the International Commission on Stratigraphy. It is up to them to decide on whether we have truly entered a new era.

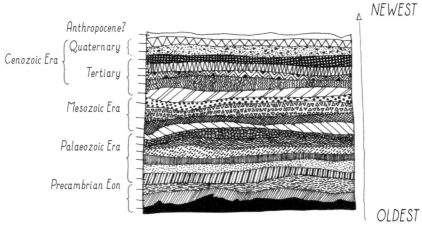

NEWEST

Anthropocene?

Cenozoic Era { Quaternary {

Tertiary

Mesozoic Era {

Palaeozoic Era {

Precambrian Eon {

OLDEST

THE EARTH

144 THE AZTECS AND THE MAYA MADE HUMAN SACRIFICES

The **Maya** lived in central America. They were a civilized people who had their own writing system, a detailed knowledge of the stars and built enormous cities. The ruins of some of those cities can still be visited today.

The Maya were constantly at war with each other. Whenever they captured enemies, it was important they were kept alive so they could be used as slaves back home. But any captured leaders weren't put to work: they were ritually sacrificed, usually at spectacular public beheadings. Later, the sacrifices became even more gruesome, when the Maya cut people's hearts out while they were still alive.

Not only men were sacrificed; sometimes the honour fell to women or children. Whenever a new king was crowned, for example, children were sacrificed during the ceremony. Historians know this because mass graves have been discovered containing the bodies of babies and infants. Mayan artworks also sometimes depict the sacrificial ceremonies themselves.

The **Aztecs** lived thousands of years after the Maya, but also made human sacrifices. Like the Maya, they often used prisoners. At the consecration of the temple in Tenochtitlan, for example, no fewer than 20,000 prisoners were forced to meet their maker. There was a great famine among the Aztecs at the time, since crops were failing due to a large disease outbreak. In addition, people were dying from bacteria and viruses introduced by the invading Europeans.

TLALOC

The Aztecs believed that they were being punished by the angry gods, who refused to let it rain so that the crops could grow. The Aztec priests were convinced that the god Tlaloc could be appeased by the tears of children, so children were first made to cry before they were sacrificed before the priest. They probably didn't need to try very hard to get the tears flowing ...

145 THE WORLD'S OLDEST TEMPLES ARE IN TURKEY

- Only twenty years ago, a farmer in Turkey discovered a very special piece of stone. It was extremely old, but had clearly been carved by human beings. Archaeologists were astounded, and the stone led to the discovery of the **Göbekli Tepe** temple complex in the Turkish region of Anatolia. The complex is an enormous religious site built 11,600 years ago, which had been buried beneath a layer of soil 3–5 metres deep.

- Many of the buildings were shaped like an oval or circle, with pillars weighing up to 50 tonnes. The columns were decorated with carvings of wild animals, including foxes, wild boars, cattle and gazelles.

- Researchers suspect that people came to visit the shrines from over 100 kilometres away, probably to ask their ancestors for good fortune when hunting and gathering food.

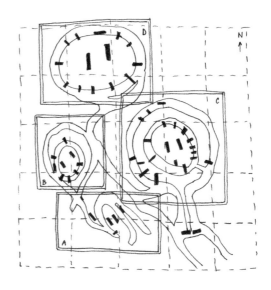

floor plan, Göbekli Tepe

146 YOUR SHOE SIZE IS DETERMINED BY A KING

If you're in Europe, you owe your shoe size to **Charlemagne** who reigned over a large part of Europe as king and emperor from 768 to 814.

Charlemagne's feet were 325 millimetres long. This size was taken as the standard, and used to produce a sizing table for shoes. The emperor was allocated size 50, and his foot length rounded up to 330 millimetres. Dividing 330 by 50 gives 6.6 millimetres, which became the official difference between one shoe size to the next.

A European whose shoe size is 37 therefore has a foot length equal to 37 × 6.6 millimetres, or 24.4 centimetres.

UK shoe sizes are based on the **barleycorn**, an old-fashioned term for one-third of an inch. A size 2 is one barleycorn larger than a size 1, and so on!

The world's tallest person, **Robert Wadlow**, wore shoes that were a European size 74. His feet were 48 centimetres long – that's nearly half a metre.

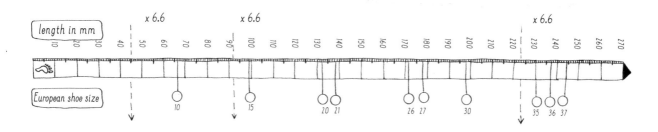

147 STUDYING PEE WAS A JOB IN THE MIDDLE AGES

Centuries ago, before the invention of modern pregnancy tests, women needed other ways to find out if they were going to have a baby. Funnily enough, the tests they used still involved urine, but not in the way you think. Women presented a sample of their urine to a **uroscoper**: a doctor who claimed to be able to determine whether a woman was pregnant just by examining her urine. Sometimes they mixed the urine with wine in order to see the results better.

Uroscopers (or 'pee-prophets') not only predicted pregnancies – they also tried to diagnose various illnesses by studying urine samples.

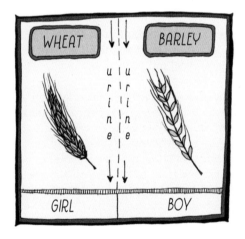

Egyptian urine test

BONUS PEE FACTS

The very first pregnancy test was developed in ancient Egypt. It was called the 'grain test', and it too involved urine. The woman was asked to urinate on grains of wheat and barley wrapped in cloth. If the barley started growing, a boy was on the way; if the wheat grew, the baby would be a girl. If nothing grew at all, the woman wasn't pregnant.

The ancient Egyptians weren't completely on the wrong track. The test was reproduced by scientists in the 1960s, and what do you know? In 70% of cases, the grain started growing if a pregnant woman urinated on it. If the woman wasn't pregnant, or if a man peed on the grain, nothing grew at all. That's because the urine of pregnant women contains certain substances that help the seeds to sprout.

ENGLISH	Monday	Tuesday	Wednesday	Thursday	Friday	Saturday	Sunday
NORSE / GERMAN		Tyr / Tiwaz	Odin / Wodan	Thor / Donar	Frigg / Frija		
LATIN	dies Lunae	dies Martis	dies Mercurii	dies Jovis	dies Veneris	dies Saturni	dies Solis
HEAVENLY BODY	moon	Mars	Mercury	Jupiter	Venus	Saturn	sun

148 THE DAYS OF THE WEEK ARE NAMED AFTER THE GODS

Have you ever wondered who named the days of the week? Well, it all begins with the Greeks and the Romans. They were the ones who divided time neatly into a system of years, months, weeks and days, which is still in use today.

To name the days, the Romans used the names they had thought up for the planets and the gods. They believed there were only seven planets: the sun (which is actually a star, but the Romans didn't know that), the moon (which isn't a planet, but they didn't know that either), Mars, Mercury, Jupiter, Venus and Saturn. These seven 'planets' together provided the names for the days of the Roman week. The names of the planets were also the names of gods.

- **Monday** was called *dies Lunae* in Latin: 'day of the moon', or Moon-day. Although the modern spelling is a little different, it is clear that we still use the same word today.

- **Tuesday** was called *dies Martis* in Latin, or the 'day of Mars'. Mars was a planet, as well as the Roman god of war. In Old High German (the language from which English evolved), the day was named after the god *Tiwaz*, or *Tyr* in Old Norse. Once you know that, it's easy to see where 'Tuesday' comes from.

- **Wednesday** was *dies Mercurii*, or 'Mercury's day' in Latin. The Germanic tribes replaced Mercury with the name of their own god *Wodan*, giving us the name 'Wednesday'.

- The same thing happened with **Thursday**. *Jovis*, or Jupiter, was both a planet and a Roman god. In Old High German, the god of thunder was *Donar*, known as *Thor* in Old Norse, which is how we ended up with 'Thor's day', or Thursday.

- **Friday** was named after Venus: *dies Veneris*. Venus was the Roman goddess of beauty and love. The Germanic tribes named the day after the goddess *Frija*, or *Frigg* in Old Norse, the first three letters of which are still in the modern name 'Friday'.

- **Saturday** is named after Saturn, which was both a planet and the Roman god of nature. There is no other name for him in Old High German, so it stayed the way it was.

- They saved the sun for last. **Sunday** is a literal translation of *dies solis*, or 'the day of the sun'.

149 THERE USED TO BE JUST TEN MONTHS IN A YEAR

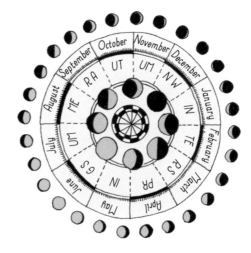

Our method for counting the **years** was invented by the ancient Greeks and Romans. But they only put ten months in the calendar: March was the first month, and December was the last. The period in between was simply called 'wintertime'. It seems like the Greeks and Romans hated winter so much, they didn't even bother to give it a proper name.

Eventually they did decide to name the winter months, and it was agreed they should be called January and February. So February officially became the end of the year, and because it was the final month, it just got whatever days were left over.

February has fewer days than the other months, in order to ensure a total of 365. For the earth to start every year in the same place relative to the sun and stars, the year needs to contain 365 days (more or less).

Februare means 'purification' in Latin, and it was the time when people cleaned their houses before starting a 'fresh' new year.

150 CASUALTIES OF WORLD WAR II

- The war between Germany and Russia took the lives of ten million Russian soldiers and fourteen million Russian citizens.

- The Russian army was also known as the **Red Army**. The soldiers weren't well-trained, and their equipment was of very poor quality. Hitler sent in three million German soldiers, who destroyed the country. Homes and farms were burned down, and factories razed to the ground. Ordinary Russians no longer had roofs over their heads, and the lack of farms meant they were also starving. The Germans were also fully prepared to kill any Russians they encountered along the way.

- According to Chinese reports, twenty million of their soldiers and citizens died during the war. The Japanese attacked the country in 1937;

the Chinese had slipshod weaponry and were poorly schooled in combat. Some even still fought with swords, which are pretty useless against enormous tanks. The Imperial Japanese army *was* very well-trained, however, and they killed a large number of soldiers and civilians.

STOP!

- The Japanese surrendered when the Americans dropped atomic bombs on the cities of **Hiroshima** and **Nagasaki**, which instantly put an end to the Second World War.

151 THE HUNS LIVED ON HORSEBACK

Nobody knows exactly where the **Huns** came from. They arrived in Europe around the fourth century CE, and forged an empire that stretched from the Ural Mountains in the east to the Rhine in the West, and from the Danube in the north to the Baltic sea in the south. According to the Romans, the Huns spent most of their time on horseback. They ate, fought, slept and held negotiations, always seated on the backs of their small, fast horses. Some accounts even say that the Huns felt dizzy if they stood on solid ground!

ZZZ   ATTACK!   YUM!

a Hun's life

The Huns formed an enormous army under **Attila the Hun,** who was their leader from 434 until 453. Attila attacked the Roman empire in both the east and the west, and also tried to conquer Gallia (modern-day France) and attacked Italy. He failed to conquer Rome, however.

Attila's nickname was 'the scourge of God'. People were terrified of him, and it was even said that 'no grass grew wherever Attila had walked.'

It is unclear exactly how Attila met his end. One story tells of a night of drunken revelry, when Attila supposedly choked on his own blood. In another legend, one of his lovers murdered him in a fit of jealous rage.

Many of the Huns returned to Asia after Attila's death, while others stayed in Europe and started families with the local population. Who knows – maybe you're a descendant of the Huns?

152 NAPOLEON WASN'T SHORT

People often think that the French emperor **Napoleon** was very short. But that's not true: Napoleon was 1.68 metres tall, quite a normal height for the time. So why did he look so tiny in all the pictures? There are several good reasons why.

- Napoleon chose his bodyguards by height: they had to be tall, in order to defend him properly. Unfortunately, their looming presence made Napoleon look shorter than he actually was.

- There's another reason why people thought Napoleon was short. The English and the French once used different units of measurement: an English 'foot' was roughly 30 centimetres, or slightly shorter than a French foot, which was 32 centimetres. The English didn't particularly like the French, and so they always gave the height of the French emperor in English feet as it made Napoleon seem shorter.

- Napoleon Bonaparte thought he was the most important man in the whole world, and proclaimed himself emperor of France. He introduced the 'Napoleonic code', a set of civil laws that are still in force in France today. He also invented the Civil Registry where all births, deaths and marriages are recorded, and introduced a universal system of measurement that included kilograms, metres and litres.

- Napoleon was said to always carry chocolate with him during battles, so that he would have enough energy to keep going. On 18 June 1815, however, he lost the **Battle of Waterloo** – perhaps he'd run out of chocolate? After that, he was banished from Europe and never returned.

BONUS NAPOLEON FACT

In France, it is still forbidden by law to name your pig 'Napoleon'.

1.68 m

Napoleon and his bodyguards

153 HATSHEPSUT WAS A FEMALE PHARAOH

Hatshepsut was a queen who lived in ancient Egypt. She was the chief wife of Pharaoh **Thutmose II**, and later became one of Egypt's rare female pharaohs. The name Hatshepsut means 'the first among women'.

Hatshepsut ruled over ancient Egypt for more than 20 years. By doing so, people thought she was behaving like a man, which is why she was often depicted with a man's upper body and wearing men's clothing. In some illustrations, she is even shown wearing a beard!

It was extremely uncommon for women to become pharaohs, but Egypt experienced a period of wealth and prosperity during her reign.

6

OUR BEAUTIFUL PLANET

154 OVER HALF THE WORLD LIVES IN ASIA

- The largest **continent** on earth is **Eurasia**. A continent is a continuous, connected piece of land surrounded by ocean. Using this definition, the earth has six continents: Eurasia (which includes Europe and Asia), Africa, North America, South America, Antarctica and Australia.

- The world is commonly divided into seven large geopolitical regions: Asia, Africa, Europe, North America, South America, Antarctica and Oceania. Using this system, a 'region' is a part of the world with its own distinctive culture and history. So continents and regions don't always share the same boundaries.

- Asia takes up around one-third of the world's habitable surface area, or roughly 44 million square kilometres. To the west, Asia shares borders with Europe and Africa. The Arctic Ocean lies to the north, the Pacific Ocean to the east, and the Indian Ocean to the south.

- Approximately 60% of the world's population lives in Asia. That's over four billion people, spread out across fifty countries. Some countries lie in multiple geographic regions: Armenia, Azerbaijan, Cyprus, Georgia, Kazakhstan, Russia and Turkey are considered to straddle both Asia and Europe; Egypt is located in both Asia and in Africa, and Indonesia and East Timor count as both Asia and Oceania.

BONUS REGION FACTS

Africa is the world's second-largest geographic region, and covers around 30 million km².

North America's surface area is around 25 million km².

South America is the fourth-largest, at 18 million km².

The surface area of Antarctica is around 14 million km².

Europe is the smallest of the continents and regions, at only 10 million km². It's only slightly larger than the whole of Canada, which is a single country in itself!

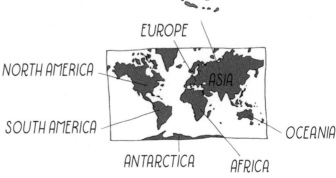

EUROPE
NORTH AMERICA
ASIA
SOUTH AMERICA
OCEANIA
ANTARCTICA
AFRICA

155 LIQUID FRESH WATER MAKES UP LESS THAN 1% OF ALL THE WATER ON EARTH

- The earth has lots of **water** – so much that our world is also known as the 'blue planet'. In total the earth has at least 1.3 billion km³ of water, spread out across the oceans, seas, rivers, lakes, groundwater, polar icecaps, and glaciers. Taken together, an estimated 70.9% of the Earth's surface is covered with water.

- Most of the earth's water is in the oceans (97%). The Pacific Ocean contains the most water: 707 million km³. The next biggest oceans are the Atlantic Ocean (323 million km³) and the Indian Ocean (284 million km³). Of course these are only estimates, as the volumes are very difficult to calculate precisely.

- The water in the oceans is salt water. To survive, humans and animals need fresh water, which makes up only a small proportion of all the water on earth (2.5%). And most of *that* water is frozen, so only 1% of all the water on earth is fresh water in liquid form. That's less than one litre in every hundred.

- Our bodies are 55–60% water, and cannot survive without it. So the preservation of our planet's rivers and lakes is literally a matter of life and death. We must take good care of them to make sure that everybody has enough to drink.

approx. 70.9% water
1% liquid fresh water

PERCENTAGE OF WATER ON EARTH

BONUS WATER FACT

One-fifth of all the fresh water on earth is contained in Lake Baikal in Russia, which freezes solid in the winter. This enormous lake is home to the Baikal seal, one of the only seal species capable of surviving in fresh water.

COUNTRY	POPULATION	SIZE
Vatican City	approx. 830	approx. 0.44 km²
Nauru	approx. 10,000	approx. 21 km²
Tuvalu	approx. 10,000	approx. 26 km²
Palau	approx. 21,000	approx. 466 km²
San Marino	approx. 30,500	approx. 61 km²

156 THE POPULATION OF THE WORLD'S SMALLEST COUNTRY CAN EASILY FIT INTO A FOOTBALL STADIUM

- The world's least populous country is Vatican City, which lies in the centre of Rome and is home to approximately 830 people. Vatican City is an independent state led by the Pope. They even have their own Euro coins.

- The islands of Nauru and Tuvalu are second and third on the list, each with about 10,000 inhabitants. Tuvalu is in the middle of the Pacific Ocean, and is one of the most isolated locations on earth. The Republic of Nauru is also in the Pacific Ocean and is part of Micronesia, a collection of over two thousand tropical islands.

- Palau, an island not far from Nauru, is home to roughly 16,000 inhabitants and is the fourth smallest country in the world.

- Lastly, the Republic of San Marino is located in the middle of Italy and is an independent country in itself, with a population of around 30,500.

The top 5 list is a little different if you look at the surface area of each country.

- Vatican City remains the smallest country in the world, with an area of 0.44 km².

- Next is Monaco, which is only 2.02 km² in size.

- Nauru (21 km²), Tuvalu (26 km²) and San Marino (61 km²) take up the last three spots on the list.

157 THE BIGGEST HAILSTONE EVER WAS ALMOST THE SIZE OF A FOOTBALL

On 23 July 2010, a heavy storm raged in Vivian, a small town in South Dakota in the United States. Things got very exciting when it started to hail, and huge – no, gigantic – **hailstones** fell from the sky, causing extensive damage.

- One of the hailstones had a diameter of 20 centimetres and weighed nearly a whole kilogram. So forget your umbrella – time to put on a helmet!

- Hailstones form in the atmosphere when small ice crystals come into contact with large, cold water droplets. In the top part of a rain cloud the temperature is about -20 °C, and that's where the ice crystals are. Lower down in the same cloud the temperature is somewhere between -10 and -20 °C. Here is where the ice-cold rain droplets form, which slowly transform into minuscule ice crystals. As the air in the cloud rises and falls, the ice crystals collide over and over with the droplets and slowly grow larger and larger. Eventually they form into

hailstones, and when they get too heavy for the rising winds to support, the stones plummet to the ground. The stronger the winds, the larger the hailstones can become before they fall.

- Slice a hailstone through its centre, and you will see that it consists of multiple layers. The milky, opaque rings are the sections that froze instantly at high altitude; the clear, transparent rings are made of liquid water that collected at lower altitudes and didn't freeze until the stone was swept higher up into the cloud.

- Hailstones can also have little lumps on them – these are smaller hailstones that have collided with the larger stone and frozen onto it.

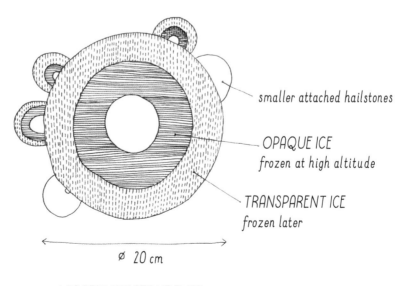

smaller attached hailstones

OPAQUE ICE
frozen at high altitude

TRANSPARENT ICE
frozen later

⌀ 20 cm

LARGEST HAILSTONE EVER

158 THE WORLD'S TALLEST MOUNTAIN NEARLY ALWAYS HAS ITS HEAD IN THE CLOUDS

- **Mount Everest** is the tallest **mountain** in the world, and is one of the Himalayan mountains on the borders of Nepal and Tibet. Its summit is a stupendous 8,848 metres above sea level. It got its name from the Royal Geographic Society, when Mr Andrew Waugh proposed naming it after Sir George Everest, who was once the president of the institute that took the original measurements of the mountain.

- The Nepalese people, of course, knew about the mountain a long time before the Royal

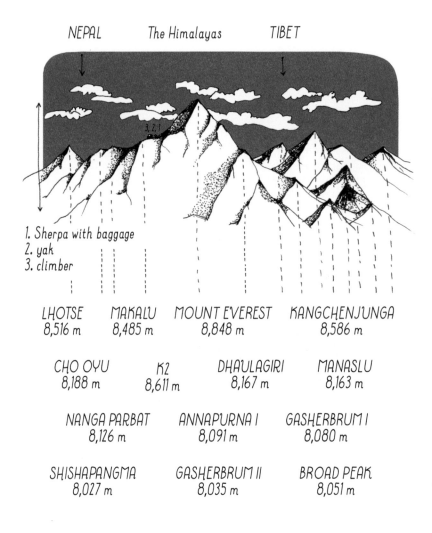

NEPAL   The Himalayas   TIBET

1. Sherpa with baggage
2. yak
3. climber

LHOTSE
8,516 m

MAKALU
8,485 m

MOUNT EVEREST
8,848 m

KANGCHENJUNGA
8,586 m

CHO OYU
8,188 m

K2
8,611 m

DHAULAGIRI
8,167 m

MANASLU
8,163 m

NANGA PARBAT
8,126 m

ANNAPURNA I
8,091 m

GASHERBRUM I
8,080 m

SHISHAPANGMA
8,027 m

GASHERBRUM II
8,035 m

BROAD PEAK
8,051 m

Geographic Society turned up. They had their own names for it, including Sagarmatha and Chomolungma.

- Many different countries attempted to work out the exact height of the mountain, and an agreement was not reached until 2010. From that point on, Everest's height was officially set at 8,848 metres.

- Each year, many mountain climbers set out to conquer Mount Everest. There are two long routes to the top: one passing through Nepal to the south-east (the standard route) and one via Tibet in the north.

- It is not entirely clear who was the first to reach the top of Mount Everest. British mountain climbers George Mallory and Andrew Irvine supposedly reached the summit together on 8 June 1924, but unfortunately they had an accident on the way down and never returned. Mallory's body was not discovered until 1999, neatly packed in the mountain ice.

- New Zealand climber Edmund Hillary and the Sherpa Tenzing Norgay were officially the first men to reach the top and return alive. They did so on 29 May 1953.

BONUS MOUNTAIN FACTS

- Climbers of Everest are always accompanied by a Sherpa, a member of the Tibetan people living to the south of the Greater Himalayas, the highest part of the Himalayan mountain range. The Sherpa are especially good climbers, carriers and mountain guides.

- The world's tallest mountain is actually not Mount Everest, but Mauna Kea in Hawaii. It measures 10,200 metres from base to summit, but the mountain fell victim to some bad luck. The bottom of it lies beneath the ocean, so its peak is 'only' 4,207 metres above sea level – and those are the only metres that count. On the plus side, Mauna Kea is more than just a mountain: it's also a dormant volcano.

- There is very little life on Mount Everest. At 6,840 metres, the only plant life left is moss, and at 6,700 metres, only one animal can still be found: a tiny species of spider called *Euophrys omnisuperstes,* or the Himalayan jumping spider.

- Yaks are often used to help carry the climbers' equipment. Yaks are pack animals that can carry up to 100 kilograms of baggage. They also have thick fur and big lungs, and can easily climb up to great heights.

- Mount Everest has already claimed many victims – almost 300 climbers have already lost their lives trying to reach the top, either by falling down the slopes or succumbing to altitude sickness. Because there is less oxygen in the air at high altitudes, climbers can experience nausea and headaches, and feel generally unwell. In some cases, they even start hallucinating and lose consciousness.

- Sadly, climbers always leave lots of rubbish behind on Mount Everest. For this reason, famous Nepalese mountain climber Apa Sherpa organized a special expedition to collect and remove thousands of kilograms of litter.

159 ASIA IS THE WORLD CHAMPION OF TALL MOUNTAINS

There are fourteen **mountains** on earth whose peaks are more than 8,000 metres above sea level. They are all situated along the ridge where two tectonic plates meet, or where the continent of Eurasia pushes against the Indian subcontinent (with countries such as Bangladesh, Pakistan, Sri Lanka and parts of Nepal, Bhutan, Myanmar and China).

1. Mount Everest: 8,848 metres
2. K2: 8,611 metres
3. Kangchenjunga: 8,586 metres
4. Lhotse: 8,516 metres
5. Makalu: 8,485 metres
6. Cho Oyu: 8,188 metres
7. Dhaulagiri: 8,167 metres
8. Manaslu: 8,163 metres
9. Nanga Parbat: 8,126 metres
10. Annapurna I: 8,091 metres
11. Gasherbrum I: 8,080 metres
12. Broad Peak: 8,051 metres
13. Gasherbrum II: 8,035 metres
14. Shishapangma: 8,027 metres

Almost all of these mountains are part of the Himalayan and Karakoram mountains – two enormous ranges extending across the border regions of Pakistan, India, China and Afghanistan.

Fact 89 contains more information on Reinhold Messner, who was the first person to climb every one of the 'eight-thousanders'.

160 THE LONGEST PLACE NAME IN EUROPE IS LLANFAIRPWLLGWYNGYLLGOGERYCH WYRNDROBWLLLLANTYSILIOGOGOGOCH …

Try pronouncing it – it's like a one-word tongue-twister! The town is situated on the island of Anglesey in **Wales**, and the inhabitants usually shorten it to Llanfair PG, or Llanfairpwll. Literally translated, the name means: 'St Mary's church in the hollow of the white hazel near to the fierce whirlpool of St Tysilio of the red cave'.

The town didn't get such a long name by accident. In 1860, the people in charge wanted the town's train station to have the longest name in the country. Their plan was to attract more tourists, who could come and have their passports stamped at the visitor centre. That's why they changed the original name of 'Llanfair Pwllgwyngyll' into the much longer Llanfairpwllgwyngyllgogerych wyrndrobwllllantysiliogogogoch. Their plan worked: even now, tourists travel there in large numbers to have their picture by the incredibly long sign at the train station.

LLANFAIRPWLLGWYN
GYLLGOGERYCH
WYRNDROBWLL
LLANTYSILIO
GOGOGOCH

HA! WE BEAT YOU!

161 ... BUT THE OFFICIAL NAME OF BANGKOK IS EVEN LONGER

- **Bangkok** is the capital city of Thailand. But the name 'Bangkok' is only the short version: officially the city is called Krung Thep Mahanakhon Amon Rattanakosin Mahinthara Ayutthaya Mahadilok Phop Noppharat Ratchathani Burirom Udomratchaniwet Mahasathan Amon Piman Awatan Sathit Sakkathattiya Witsanukam Prasit. Imagine trying to fit that on a signpost! The name means 'The city of angels, the great city, the residence of the Emerald Buddha, the impregnable city (unlike Ayutthaya) of God Indra, the grand capital of the world endowed with nine precious gems, the happy city, abounding in an enormous Royal Palace that resembles the heavenly abode where reigns the reincarnated god, a city given by Indra and built by Vishnukarn.' What a mouthful! And all the schoolchildren in Bangkok need to learn it off by heart!

- The second-longest place name in the world is the village of Tetaumatawhakatangihan gakoauaotamateaurehaeaturipukapihima unga-horonukupokaiwhenuaakitanarahu in New Zealand. The name comes from the Maori, the original inhabitants of New Zealand, and it means 'The summit where Tamatea – the man with the large knees, the slider, climber of mountains and land-swallower who travelled about – played his nose-flute to his beloved.' A little long-winded perhaps, but a very beautiful name nonetheless!

162 LIGHTNING BOLTS ARE SUPER HOT!

- Inside storm clouds, tiny ice crystals are constantly moving from top to bottom and vice versa. The friction of this up-and-down motion eventually means that the top of the cloud becomes positively charged, and the bottom becomes negatively charged.

- Most **lightning** flashes happen inside clouds themselves. But sometimes the ground beneath a cloud takes on a positive charge, due to the negatively charged storm cloud above it.

- If the difference in polarity between the earth and the cloud becomes too great, electrons travel from the lower, negatively charged part of the cloud towards the ground. This movement of electrons is called a 'leader'. If the electrons reach earth, they cause a bolt of lightning. If you see a lightning bolt with various branches, that means they are running from the earth to the cloud, and not the other way around. Only one-fifth of all lightning flashes occur between the clouds and the ground.

- Lightning is incredibly hot and can reach temperatures of up to 30,000 °C – that's five times hotter than the surface of the sun.

- Because of the intense heat, the air surrounding the lightning bolt expands very quickly, creating a loud explosion in the atmosphere that reaches our ears as thunder.

163 SUMMER EQUALS STORMY WEATHER

The hotter it is outside, the greater the chance of **stormy** weather.

- Warm weather produces small clouds with fluffy edges. These are called *cumulus humilis*.

- These clouds can grow into enormous, puffy white clouds called *cumulus mediocris*.

- Sometimes they take on a more menacing colour. That means they have become *cumulus congestus* clouds.

- Rain, or 'precipitation', doesn't form until the cloud takes on the characteristic 'cauliflower' appearance of rain clouds. These clouds are called *cumulonimbus*: they can sometimes reach altitudes of 10–20 kilometres, and are very dark at the bottom. There is lots of activity inside a cumulonimbus cloud – vertical currents in both directions can produce small balls of ice, which fall to the earth as hailstones.

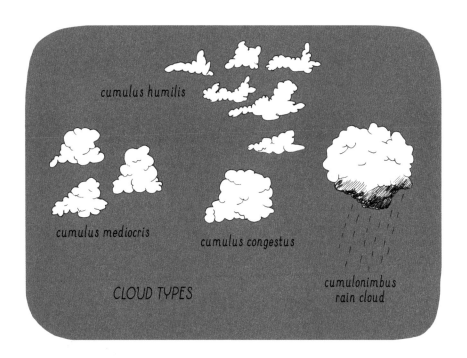

cumulus humilis

cumulus mediocris

cumulus congestus

cumulonimbus
rain cloud

CLOUD TYPES

- Storm clouds can occasionally be enormous, covering areas of up to 5,000 km². That's when you need to be careful, since air pressure can drop and cause a major storm.

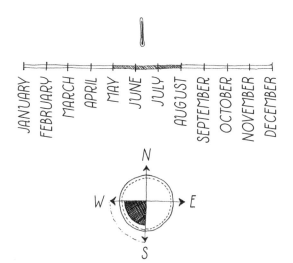

BONUS STORM FACTS

On average, lightning strikes the earth a hundred times per second.

The Empire State Building, a tall skyscraper in New York City, is struck by lightning 23 times a year on average.

Lightning bolts travel at 60,000 kilometres per second.

If lightning strikes ground that's rich in quartz, it can produce what is called a fulgurite – a tube-shaped column of molten sand in the shape of a lightning bolt. They occur mostly in soil with a high sand content.

164 OCEANIA IS HOME TO SOME REALLY STRANGE CREATURES

Oceania is the world's smallest continent, and includes Australia, New Zealand and a bunch of smaller islands. Because the islands in Oceania are so isolated, this part of the world is home to many animal species that are found nowhere else on earth.

The area's unique creatures include ordinary mammals (those with a womb that give birth to live young), marsupials (with a pouch), and even mammals that lay eggs (called monotremes). But because they all have mammary glands and suckle their young, they all fall under the category of mammals. There are also many unique bird species in the region.

ORDINARY MAMMALS

- Dingoes are an Australian species of wild dog, and probably evolved from Indian wolves. They reproduce several times a year and live in packs, just like wolves do.

- The grey-headed flying fox is an ace flier: it's a bat with a wingspan up to a metre wide. They normally appear at dusk, when they leave their hiding places in search of food.

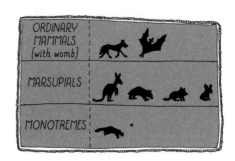

MARSUPIALS

- The kangaroo is the national symbol of Australia, where more than fifty million kangaroos live, divided into over 60 species. They are marsupials with incredibly long hind feet that enable them to jump around with enormous bounds. The largest species is the red kangaroo, which can weigh up to 90 kilograms. Its young, however, are not much longer than a centimetre when they are born – after emerging, they first crawl into their mother's pouch, where they continue to develop for about nine months.

- The wombat's pouch faces backwards. Wombats dig burrows in the ground, so if their pouch faced the front it would become full of sand and dirt, and its young would suffocate and die.

- Tasmanian devils can only be found in Tasmania, an island off the south coast of the Australian mainland. They are small animals with black-and-white fur that live among the boulders in rocky areas. The animals unfortunately fell prey to a serious epidemic and nearly became extinct, but thankfully the Australians have now set up breeding programmes for Tasmanian devils, allowing their numbers to increase once more. The animal's name is no coincidence – they are very fierce and really do fight like the devil!

- Koalas may very well be the cutest animals on earth: their round, fluffy heads make them look just like teddy bears. Still it's wiser to keep a safe distance, since both Mr and Mrs Koala have sharp claws and have been known to bite. But that only happens when they're awake, which isn't very often – koalas usually sleep in trees for around 22 hours a day!

MONOTREMES: EGG-LAYING MAMMALS

- The platypus is one of the most curious animals in the world. It is a monotreme, or a mammal that lays eggs. The platypus looks a bit like it has been cobbled together using other animal parts: it has a body like a mole, but the tail of a beaver and the beak of a duck!

BIRDS

- The southern cassowary can grow up to 190 centimetres tall and weigh up to 85 kilos. It has a blue neck, and a glorious crest on top of its head. Because of its size, it is a flightless bird.

165 WIND IS CAUSED BY THE SUN

Sounds weird, right? Read on to find out how.

- **Wind** is created when air moves from one place to another. But this doesn't just happen randomly.

- To get wind, you need the sun. The sun heats up the air; as the air gets hotter, it rises. Just think of a hot-air balloon, which ascends into the sky when the air inside it is heated up.

- New air must come in to replace the air that has risen up. This air will always be cooler than the air that moved upwards. So as the hot air rises, the cooler air flows in to replace it – this is the sideways motion that we perceive as wind.

- Air flowing at very high speeds can cause a storm or a hurricane. That's when large amounts of hot air rise very suddenly, and are replaced by powerful gushes of cold air. All that air moving at once results in gale-force winds.

- The air around us is constantly in motion, always blowing this way and that. That's why the weather is always changing from day to day!

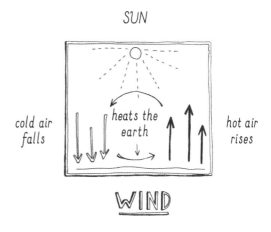

166 THE NILE IS THE LONGEST RIVER IN THE WORLD

The **Nile** is 6,650 kilometres long. The **Amazon** is a very close second at 6,400 kilometres, but does win the prize for the river containing the most water on earth.

- The source of the Nile was unknown for a long time. Now we know that in fact it has two sources. The Blue Nile originates from Lake Tana in Ethiopia, while the White Nile starts in Lake Victoria: a lake that is so large, parts of it lie in three different African countries (Uganda, Kenya and Tanzania). The two branches of the river come together in Khartoum, the capital city of Sudan. From there, the Nile's course continues through Egypt, where it empties into the Mediterranean Sea.

- The Amazon is in South America, and originates high in the mountains of Peru. It flows through Brazil, and eventually empties into the Atlantic Ocean. A long section of the river flows through the Amazon rainforest, where it can become up to 40 kilometres wide during the rainy season. By the time it reaches the Atlantic, the Amazon contains the water from 1,100 smaller rivers (called 'tributaries').

BONUS AMAZON FACT

The explorer **Francisco de Orellana** was sailing along the river, when poison arrows suddenly flew at his ships. To Francisco's surprise, the arrows were being shot by women. He called them 'Amazons', after the female warriors of Greek mythology, and the river has been known by that name ever since.

167 HURRICANES USED TO BE NAMED AFTER WOMEN

Hurricanes are storms with a wind speed of over 12 knots. Another name for a hurricane is a cyclone or typhoon.

- Hurricanes originate in tropical or sub-tropical areas, and are always made up of three parts: the eye, the eye wall and the rain bands. The eye is the centre of the hurricane and is usually 30–65 kilometres wide, but can sometimes be as wide as 200 kilometres. The eye of the storm is peaceful – there is no wind and it is eerily still.

- The eye is surrounded by the eye wall, where there is lots of rain and incredibly high winds. The wall is the part of the hurricane that causes the most damage.

- The eye wall is surrounded by the rain bands, where there is both rain and wind, but less than inside the actual wall.

- Hurricanes occur in particular regions of the world, and form at certain times of year. These times are referred to as 'hurricane season'.

- Humans have been naming hurricanes for a long time. Originally they used names of people they didn't like, or the name-days of saints on which the hurricane occurred. From 1953 on, only women's names were used, based on the unfair idea that 'hurricanes were as unpredictable as women'. The names were given in alphabetical order each year.

- The World Meteorological Organization (which named the hurricanes) eventually realized that using only women's names for devastating storms wasn't particularly nice, so since 1979, men's and women's names have been used alternately. Six years' worth of lists have been drawn up, which are re-used in a cycle, so the same names crop up every six years. Names beginning with the letters Q, U, X, Y and Z are not chosen.

- In 2020, the names of the hurricanes were: Arthur, Bertha, Cristobal, Dolly, Edouard, Fay, Gonzalo, Hanna, Isaias, Josephine, Kyle, Laura, Marco, Nana, Omar, Paulette, Rene, Sally, Teddy, Vicky and Wilfred.

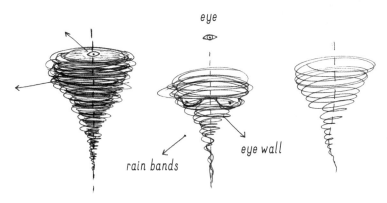

eye

rain bands

eye wall

PARTS OF A HURRICANE

168 THE OCEAN FLOOR IS MADE OF PLASTIC

At least, that's what it looks like. Every square kilometre of the **ocean floor** is covered in no less than 70 kilos of **plastic waste**. Of all the plastic that ends up in the sea, 80% flows in from the land and includes plastic bottles, bags and other forms of packaging.

The ocean currents carry a very large proportion of the plastic (70%) to an area called the 'Great Pacific Garbage Patch' or the 'Pacific Trash Vortex', which has been estimated at three times the size of Spain. The plastic is extremely harmful to animals in the ocean, as they can easily choke or become trapped in it. The plastic swallowed by fish, tortoises, seals and other marine animals can cause digestive problems, illness or even death.

Animals can also get stuck inside pieces of plastic, sustaining deep cuts or other injuries. Sometimes they become so entangled that they drown, starve or can no longer swim properly, making them easy prey for other animals.

Want to help reduce the amount of plastic in the oceans? Then help to keep the beaches tidy: on average, every square kilometre of beach contains around two tonnes of plastic. The sea and the shore are constantly swapping their rubbish, in a sense. So keeping the beaches clean helps to keep the water clean!

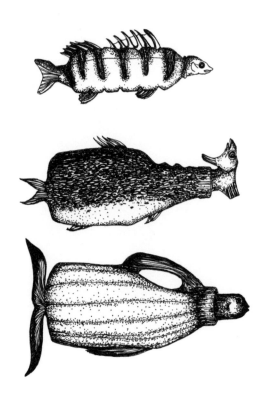

BONUS PLASTIC FACTS

Plastic doesn't decompose. But the movement of the ocean does break it up into smaller pieces, forming a kind of plastic layer on the surface that can be very problematic. To help discourage the use of plastic, many supermarkets now charge for plastic bags. So bringing your own shopping bag doesn't just help save the planet, but saves you money as well!

Thankfully, there are large companies helping to create solutions. Do you know those pieces of plastic used to hold cans together? They are like six plastic rings all joined up, with one can fitting into each ring. These 'six-pack rings' have already wreaked havoc on marine life. A brewery in the United States, called the Saltwater Brewery, has invented a solution: edible six-pack rings made of organic, compostable products such as wheat and barley. Not only do the rings eventually dissolve in water, they can also be eaten by many animals in the ocean. Now that's smart!

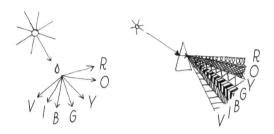

169 RAINBOWS HAVE NO BEGINNING AND NO END

- **Rainbows** are actually shaped like circles, which have no beginning and no end. So when you look at a rainbow, you're actually only seeing half of it – the other half lies below the horizon. Only when viewed from a mountaintop or an aeroplane, when the earth isn't in the way, can the entire circular rainbow be seen.

- Rainbows appear when the sun shines during rainy or humid weather. Normally sunlight reaches our eyes as white or yellow light, but it actually includes many different colours that together make up the 'visible spectrum'. When the sun shines through rain, the droplets break up the light into its separate colours, making them visible to our eyes.

- The colours always appear in the same order: red, orange, yellow, green, blue, indigo, violet. The first letter of each colour spells a funny name – ROY G. BIV – making the order easy to remember.

- Very rarely, a double rainbow will appear, one above the other. This is only possible when the sunlight hits the raindrops in a special way. The second rainbow is always less clear than the first one, and in this case the order of colours is reversed.

Now that you know a rainbow is a circle, you understand why there can be no pot of gold waiting at the end!

WOW!

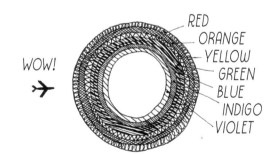

RED
ORANGE
YELLOW
GREEN
BLUE
INDIGO
VIOLET

My name is Ichthy, not Nessie!

Ichthyosaurus

170 THERE'S A MONSTER IN SCOTLAND (BUT NOT IN LOCH NESS)

You've probably heard the legend of the **Loch Ness Monster**: a huge dinosaur-like creature supposedly hiding somewhere in the depths of Loch Ness, a huge lake in Scotland. The monster (or 'Nessie' as she's sometimes called) is most probably a myth. Tourists still travel in their thousands to Loch Ness in the hopes of getting a glimpse, but scientists are now pretty certain that there's no dinosaur swimming around in the lake.

Still, a real monster did once live in Scotland. Admittedly, it was 170 million years ago, at a time when our planet was still home to many enormous land and sea-dwelling creatures.

The Scottish monster was a marine reptile, or Icthyosaurus: it was around 4 metres long, with a round head and hundreds of razor-sharp teeth in its jaws. Not something you want to run into when you're taking a swim!

The monster's remains were discovered in 1966 on the Isle of Skye, trapped inside layers of rock that took a long time for archaeologists to excavate. Ichthyosaurus looked a little bit like a dolphin, but was nowhere near as friendly.

171 THE 'STEAMBOAT GEYSER' IS TALLER THAN A FIFTEEN-STOREY BUILDING

- **Geysers** are an impressive natural phenomenon. At some places on earth, water is heated up by geothermal energy from the ground. The result is often an ordinary hot spring where the water bubbles up slowly to

the surface, creating a nice pool where you can enjoy a warm bath. Occasionally, however, the water boils and quickly expands, shooting up through vents, many metres into the air. These vertical hot-water jets are called geysers.

- There are six main regions in the world where geysers form: the United States, Iceland, New Zealand, Russia, Chile and Alaska. At other places in the world, geysers only occur individually, not in groups.

- Yellowstone National Park in the United States has the most geysers of any region in the world, with hundreds of places where the water occasionally shoots out of the ground with tremendous force. Yellowstone also has the world's tallest geyser: named the 'Steamboat Geyser', its jet of water can reach heights of up to 90 metres. Steamboat is not always active, however, and the wait for a water jet ranges from four days to fifty years!

- Luckily, the park also contains another, far more active geyser. Nicknamed 'Old Faithful', it shoots out a water jet roughly every thirty minutes. It may be less impressive than Steamboat, but it's certainly far more reliable.

WHOOSHHH!

WHOOSH!

172 EUROPE'S OLDEST LIVING INHABITANT IS ... A PINE TREE

The oldest living thing in Europe is over 1,075 years old. It's a **Bosnian pine tree**, and grows in Greece.

HELLO, OLD FRIEND!

1,075 years

Adonis

- Tree experts drilled a hole into the tree and removed a piece of its trunk. By counting the rings, they worked out exactly how old it was.

- The tree has certainly lived through some troubled times. Storms and wars have raged around it, yet still it remains standing.

- The researchers have named the tree 'Adonis', which means 'handsome one'.

- The tree stands high up in the Pindus mountains, surrounded by a few friends who have also been around for more than a thousand years. Imagine if trees could talk! The stories these ones could tell...

173 THE EARTH IS WARMING UP FASTER THAN EVER BEFORE

The **climate** on earth has changed a lot over the course of its history. There have been ice ages, droughts, and also periods of thousands or millions of years when the temperature was above average. That's why some people think the climate-change debate is all a bunch of nonsense, saying that it's a natural process and that humans can't do anything to stop it. Most scientists, however, now agree that there's more going on than just a 'natural process'. The earth is currently warming up much faster than ever before, and not because of volcanic eruptions or changes to the sun's activity. The climate is changing because humans are changing it.

- Human civilization needs energy. Lots of energy. We use it to drive our cars, travel by aeroplane, generate light, heat our homes and charge our phones. All these new machines mean we use much more energy than we used to. To generate the energy, we need fuel. Aeroplanes can only fly on a full tank of kerosene. Cars need petrol. Natural gas, coal or nuclear power is used to generate the electricity to power your computer. Burning certain types of fuels – called 'fossil fuels' – produces greenhouse gases and releases them into the atmosphere. One such gas is carbon dioxide, which prevents much of the sun's energy from reflecting back out into space, trapping it in our atmosphere. That's why the planet is heating up.

- You might think this sounds all right: nice warm weather means we could go out for a swim every day! But things aren't that simple. Rising temperatures mean rising sea levels, which will create more serious floods. Other places will suffer droughts, where no food can grow anymore. Weather conditions will also become more extreme, resulting in heavy rainfall or devastating hurricanes. All of this will make the earth less habitable.

- Governments are therefore talking about ways to solve the climate problem, and making agreements to reduce the amount of carbon dioxide in the atmosphere.

You can do your bit too!

- Try to use less energy. Turn off the light when you leave the room, or set the thermostat a few degrees lower.

- Re-using household objects helps too. Everything you buy takes energy to make – so the less we buy, the less will get made!

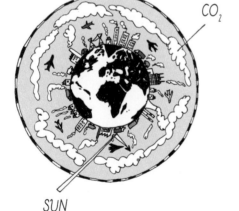

CO$_2$

SUN

- Try to eat more locally produced foods. Aeroplanes loaded with apples from Argentina use incredible amounts of energy, but apples from your backyard taste just as good!

- If you really want to help the environment, eat less meat. Cows need to eat a lot, and many forests are chopped down to provide room for them that would otherwise be helping to reduce the amount of carbon dioxide in the air. Cows also produce a lot of methane, an even stronger greenhouse gas than carbon dioxide. So eating a few vegetarian meals a week is a good idea.

174 THERE ARE MORE MEN THAN WOMEN ON EARTH

In 2017, there were **7.5 billion people** on our planet. According to the United Nations census data, there are 100 women for every 102 men on earth.

In reality, there are only 76 countries where men are in the majority. In 119 other countries, the women outnumber the men.

MORE MEN THAN WOMEN
Of the countries where the men outnumber the women, China and India come out on top. For a long time, Chinese couples were only permitted to have one son or daughter, under a government regulation called the 'one-child policy'. It was introduced because otherwise the Chinese population would expand too quickly. Because many people in China prefer sons to daughters, men now outnumber women in China by 33.5 million. In India, too, there is a preference for sons, and for this reason there are 37 million more men in India than women.

The same applies to many countries in the Middle East. In Qatar, for example, only one-quarter of the population is female. That's because so many men travel there to work in construction.

MORE WOMEN THAN MEN
In the United Kingdom, there are slightly more women than men. The same is true of most European countries.

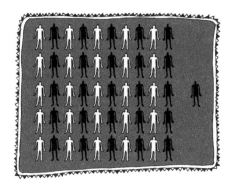

7.5 billion people on Earth – but slightly more men

175 CANADA HAS THE LONGEST SEASIDE WALKS

- Do you enjoy walking by the seaside? Then you definitely need to visit Canada, as it has a whopping 202,080 kilometres of **coastline**.

- Sadly, they're not all sandy beaches where you can spread out a towel and catch some rays. Most of Canada's coastline is fairly rugged

terrain, and temperatures in the north are freezing cold. But don't worry! That's a great place to do some whale-spotting.

- Canada is flanked by the Pacific Ocean in the west and the Atlantic Ocean in the east. To the north is the icy Arctic Ocean. But Canada isn't

just surrounded by salt water: the country also has plenty of fresh water. In fact, 20% of all the world's fresh water is contained in Canada's lakes, rivers and glaciers.

- Remember, Canada is an enormous country. It's forty times bigger than the United Kingdom, and the second-largest inhabited country in the world. Only Russia is bigger.

- The entire world has 1,162,306 kilometres of coastline. The other countries in the top 5 are Indonesia (54,716 km), Russia (37,653 km), the Philippines (36,289 km) and Japan (29,751 km).

176 THE WORLD'S BIGGEST WATERFALLS ARE IN SOUTH AMERICA

- The Iguaçu **waterfalls** are incredibly big and imposing, and lie on the border between Brazil and Argentina. The name given to the falls by the local population is no surprise: 'Iguaçu' means 'great water' in Guaraní, the language of the region's original inhabitants.

- If the old legends are to be believed, the waterfalls are the result of an old love story. A young girl, Naipi, had been chosen as a sacrifice to the divine water snake M'Moy. She wasn't looking forward to it, of course, so instead of lying on the altar, she tried to run away with her beloved, Tarobá. The water snake chased after the lovers and burrowed itself into the ground, creating the chasm with the water gushing over it. It transformed Naipi into a stone that would forever roll back and forth in the waterfall. Tarobá turned into a tree on the bank, so the two lovers could still see each other, but would never be together.

- Iguaçu has between 250 and 300 separate waterfalls, depending on the amount of water

IGUAÇU

flowing through the Iguaçu river. Altogether the falls are 2.7 kilometres across and 82 metres deep. The most impressive part of the falls is the Devil's Throat (*Garganta do Diabo*), a U-shaped waterfall where the water crashes down with torrential force.

- Want to see some amazing waterfalls, but don't want to travel so far? Then why not visit Vinnufossen in Norway, which is the largest waterfall in Europe.

177 IN CHILE THERE'S AN EARTHQUAKE NEARLY EVERY WEEK

- **Chile** is a long, thin country in South America, extending from the southern tip of the continent up along the west coast to Peru in the north. Its coastline is 6,435 kilometres long, and at its widest point, Chile is only 350 kilometres across.

- Chile lies on the edge of the South American continental plate, which is always moving in a particular direction. It also borders the Nazca plate, which moves in the opposite direction. These two opposing continental plates cause regular **earthquakes**.

- The Chileans are used to this, and so small earthquakes don't bother them anymore. They even have different names for different types of earthquakes.

- Now and again, Chile does experience terrible earthquakes. The Valdivia earthquake in 1960 was the worst on record, measuring 9.5 on the Richter scale. Some cities in Chile were wiped completely off the map, and rivers even changed their course. To make matters worse, Puyehue volcano also erupted! The quake caused a tsunami that engulfed large parts of the country. But the number of casualties was lower than might have been expected; only around 5,000 people lost their lives. The reason for the 'limited' death toll was the fact that there had been a less severe earthquake shortly before, and many Chileans had fled their homes and sought refuge in the mountains.

- Nowadays, **seismologists** try to predict tsunamis and earthquakes as best they can. Whenever a major quake is expected, they send warning messages to all residents in the region, with instructions on how to prepare.

CHILE

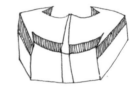

DIVERGENT BOUNDARY
chance of minor earthquakes

TRANSFORM BOUNDARY
chance of major earthquakes

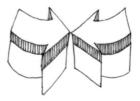

CONVERGENT BOUNDARY
large chance of major earthquakes

178 MILLIONS OF ANIMALS STILL HAVEN'T BEEN DISCOVERED

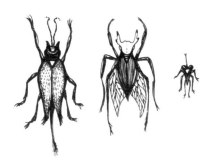

undiscovered species

Want to know what **animals** haven't been discovered yet? That's of a tough question to answer, since undiscovered animals are, well... undiscovered.

So how do scientists know that they exist?

- Tropical rainforests are home to thousands upon thousands of insects – just wander through with a butterfly net and you're sure to bag oodles of them. Next, ask a beetle expert, a butterfly expert, and a few other experts to examine your catch. They will undoubtedly recognize a few species straight away and be able to identify them, but there will also be some they're not so sure about. There might be one bug that looks a lot like another species, but isn't exactly the same. Maybe it's a new sub-species?

- The experts will then head to the library or use the internet to research the odd-looking bug, and perhaps even seek advice from their colleagues all around the world.

- Even after all the world's experts have examined the contents of your net, you can be sure that there will still be some critters that nobody recognizes exactly. They will need to be studied in more detail.

- Of course, bigger animals can't be captured by running through the forest with a net. Most of the larger animal species have already been discovered, although new ones do surface from time to time. Divers often encounter deep-sea fish that they've never seen before. They send submersible craft (like tiny submarines) down to the ocean floor. They are equipped with strong lights, since it's pitch-black down there in the murky depths. If ever they find something unfamiliar, they need to try to catch the new fish or animal and bring it to the surface so they can be sure it's definitely a new species.

- Scientists estimate that the earth is home to 8.7 million animal species, a little over one million of which have already been discovered. If we do the maths, that means that about 86% of all land species and 91% of marine species are still yet to be found. Some species even go extinct before we have a chance to identify them.

So, want to become a biologist? There's still plenty of work to be done!

179 KRAKATOA ERUPTED WITH THE FORCE OF FOUR ATOM BOMBS

Krakatoa is an **active volcano** in Indonesia, located in the Sunda Strait between the islands of Java and Sumatra. On 27 August 1883, it erupted with the explosive power of around 200 megatons of TNT – that's four times more powerful than the biggest atom bomb. Krakatoa's eruption is still one of the largest in recorded history.

- There were four explosions on that day in August, which were of unprecedented strength and caused incalculable damage.

- Two-thirds of the island was blown to pieces; 36,000 people died, and cities and villages on both Java and Sumatra were wiped away by the resulting tsunami. The boom of the explosion could be heard thousands of kilometres away in Australia.

- The eruption produced such an enormous cloud of dust that the sunlight couldn't penetrate it.

That's why the average temperatures on earth dropped by 1.2 degrees that year.

- The mountain that once stood there blew up, and disappeared underwater.

- Suddenly, in 1932, more ash and sulphur began emanating from a new mountain, and a new island was created. The island was named **Anak Krakatua**, or 'child of Krakatoa'. Thus a new volcano was born, and on days when it's not dangerously active, tourists can even visit the smoking crater accompanied by a guide.

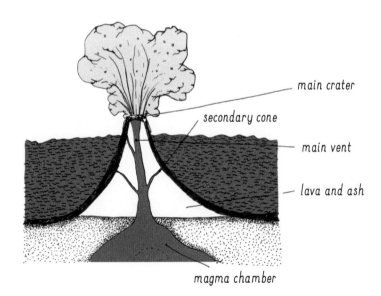

main crater

secondary cone

main vent

lava and ash

magma chamber

INSIDE THE VOLCANO

180 BELGIUM BOASTS THE BIGGEST LOCK

No, we're not talking about the kind of **lock** that requires a key. This lock is a piece of water technology, that allows ships to pass between two bodies of water that are not at the same height. Another name for a lock is a 'sluice'. It ensures a level surface for the ship to float across, and means the water levels can be adjusted while the ship is stationary.

- The biggest lock in the world is in the province of Antwerp in Belgium. It's called the Kieldrecht Lock (or the Deurganck Dock Lock). It's half a kilometre long, 68 metres wide and 17.8 metres deep, and allows enormous ships to pass from the river Scheldt into the port of Antwerp.

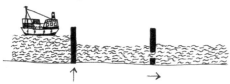

KIELDRECHT LOCK

- Building Kieldrecht Lock meant excavating nearly 10 million cubic metres of soil. The lock was officially opened in 2016 by King Philip of Belgium.

- The world's second-largest lock is also in Antwerp, and is known as the Berendrecht Lock. Its length and width are the same as those of the Kieldrecht Lock, but it is a little shallower (13.5 metres).

- But records are made to be broken, even when it comes to locks. A new ocean lock is currently under construction in Ijmuiden in the Netherlands, which is 500 metres long, 70 metres wide and 18 metres deep. Construction began in 2016 and is scheduled for completion in 2022. But until then, the Kieldrecht Lock will remain the biggest in the world.

181 THE SALTIEST WATER IS IN ANTARCTICA

The water in the Don Juan Pond in the McMurdo Dry Valleys in **Antarctica** is so **salty** that it never freezes – even at temperatures of -50 °C, the water remains liquid. Although Don Juan Pond is only 15 centimetres deep, and the water consists of about 33% salt.

The pond was discovered in 1961 by two pilots. Their names were Donald Roe and John Hickey, and their first names – Don and John (or Juan) – were used to give the pond its name.

When it was first discovered, some species of algae and fungus were found living in it. Now it's so salty that nothing can live in it anymore.

Some scientists believe that if we ever find water on other planets, it might resemble the water in Don Juan Pond.

SOUTH POLE

Don Juan Pond
77° 33' 55" S
161° 11' 26" E

182 'EARTH OVERSHOOT DAY' GETS EARLIER EVERY YEAR

The longer you shower, the quicker the water runs out. The more you eat, the faster your food runs out. If you leave your laptop on all the time, the battery will die sooner.

The earth provides us with all the resources we need to survive, and more. But those resources are running out a tiny bit sooner every year. The day on which the Earth's annual resources expire is called **Earth Overshoot Day**.

Earth Overshoot Day happens on the day when humans have used up all of the resources that the earth can produce in a year. After that day, we start 'borrowing' from the earth and live on the additional reserves that the earth has built up over time. Luckily these reserves are large, and it doesn't affect us very much right now. But that can't go on forever.

Once the reserves are all gone, there will be nothing left for us to eat or drink.

- In 1987, Earth Overshoot Day fell on 19 December. By 2020, it had crept forward to 22 August.

- Not everybody uses up resources at the same rate. In some countries, the inhabitants consume very little; in others, people use far more than they really need. The amount of resources you use to live your life is called your 'ecological footprint'.

- The average ecological footprint in the United States is extremely large. If everyone in the world lived like the Americans, we would need five earths to produce enough food and drink for everybody!

- Curious about your own ecological footprint? There are lots of websites that will calculate it for you, and where you can find tips on how to reduce it.

183 THERE'S A RAINBOW RIVER IN COLOMBIA

The **Caño Cristales** is a **river** winding through the ancient forests of Colombia in South America.

- The river is about 100 kilometres long. For most of the year it looks like an ordinary river. But everything changes in July, when the Caño Cristales becomes a magnificent and brightly coloured fairy-tale stream.

- July is the Colombian dry season. That's when the water levels drop, allowing the river's mosses and algae to absorb more sunlight and grow much faster than normal.

- There's a plant growing in the river called *Macarenia clavigera*, which turns a fiery red colour when it blooms. The deep red forms a stark contrast with the river's clear blue waters and bright green mosses. The river is framed by the shore's glistening black rocks and yellow sands, making the scene even more beautiful.

Caño Cristales

7

ALL AROUND
THE WORLD

184 THE WORLD'S TALLEST BUILDING IS IN DUBAI

- The **Burj Khalifa** is 828 metres tall, making it officially the world's **tallest building**. For the time being, at least – there are already plans elsewhere to build skyscrapers over a kilometre high. Construction of the Burj Khalifa started in 2004. It took six years, and was opened on 4 January 2010 with a magnificent fireworks display. The tower contains offices, apartments and a large hotel – the 78th floor even has a swimming pool.

- Shanghai Tower in Shanghai, China occupies second place at 632 metres tall, and close behind in third position is the 601-metre Abraj Al Bait tower in Mecca, Saudi Arabia.

- The tallest building in Europe is the Lakhta Center in St Petersburg, at 462.5 metres. In second place is the Federation Tower in Moscow, at 373.7 metres. The third-, fourth- and fifth-highest buildings are also in Moscow. In sixth place is The Shard in London, which measures 310 metres.

BONUS FACT

A sculpture of the Burj Khalifa made by master chocolatier Andrew Farrugia also broke a record. He used no less than 4.2 tonnes of chocolate to build an edible, 13.5-metre-tall replica of the tower in Dubai. Andrew Farrugia's creation made it into the *Guinness Book of Records* as the tallest chocolate structure ever built.

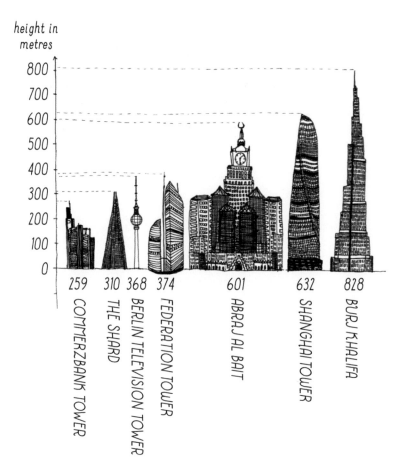

height in metres

800 700 600 500 400 300 200 100 0

259 — COMMERZBANK TOWER
310 — THE SHARD
368 — BERLIN TELEVISION TOWER
374 — FEDERATION TOWER
601 — ABRAJ AL BAIT
632 — SHANGHAI TOWER
828 — BURJ KHALIFA

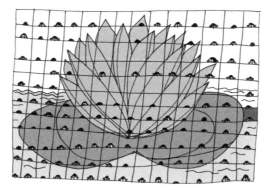

OOPS!

185 FANCY A HOLIDAY IN NORTH KOREA? WELL, THINK AGAIN!

North Korea is one of Asia's most interesting countries. Its official name is the Democratic People's Republic of Korea, but the 'democratic' part in the name doesn't mean what it usually means to us. The country was created in 1948, when Korea was divided in two.

- Fewer than 100,000 tourists visit North Korea each year. Most of them come from China, and only 5,000 are admitted annually from the West. Those who do visit are not allowed to photograph whatever they like, and they usually have an official guide with them at all times.

- The leaders in power in North Korea make all the decisions; people are only allowed to watch TV programmes made by the government, for example. They also have no access to the internet. They do have their own national 'intranet', which again provides information issued by the government.

- Every year in August and September, North Korea holds the Mass Games, also referred to as the Arirang Festival. During this spectacular event, it is compulsory for the Korean population to pay tribute to their leaders and the political party. No fewer than 80,000 people take part in the extravaganza, and train hard all year to make sure their movements are perfectly synchronized. There's dancing, gymnastics and song, and children as young as five take part.

- The festive scenery is provided by 20,000 students holding up pieces of coloured cardboard, which allows the background to keep constantly changing. The show always ends with a call for world peace.

- Want to see the Games yourself? Just search YouTube using the terms 'Arirang' and 'North Korea'. Be sure to watch the background carefully – it may look like a large television screen, but it really is made up of people holding coloured cardboard sheets!

186 PARAGUAY IS THE ONLY COUNTRY WHOSE FLAG HAS TWO DIFFERENT SIDES

Most of the Paraguayan **flag** is made up of horizontal red, white and blue stripes. Red stands for justice, white for peace, and blue for freedom.

The white stripe also contains an emblem. On one side it is a coat of arms, but the other side shows a lion and the nation's motto *Paz y Justicia* (Peace and Justice). All other countries have flags that are the same on both sides.

BONUS FLAG FACTS

The Austrian flag is the oldest national flag in the world still in use today. Like the Paraguayan flag (and many others in the world), it has three horizontal stripes: in this case, red at the top and bottom, and white in the middle.

The flag of the United States is sometimes called the Star-Spangled Banner, Old Glory or the Stars and Stripes.

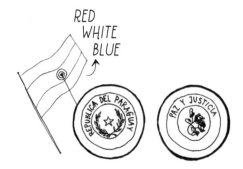

187 IN CHINA THERE ARE ALMOST NO FILMS ABOUT TIME TRAVEL

Have you ever seen *Back to the Future*, a movie showing the story of Marty McFly and Doc Brown's adventures through time? Then chances are you don't live in **China**, where movies about time travel are frowned upon.

The Chinese government thinks that films about time travel have a negative influence, and give people the wrong impression about history. They are also considered too 'western', and the government in China would prefer its people to watch Chinese movies.

left

right

KEEP RIGHT, SWINE!

188 ONLY 75 OF THE WORLD'S COUNTRIES DRIVE ON THE LEFT

In the **United Kingdom**, driving on the left seems totally normal. But there are actually only 75 countries where cars drive on the left – that's less than 40% of the world's countries, putting the UK in the minority.

You may already know some other countries where driving on the left is common – Ireland, for example. But did you know that cars in Japan, Thailand, Australia, South Africa, New Zealand, Australia and many other smaller countries also drive on the left? When in a foreign country you should always look extra carefully when crossing the street – old habits are hard to break!

In countries where the traffic is on the right, the road rules are about the same as for driving on the left. The only major differences are that you overtake on the left, and roundabouts go in the opposite direction.

- Before cars existed, people travelled on horseback and everyone kept to the left. This is because men often carried swords, and as most people are right-handed, they wielded their swords on their right side. To fend off an attack, it was easier to travel on the left.

- When the horse and carriage became more fashionable, traffic in most countries shifted to the right, as that made it easier for the driver to control the horses.

- In France, people on horseback kept to the left, while pedestrians walked on the right. Napoleon decreed that all military traffic – horses included – should travel on the right, and he ensured that the practice spread.

- Until 1967, traffic in Sweden was still on the left. But because all of its neighbouring countries had switched to the right, the Swedish government decided they should too.

> ### BONUS TRAFFIC FACT
>
> The Japanese drive on the left because their Samurai warriors carried their swords on that side. If two samurai ever passed each other and their swords made contact, it might have led to a duel. So to help keep the peace, they decided to pass each other on the right instead.

189 THE WORLD'S LARGEST PYRAMID IS IN MEXICO

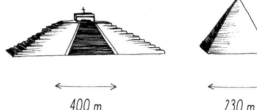

PYRAMID-BUILDING CONTEST

140 m

400 m
Cholula

230 m
Giza

Lots of people think that the Great Pyramid of Giza in Egypt is the world's largest **pyramid**, but that's not true. The honour goes to the Great Pyramid of Cholula in **Mexico**.

- At 140 metres, the Great Pyramid of Giza might be the world's *tallest* pyramid, but its base is only 230 metres wide. Its Mexican counterpart is quite a bit shorter (only 55 metres), but it is 400 metres wide at its base.

- The construction of the Mexican pyramid began around 300 BCE, and it wasn't completely finished until the 9th century CE. So it took an amazing twelve centuries to build!

- The Great Pyramid of Cholula was once dedicated to the Aztec god Quetzalcoatl (the 'feathered serpent'). Nowadays it looks like a natural hill with a church on the top, which was built by the Spanish during the colonial times. That's why the Pyramid of Cholula is now also a Catholic pilgrimage site.

190 YOUR RIGHT HAND RULES IN INDIA

In **India**, people use their right hand for most day-to-day things. The left hand is reserved for wiping your bottom after going to the toilet, so it is considered 'impure'.

When eating food with their fingers, people in India use only their right hand. They are disgusted by people eating with their left hand – to them, using their 'dirty' hand is a sign of disrespect for both food and the body.

When handing over or receiving objects in India, be sure to only use your right hand. Pointing is always very impolite, regardless of which hand you use. Instead, people here always use their chin to point to things.

What if you're left-handed? Well, that's a pity. It might be hard, but you just have to adapt.

CAUTION!

BONUS INDIA FACTS

People in India often show agreement by tilting their heads from side to side.

To greet somebody, put your palms together and place your thumbs against your forehead. The higher up you hold them, the more respect you show for the other person.

Cows are sacred creatures in the Hindu faith. That's why you must never push a cow aside in India, even if it gets in your way!

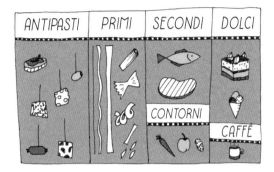

191 ITALIANS WORK THEIR WAY THROUGH THE ENTIRE MENU

Think the **Italians** only ever eat pizza or pasta? Well, think again: pizza and pasta are only a tiny part of a full Italian meal. Traditionally, Italians follow a strict series of courses when they sit down to eat.

- A proper Italian meal begins with **antipasti** – small bits of finger-food including Italian cheeses, meats, crispy bread and pickled vegetables or small salads.

- Next come the **primi**, or 'first dishes.' Primi might be risotto, or pasta with sauce. If you've ordered spaghetti or another kind of pasta, be sure to use only your fork when eating. Using a knife is bad manners.

- The **secondi** are the 'main courses', and consist of a piece of meat or fish on a plate. That's it, unless you order some **contorni** or side dishes to go with it: some potatoes perhaps,

or maybe vegetables. Pasta is not included among the secondi.

- Pizza is often available as secondi, but you can also enjoy a slice for lunch, or as a snack.

- A full meal ends with **dolci**, or 'sweets.' Dolci is the perfect time for a delicious **tiramisù**, a type of creamy dessert.

After dolci, diners will often enjoy some **caffè** or coffee. But be warned: after about eleven in the morning, most Italians drink only black coffee. Coffee with milk is frowned on after midday!

192 THE REPUBLIC OF NAURU HAS NO CAPITAL CITY

Nauru is an island in the Pacific Ocean, and is home to about 10,000 people. In 1968, it became an independent republic.

- The island has a surface area of 21 square kilometres, making it the world's smallest island nation.

- It is surrounded by magnificent coral reefs.

- Nauru has no capital city. The government buildings are located in Yaren, but that's not the official capital.

- Nauru has no army either. Nor does it need one, as the island has never had any enemies!

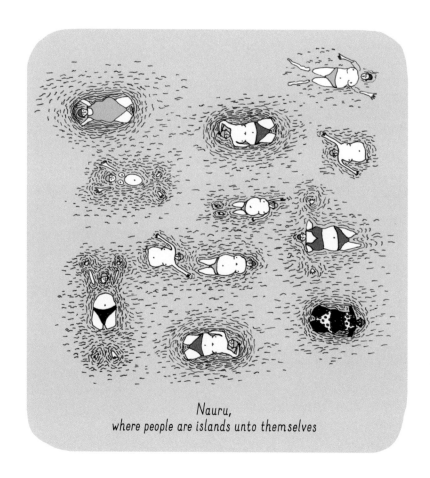

Nauru,
where people are islands unto themselves

193 THE ISLAND OF NIUE USES MICKEY MOUSE MONEY

The island of **Niue** in the Pacific Ocean has only 1,600 inhabitants. Getting there is quite a journey, but it's well worth the trip! Niue has something very special indeed.

In 2014, the island created its own new coins. One side depicts Queen Elizabeth II, the official head of state, and the other side shows pictures of Disney figures – so you can actually pay for things with coins that have Mickey Mouse, Goofy, Pluto or Minnie Mouse on them!

The coins were made mostly for tourists; thankfully you can also pay using 'ordinary' money. The special coins are made of pure gold and silver, which creates a problem: the material the coins are made of is worth far more than whatever you can buy with them, so people tend to save them rather than using them as currency. Collectors travel to the island just to get their hands on one of these coins!

The island had already issued special coins three years earlier in 2011, with *Star Wars* characters on the back.

194 DANCING USED TO BE A CRIME IN SWEDEN

In the not-so-distant past, **Swedish** people had to watch out when dancing in a café or restaurant. Until 2016 it was illegal, and dancing was only allowed if the venue had a proper permit. Business owners without a dancing permit who allowed people to dance could be fined lots of money.

DANCE! SHAKE SHAKE

permit applies to humans only!

- The law against dancing was created in the 1930s, when it was believed that dancing got people too excited and there were fears of unrest and civil disturbances.

- Over twenty campaigns were launched to try to lift the ban. But each time, the government fought to keep the law and were supported by the police. Finally, in 2016, the law was repealed.

- A similar ban on dancing applied to businesses in Japan until 2015. Even in places that had permits, dancing had to stop at midnight. Then the Japanese musician Ryuichi Sakamoto started a petition to abolish the law. He collected 150,000 signatures and was successful. Now the Japanese are free to let their hair down whenever they like!

195 IT'S RUDE TO POINT WITH CHOPSTICKS

In **China**, forks and knives are usually only used in the kitchen – at the table, most people eat using wooden sticks called **chopsticks**. They also use porcelain spoons, but only when eating soup.

- The two chopsticks are both held in the right hand. Place the lower one in the gap between your thumb and forefinger, and hold it firmly in place with your ring finger (the one next to your pinkie). The lower chopstick never moves.

- Now hold the other chopstick with your thumb, index and middle fingers (as though holding a pen), and move it up and down to grip pieces of food between the two sticks, raising them from your plate to your mouth. It may take practice, but it's not very difficult. You can also bring the bowl closer to your mouth if that's easier.

- When you've finished eating (or when taking a break), lay the chopsticks on the special holder beside your bowl or plate.

- Never point at people with chopsticks at the table – that's considered very rude.

- Avoid standing the chopsticks up vertically in your bowl of rice. In China, this is seen as a reference to death.

- It's also considered very impolite to stab food with your chopsticks, or to lick them clean.

- Lastly, never use your chopsticks to give anybody else a piece of food.

196 UNLUCKY NUMBERS VARY FROM COUNTRY TO COUNTRY

Are you the kind of person who stays in bed all day on Friday the 13th in case bad things happen to you? If you are **superstitious**, then you might believe that the number thirteen brings bad luck.

- Thirteen is only considered unlucky in Europe, America and a few Asian countries.

- The reason thirteen is thought to be unlucky is because twelve is considered to be a perfect number – just think of the twelve apostles, or the fact that there are twelve months in a year. But thirteen is one higher than twelve, making it 'more than perfect'. That's impossible, and is therefore linked with the idea of bad luck!

- Some people take the superstition about the number thirteen to ridiculous lengths. There are hotels that have no thirteenth floor, for example, and which use the numbers 12A and 12B instead. Christ was nailed to the cross on a Friday, so in combination with the number thirteen, Fridays seem especially bad.

- Another possible explanation is that Friday was always the day when Romans executed prisoners who had been sentenced to death.

- Other people suggest that Friday was the day when witches gathered to do their mischief.

- Funnily enough, there are no more accidents on Friday the 13th than on other days. On the contrary: there are actually fewer! Perhaps it's because superstitious people are especially careful on that day, or they stay at home instead of going to work.

- If you are super-afraid of the number thirteen, you may suffer from what is called *triskaidekaphobia*. In that case it can be useful to know that unlucky numbers and days are very different all over the world.

BONUS BAD-LUCK FACTS

In Spain and many South American countries, Tuesday the 13th is considered a bad-luck day, not Friday.

Italians, on the other hand, are scared of the number seventeen. Expressed in Roman numerals, the number is written XVII, which can be rearranged into the Latin word *vixi*, or 'I have lived' (in other words: I'm dead now).

In Asia, the number four is the unluckiest number, since in Japanese and Chinese the number sounds very similar to the word for 'death'. For the same reason, the Japanese tend to avoid the number nine, as it sounds like the word for 'pain'.

No discussion of unlucky numbers would be complete without the number 666 or the 'number of the beast'. In the Bible, the 'beast' is always a reference to the devil. So wherever you see the number 666, the devil is supposedly never far away.

However, fear of certain numbers is only a superstition, and superstitions make your life more difficult. Our suggestion is just to ignore these numbers instead of being afraid of them.

OW!

EEEK!

AAH!

BAH-HA-HA!

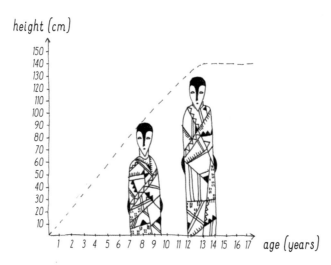

height (cm)

150
140
130
120
110
100
90
80
70
60
50
40
30
20
10

1 2 3 4 5 6 7 8 9 10 11 12 13 14 15 16 17   age (years)

197 PYGMY PEOPLE SOMETIMES STOP GROWING AT AGE TWELVE

Pygmy peoples are a set of tribes who live in the rainforests of **Central Africa**.

- The best-known pygmy tribes are the Aka, Baka, Mbuti and Tua.

- For food, traditional pygmy tribes collect honey, nuts and fruits, and hunt various kinds of small animals. They also build huts out of leaves.

- The most striking thing about pygmy peoples is their height. The men are usually no taller than 150 centimetres, and they stop growing at around the age of twelve.

- Scientists believe that people from pygmy tribes may stop growing early because their immune systems need to battle many diseases and infections in the rainforest. These extra pressures mean their bodies have little energy left for growing.

- Pygmy people are also famous for their music, which plays a big part in everyday life. It includes polyphonic singing, which is a way of singing two notes at the same time!

198 IRANIANS ARE OFFENDED BY A THUMBS-UP

If your **Iranian** friend has done something amazing and you give an enthusiastic **thumbs-up** to show your support, there's a chance you might not stay friends much longer.

THUMBS-UP
In Western countries, a thumbs-up is a very positive gesture. But in Iran, Afghanistan, Latin America and West Africa, it's a serious insult.

THUMB AGAINST FOREFINGER
Now that you know, you might want to be more careful, perhaps putting your thumb and forefinger together to say everything's 'OK'.

- Unfortunately, your French, Moroccan and Tunisian friends won't appreciate it. They'll think you're calling them a 'zero', meaning you think they're worthless and good-for-nothing.

- It's also an impolite gesture in South America, and many southern European countries.

- In Japan, the symbol means you want to receive your change in coins.

- In Korea the sign simply means 'money'.

OTHER SIGNS
- Have you ever seen someone make the 'sign of the horns'? That's when the index and pinkie fingers are pointing up and the other three are curved inward. In the west, the sign is extremely popular at rock concerts. But be careful with it in Italy, Brazil, Colombia, Portugal and Spain, where the gesture is a serious insult. There, the 'sign of the horns' is used to tell people their partner is cheating on them. In Italy you can receive a fine of 50 euros for making it.

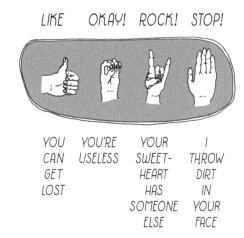

LIKE   OKAY!   ROCK!   STOP!

YOU CAN GET LOST   YOU'RE USELESS   YOUR SWEET-HEART HAS SOMEONE ELSE   I THROW DIRT IN YOUR FACE

- Do you ever try to tell people to 'stop' by holding up your hand with an open palm? Be careful with that in Greece! There, it's an insult meaning 'I throw dirt in your face'.

- We'll finish with head-shaking. In the west, shaking your head to the left and right means 'no'. But in Bulgaria and Greece it means the opposite. And that's not all: in English-speaking countries, an up-and-down nod means 'yes', but in Greece and some Arabic countries it means 'no'. And to say 'yes' in India, you need to tilt your head from side to side. Confused yet?

So be sure to learn some local 'sign language' before heading to a different country. It might save you some trouble...

RESPECTOMETER

199 DON'T SHAKE HANDS IN JAPAN

Japanese people are often uncomfortable with the idea of touching strangers. So instead of shaking hands, they bow as a sign of respect.

For example, imagine you're attending a Japanese school. As a student, you must always be the first to bow to the teachers. Not only that, but you must also bow the deepest. The highest-ranked person will also bow, but less deeply.

Women place their hands lightly on their thighs when bowing, while men let their arms hang by their sides. The bow is performed from the waist.

When you're in the middle of a bow, never look at the face of the person you're bowing to – it might make you seem rude.

BONUS JAPAN FACTS

- Be sure to wear nice clean socks when visiting friends in Japan. It's customary to remove your shoes when entering a Japanese home, and you will be given a pair of special slippers to wear inside. That's why it's best to make sure you're not wearing worn-out old socks with enormous holes!

- The same applies in traditional Japanese restaurants, where the waiter will look after your shoes and give you a pair of slippers.

- Special slippers are available when using the toilet, and will always be waiting by the bathroom door. The 'toilet slippers' will be a different colour, so be sure to swap them for your normal 'house slippers' before returning to your hosts.

- Never give white flowers when visiting a Japanese home, as white flowers are only used at funerals. Gifts must not be wrapped in white, black or grey paper – those are all colours reserved for funerals. If you give your hosts a gift, they usually won't open it until after you've left.

- Never lie down after a meal in Japan. According to superstition, you run the risk of turning into a cow!

200 THE 'ISLAND OF DEAD DOLLS' IS ONE OF THE CREEPIEST PLACES ON EARTH

In **Mexico**, not far from the centre of Mexico City, you will find the 'Island of Dead Dolls'. It's a tiny little island in a national park, completely surrounded by canals.

- Hundreds of dolls hang in the island's trees. Some are still intact, but others are tattered, damaged or missing limbs. It's quite a terrifying sight, and people are convinced that the island is full of ghosts. The Island of Dead Dolls is certainly one of the creepiest places on earth.

- But how did the dolls get there in the first place? Here's the story: a man named Julian Santana Berrera once lived on the tiny island, and his job was to keep everything tidy. One day, a little girl's body washed up on the shore – she had drowned, but nobody knew exactly how or where she had come from.

- Several days later, Julian found a small doll in one of the canals surrounding the island. It had probably belonged to the little girl, and Julian hung it up in a tree as a sign of respect.

- From that moment on, Julian became obsessed with the spirit of the little girl. He went in search of even more dolls to try to appease her ghost, and hung them up in the island's trees.

- Julian kept expanding his collection, and after fifty years the entire island was full of dolls. But they weren't pretty ones: they were often dirty, broken or missing body parts.

BOO!

the Island of Dead Dolls

- Julian eventually drowned in the same place where the little girl had been found, and the people of Mexico now believe that his ghost haunts the island too.

- Most tourists don't seem worried, however, and there are many who enjoy visiting the island. Some even hang their own dolls in the trees.

201 AUSTRALIA WAS ONCE CALLED 'NEW HOLLAND'

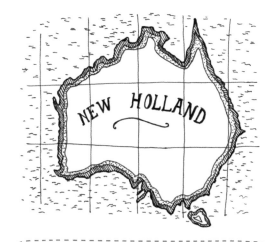

Open up a seventeenth-century atlas, and you'll notice that way back in the beginning, **Australia** was called 'New Holland'. A Dutch explorer named Abel Tasman was the one who gave the country that name, in 1644. It caught on, and was used by many other seafarers and cartographers (map-makers) from the same period.

In 1770, Great Britain colonized part of Australia and named it 'New South Wales'. Only the regions not occupied by the English were still known as 'New Holland', and it wasn't until the nineteenth century that the country was given the name it uses today.

BONUS FACT

The island of **Tasmania** was named after Abel Tasman, but not until many years after he arrived there. The island is now part of the Commonwealth of Australia, and lies around 240 kilometres off the coast of the Australian mainland.

202 WANT TO VISIT HELL? GO TO FENGDU

On the banks of the Yangtze river in China lies the city of **Fengdu**, also called the Ghost City.

- Long ago there were two army officers, Yin and Wang, who came to Fengdu to practise Taoism. Their two names together form the word 'Yinwang', which means 'the king of hell' in Chinese. According to legend, the two men became immortal and stayed living in Fengdu.

- Lots of temples were built on Ming mountain where Yin and Wang lived. Demons and other scary creatures were depicted in and around the temples as a tribute to the king of hell, along with paintings and statues of people being tortured. Because of all its eerie artwork, some Chinese people say that Fengdu offers a glimpse of what hell must look like.

- According to Chinese beliefs, people who die must complete three trials before passing into the next life:

1. First, they must cross the Bridge of Helplessness. This bridge was constructed in Fengdu during the Ming dynasty, and is a test of good and evil. The bridge connects the living world to the spirit world: those who have done no wrong can cross the bridge unharmed, but evildoers will fall through it, plummeting into the water below the bridge.

2. The second test is the Ghost-Torturing Pass, where souls entering the underworld are judged by Yama, the king of hell.

3. Those who pass the first two tests will arrive at Tianzi Palace, where the requirement is to stand on one leg on a special rock for three minutes. Good people will pass the test without a problem, while baddies may lose their balance and fall down into hell.

203 THE WORLD'S FASTEST ROLLER COASTER IS IN ABU DHABI

Are you a roller coaster fiend? Like it fast and furious? Then you really should visit Ferrari World in **Abu Dhabi** in the United Arab Emirates. It's the world's largest indoor amusement park, and contains twenty attractions that are all racing-car themed. The Formula Rossa roller coaster reaches a top speed of 239 kilometres per hour. The only way it can achieve such high speeds is by using the same system that launches planes from an aircraft carrier. The coaster reaches full speed in five seconds flat, and the carriages look like Ferrari cars. Passengers must wear goggles to keep the sand out of their eyes (the Formula Rossa is outside, unlike the rest of the park, which is indoors).

> **BONUS FENGDU FACT**
>
> In the hills surrounding Fengdu, there is a gigantic stone statue of an enormous man. His body is spread out across the hill, and according to the *Guinness Book of Records*, it's the largest statue ever to be carved out of rock. It's so big in fact – 138 metres tall and 217 metres wide – that it can be seen from a long way away.

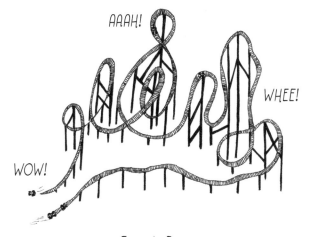

Formula Rossa

If you prefer height to speed, the world's tallest coaster can be ridden at Six Flags Great Adventure in Jackson, New Jersey. It's called Kingda Ka, is 139 metres tall and reaches a top speed of 206 kilometres per hour, making it the second-fastest roller coaster in the world.

Machu Picchu

204 MACHU PICCHU IS ONE OF THE GREAT WONDERS OF THE WORLD

High up in the Andes mountains in **Peru** lies **Machu Picchu**, the hidden city of the Incas.

- The city was never discovered by the Spanish, so it was spared the destruction wrought on many other ancient cities. It wasn't visited by westerners until 1911, when a professor named Hiram Bingham was led there by a local guide.

- Machu Picchu is the best place on earth to study Incan history, and was probably built around the year 1450.

- Scholars aren't sure why the Incas built a city so high up. It's hard to get to, and there are no other cities close by. There are theories that Machu Picchu was a country residence for kings, or that the site had religious significance.

- The city is divided into three areas: residential buildings (houses), a zone reserved for the nobility, and an area for holding religious services. The city could accommodate around 750–1,000 residents, and the religious quarter included shrines to many gods and goddesses, including those of the sun and moon.

- It's a miracle that the Incas succeeded in building a city at such high altitude, since they didn't have any wheeled vehicles they could use to transport the heavy building materials!

- The city is open to tourists. To ensure that tourism causes as little damage to the site as possible, and that it remains preserved for the future, all tourists must be accompanied by a special guide.

205 RAPA NUI IS COVERED IN HUGE STATUES

Rapa Nui is an island in the Pacific Ocean, also called Easter Island. Officially it belongs to **Chile**, but it's a long way from Chile's coast. The island is most famous for its hundreds of statues, known as 'moai'.

- The statues can be up to 10 metres tall, and some of them weigh over 80 tonnes. They are carved out of volcanic rock.

- The moai are located on a hillside, and most face inland towards the centre of the island. Only seven of them face the sea.

- According to old legends, the moai are the deceased ancestors of the island's first inhabitants, and offer prayers of fertility to the gods on behalf of the island and its people.

- For a long time, historians were puzzled as to how the island's original inhabitants managed to transport the statues. The moai were all carved in the same place, and then moved many kilometres away without the aid of wheels, cranes or even work animals!

- Archaeologists believe that the moai were specially constructed so they could be transported using only manpower and ropes. The ropes were attached to the statue's head and used to 'shuffle' the statue to its final location, a technique made possible by the statue's unique shape.

- Researchers tried it out this idea, and they succeeded in using the technique to move a statue weighing 5 tonnes.

- Some of the present-day islanders think differently, and refuse to believe the scientists' theories. They say the statues simply walked over to wherever they are standing now.

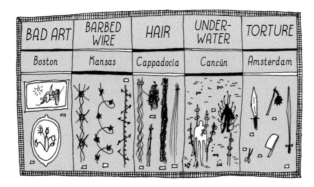

STRANGE MUSEUMS OF THE WORLD

206 BOSTON HAS A MUSEUM OF BAD ART

- That's even the museum's official name: **MOBA**, or the **Museum of Bad Art**. It's dedicated exclusively to 'ugly' paintings, and the collection ranges from portraits and landscapes to more abstract works. Some don't even look that bad – visit www.museumofbadart.org and decide for yourself. Maybe they might even agree to display some of your own paintings!

- MOBA is not the only weird museum on earth. The **Barbed Wire Museum** in Kansas can teach you everything you need to know about barbed wire. With more than two thousand different types on display, the museum also offers plenty of information on the history of the United States, which seems very closely intertwined with the history of barbed wire.

- Barbed wire doesn't grab you? Then why not try the **Hair Museum** of Avanos in Cappadocia, Turkey. Thirty years ago, a Turkish potter was devastated when his dear girlfriend had to move away. To help him feel better, he asked for a lock of her hair to remember her by.

Other women followed, and the potter got a taste for collecting locks of hair. So he just kept on going. Now there are sixteen thousand locks of hair hanging in his museum, each accompanied by a touching description of whose hair it is, and how he came to possess it.

- The **Underwater Museum of Art** in the Mexican city of Cancún is literally a different world: its five hundred sculptures stand on the ocean floor, where they are slowly but surely disappearing under layers of coral. Oh, we forgot to mention: a diving licence is required to visit the museum!

- If you're a horror fan, then you might enjoy the **Torture Museum** in Amsterdam. Guillotines, head crushers, racks, choke pears and iron spiders are all on gruesome display, complete with detailed instructions for use. There are also illustrations that clearly depict how the torture was performed. It might not be your idea of a dream outing, but it will certainly give you nightmares!

Australia's underground city is called **Coober Pedy**. It's a relatively isolated place, the nearest town being roughly 850 kilometres away.

Originally, Coober Pedy was an ordinary mining town where opals (a kind of gemstone used to make jewelry) were extracted from the ground. But the city was hot – far too hot. Summer temperatures could soar above 40 °C, and so the miners began sleeping down in the mines, where it was cooler. It was so pleasant in fact, they began expanding the city underground. The area was also nearly devoid of trees, so there was no wood for building houses anyway.

Coober Pedy now has over 1,500 underground homes. Air circulation is provided by holes in the roof, and some houses have swimming pools! The town even has churches and a bar. Why not give the underground lifestyle a go?

Coober Pedy

8

THE WONDERFUL WORLD OF SCIENCE

208 ASTRONAUTS PEE INTO VACUUM CLEANERS

As you probably already know, gravity is the force that pulls everything towards the centre of the earth. It's **gravity** that stops you from floating away, and that keeps both your feet on the ground.

- Gravity gets weaker the further away from earth you are, but it never disappears completely. It's gravity that keeps the moon revolving in an orbit around the earth.

- The same principle applies to orbiting spacecraft. The spacecraft is actually moving so fast that it wants to escape, but gravity is what keeps it close to the earth. The two forces – gravity and the spacecraft's speed – cancel each other out, which means that the astronauts and their spaceship are 'falling' at a constant speed *around* the earth. So even though gravity is still acting on them, they are effectively 'weightless' (in the same way that you are weightless if you plummet to the earth in an aeroplane or elevator).

- This weightlessness makes everything in space seem to float around – even in the toilet. Imagine that, coming face-to-face with floating drops of pee or poo!

- Luckily, some bright sparks invented a special kind of vacuum cleaner to solve the problem. Male astronauts need to attach a special hose that sucks all the pee into a tank. For number twos, and for use by female astronauts, there's a special kind of toilet seat that neatly vacuums everything away.

- Using the equipment is more complicated than it sounds. First of all the astronauts need to sit tight on the seat: they float over to it (no gravity, remember?) and strap themselves down using special belts. Of course they need to remember to actually turn the vacuum on, otherwise whatever they leave behind will escape as soon as they leave the toilet.

- Sometimes astronauts need to work outside the space station. In that case, they put on a nappy.

Perhaps an astronaut's life doesn't seem quite so appealing anymore...

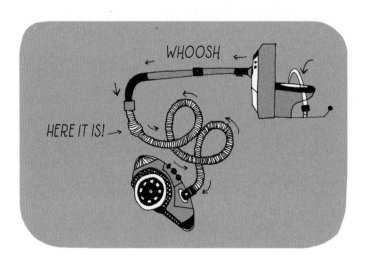

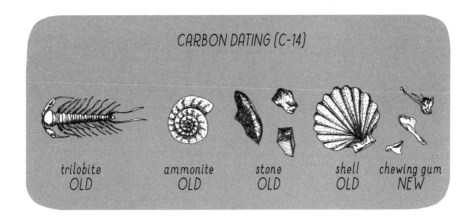

CARBON DATING (C-14)

trilobite
OLD

ammonite
OLD

stone
OLD

shell
OLD

chewing gum
NEW

209 MACHINES CAN TELL YOU EXACTLY HOW OLD BONES ARE

Say you've discovered an old **bone** in a forest, and you want to find out how old it is. Who knows – it might even be from a mammoth!

To figure it out, you could ask a **palaeontologist** to take a look. Palaeontologists are scientists who study what the world was like long before recorded history.

- First, the palaeontologist will look at the other objects surrounding the bone. If certain types of rock or shells can be found nearby, then they will already have an idea of how old the bone is.

- For an extremely accurate estimate, the bone's age can be determined by a special machine that measures the amount of radioactive carbon (C-14) inside. Radioactive carbon occurs everywhere on earth in very small amounts, and it breaks down very slowly in bones. The less C-14 is found in a bone, the older it is. The machine can determine the age of bones going back over 50,000 years, and the technique is called 'C-14 dating' or 'carbon dating'.

BONUS CARBON FACT

Carbon dating was invented in the year 1949 by **Willard Frank Libby** and colleagues, who received the Nobel Prize for Chemistry in 1960. The Nobel Prize is an award given to researchers who make ground-breaking discoveries in the fields of physics, chemistry, physiology or medicine. There are also Nobel Prizes for peace and for literature.

210 ALL THE WORLD'S BACTERIA WEIGH MORE THAN ALL THE WORLD'S MAMMALS

- **Bacteria** are animals made of only one cell, and they belong to the category of **single-celled organisms**. Bacteria are extremely small (measuring 0.005–0.001 mm across) and can't be seen with the naked eye. But bacteria are literally everywhere.

- People often think bacteria are just nasty germs that make you sick. But that's not true: there are bacteria in the air, in the water, in the ground and inside your body. But before you reach for the disinfectant, you should know that the bacteria are there for a reason. We need them to survive.

- The bacteria on your skin, for example, are called your 'skin flora'. The good bacteria compete with the bad bacteria, making them less likely to gain the upper hand and cause disease. So they act a bit like a protective shield, and help to keep your skin healthy.

- Your intestines are also teeming with healthy bacteria, called your 'intestinal flora'. They keep the nasty bacteria off your intestinal wall, and help to digest your food. Here's how: before being digested, your food first needs to be broken up into tiny pieces. That work is done by small molecules called enzymes, which are emitted by the intestinal walls. Your intestines are where all the food you eat is absorbed for use as energy, and to provide the building blocks for cells. Bacteria have no intestines – but they do produce enzymes. Some of them are used to digest their own food, but the rest help us to digest our own.

- Bacteria are all over the place, but there's no need to be afraid! All the bacteria on Earth would weigh more than all the mammals put together. So if all bacteria were dangerous, humankind would have died out long ago.

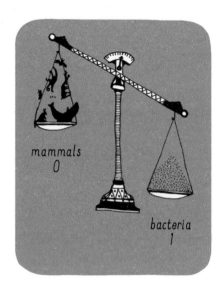

mammals
0

bacteria
1

BONUS BACTERIA FACT

Did you know that certain bacteria can be used as street lights? Scientists are currently running tests on special bacteria found in squid, which emit light. They put the bacteria in a transparent bag along with some food, and the bacteria stay lit up for three days!

space

sea

211 HUMANS HAVE EXPLORED SPACE MORE THAN THE OCEAN FLOOR

The **moon** is about 385,000 kilometres from earth. That's pretty far. Yet twelve astronauts have already walked on the moon's surface, and many more space travellers have been sent to various space stations.

The deep sea is right here on earth, so you might think that lots of people have already taken a look down there. But that's not so.

- Less than 10% of all the **oceans** on earth have been explored. Perhaps that's not so strange, when you consider that 70% of the earth is covered in water – that's a big area!

- On average, the ocean is 4,300 metres deep.

- The deepest known point on the ocean floor lies 10,900 metres below sea level. It was named **Challenger Deep**, after the exploratory vessel that discovered it (the *Challenger*). Challenger Deep is a chasm in the Mariana Trench in the western Pacific Ocean.

- There are reports of a deeper known point dubbed the Mariana Hollow, which was discovered by a Russian ship called the *Vitjaz*. The depth has only been measured once until now, and so its accuracy is contested. The existing measurement was taken by lowering a sonar kit down from the ship, using a rope.

- Scientists were astonished to discover creatures living so far down: several unique fish species were swimming around, and there were even shrimp crawling over the rocky ocean floor. Reason enough to visit more often!

212 DRAINWATER DOESN'T FLOW THE OTHER WAY IN THE SOUTHERN HEMISPHERE

Perhaps you've heard people claim that water in the northern hemisphere swirls anti-clockwise down the **drain**, while it flows clockwise in the southern hemisphere? They say the phenomenon is due to the 'Coriolis effect'.

While the Coriolis effect does exist, it's extremely weak and only noticeable across enormous distances. It causes ocean currents and winds to bend, for example, and it creates large-scale spiral movements.

Toilets, sinks and baths are far too small for the effect to be noticeable.

At tourist locations along the equator, con artists still use clever tricks to 'demonstrate' the effect and fool people – they even earn money doing it. But now you know better!

213 PAINKILLERS DON'T KNOW WHERE THE PAIN IS

Imagine you have a terrible toothache and your mum gives you a **painkiller**. How does that little pill know that it's your tooth that hurts, and not something else like your toe?

- Actually, the pill doesn't know anything at all. Painkillers are usually taken with a glass of water, and the painkilling substance passes through your stomach and intestines, into your bloodstream.

- Once in the blood, the painkiller starts a journey through your entire body. Pain is experienced when special signals are sent via the nerves to the brain. The chemical in the painkiller prevents these annoying signals from reaching the brain, so you aren't aware of the pain anymore.

- Because the drug is everywhere in your body, there's a good chance that not only

your toothache will disappear, but also the pain in your muscles from yesterday's exercise, or even a headache if you have one.

- As long as your brain never gets the pain signals, you won't feel any pain.

- So painkillers don't take away the source of the pain, and they don't help you get any better. All they do is block the signals being sent to your brain, and they do that everywhere in your entire body.

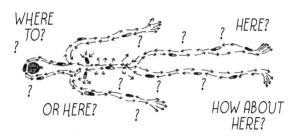

214 THE LOWEST TEMPERATURE EVER MEASURED ON EARTH IS -89.2 °C
(THAT'S TWICE AS COLD AS THE WORLD'S COLDEST DEEP-FREEZE)

The Russian city of Vostok is cold. Horribly cold. That's why Vostok is also the name of the weather station at the **South Pole**, where the average winter temperature is around -65 °C. Thankfully, in summer things warm up to a more comfortable -30 °C.

Vostok weather station is where the lowest ever temperature on earth was measured, on 21 July 1983. The thermometer read -89.2 °C, which is twice as cold as a four-star deep-freeze with a minimum temperature of -40 °C.

But hang on – how could it be so cold in July? Well, in the northern hemisphere July is in the middle of summer, but south of the equator the seasons are reversed, and July is actually in the middle of winter.

If you prefer the heat, then maybe book a trip to the Middle East, North Africa or Death Valley – all places where the world's heat records have been broken at some time or other.

On 10 July 1913, blistering heat was measured in Death Valley when temperatures rose to 56.7 °C. Several years later, the record was broken in Al Aziziyah in Libya, where a temperature of 57.7 °C was measured on 13 September 1922. But meteorologists question whether these measurements were taken correctly, as the equipment used was not as advanced as it is today. Experts agreed, however, that the 54 °C measured in the summer of 2016 in Mitribah, Kuwait was the highest temperature ever recorded. Then, in August 2020, a record high of 54.4 °C was measured in Death Valley in the USA.

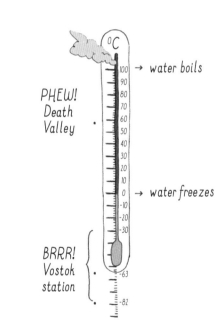

215 AN ENTIRE LIBRARY CAN FIT ONTO A USB STICK

A **USB stick** might be only a few centimetres long, but if its capacity is large enough, an entire **library** can fit onto it. A one-terabyte (1TB) stick can store the text of one million two-hundred-page books. One terabyte is equal to a thousand gigabytes, or 1,000,000,000,000 bytes.

The world's biggest library is the Library of Congress in Washington, United States. It has 38 million books, all of which would fit onto

38 memory sticks of 1TB each, which could easily fit into a desk drawer!

USB sticks and storage drives are two types of 'storage media'. These media are getting smaller and smaller, while their capacity is getting larger and larger. An old 3.5-inch floppy disk could only store 1.44 megabytes of information; a DVD can store up to 4.7 gigabytes, and there are now USB sticks that can hold up to 2 terabytes.

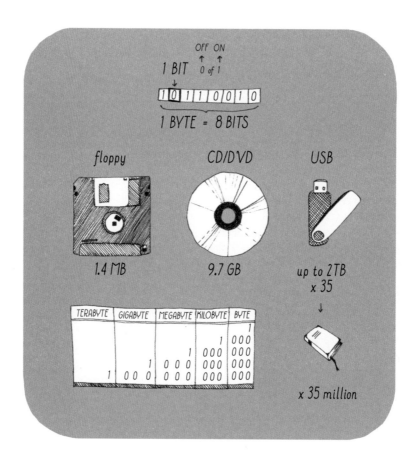

OFF ON

1 BIT   0 of 1

1 0 1 1 0 0 1 0

1 BYTE = 8 BITS

floppy — 1.4 MB

CD/DVD — 9.7 GB

USB — up to 2TB x 35

x 35 million

TERABYTE	GIGABYTE	MEGABYTE	KILOBYTE	BYTE
				1
			1	000
		1	000	000
	1	000	000	000
1	000	000	000	000

Computers have become more and more powerful over the years too. The world's first computer – ENIAC – was built in 1946. It took up 167 square metres of floor space, and could make 5,000 calculations per second.

Compare ENIAC to the world's fastest modern supercomputer: Summit in the United States is capable of 143.5 quadrillion (or a billion billion) calculations per second. Summit fills just over 520 square metres of floor space – or about two tennis courts – and weighs over 320 tonnes. That's more than a commercial aeroplane!

216 WATCH OUT! FARTS ARE FLAMMABLE

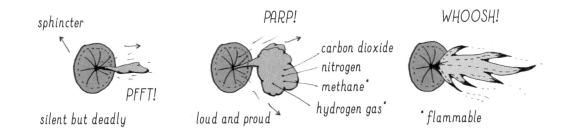

sphincter

PFFT!

silent but deadly

PARP!

carbon dioxide
nitrogen
methane *
hydrogen gas *

loud and proud

WHOOSH!

* flammable

Ever wondered what **farts** actually are? Put simply, they are just gases leaving your body. There are different types: the 'silent but deadly' type doesn't make much sound, but can easily clear a room with its stench. Then there are 'trumpet farts', which exit with a loud noise and make the windows rattle. The sound of a fart is made by the sphincter – the circular muscle surrounding the anus – which vibrates as the gas escapes. Sphincters are a type of muscle used by the body to seal off hollow organs. In this case, the organ is your intestines.

Farts can contain various gases. The bacteria in your intestines that help digest your food produce hydrogen gas, methane and carbon dioxide. It's the methane and hydrogen that make your farts flammable.

We don't recommend trying it out – you could end up with a bottom covered in blisters!

BONUS FART FACTS

The stinkiest farts contain sulphur, which generally comes from eating eggs or meat.

A 'flatulist' is someone who can do farts on command, and who enjoys demonstrating their ability to others. Some flatulists are even performing artists, and develop entire stage acts around their unique talent. Mr Methane (Paul Oldfield) and *Le Pétomane* (Joseph Pujol) were both famous flatulists.

Herrings use farts to communicate with each other.

217 PIGEONS HAVE AN INBUILT GPS

If you release a **pigeon** hundreds of kilometres away from its coop, it will always be able to find its way back home **again**. That's because pigeons (as well as some other birds) have a sort of inbuilt GPS system.

- Scientists still don't fully understand exactly how the pigeons do this. Nerve cells have been discovered inside pigeons' brains that can detect the strength and polarity of the earth's magnetic field, which is probably how the birds always know roughly where they are. They are constantly creating a mental map of their surroundings, and that's how they find their way back home.

- More recent research has revealed that pigeons probably also use the wind and scents to draw the map in their mind. Analysing the direction and smell of the wind helps them find their coop even faster.

- Because pigeons can always fly back home, contests are held among pigeon fanciers who breed pigeons especially to hold races. The birds are loaded into enormous baskets and transported hundreds of kilometres away, sometimes even in specially outfitted lorries or trucks. Then they are released, and the pigeon that makes it home first is the winner.

- Prize pigeons can be worth a lot of money. The most valuable pigeon ever was a Belgian racing pigeon called Armando, which was sold to a Chinese buyer in 2019 for $1.4 million!

PLEASE MAKE A U-TURN

BONUS PIGEON FACT

Pigeon racing is especially popular in Germany, the Netherlands and Belgium. Each year, various national and international races are held from April to September. Young pigeons must take part in five races a year; older birds are limited to a maximum of fourteen.

Many animal rights activists oppose pigeon racing. Birds can sometimes get lost and end up in a strange city, where they join the ranks of the local city birds. Other birds are less fortunate still, and can die if they end up in bad weather.

Racing pigeons must also be in excellent physical condition in order to cover the vast distances demanded of them. Many breeders attempt to strengthen their pigeons through 'doping', and the weakest birds are usually removed from the nest early and killed.

218 UGH, THERE'S LIVE FUNGUS IN YOUR BREAD!

- To make bread rise so it's light and fluffy, **yeast** is necessary. Yeast is also what gives different breads their unique flavours. When bread is baked, the yeast converts sugars into bubbles of carbon dioxide gas, which are what make the bread so fluffy and tasty.

- Yeast is also used to make beer and wine, and is what produces the alcohol in these drinks.

- But did you know that yeast is a living thing? It's a single-celled fungus that grows best at temperatures from 15–30 °C, which is why it always needs to be mixed with lukewarm water.

strong yeast

You may never look at your sandwich the same way again!

219 AIR BUBBLES CAN FORM IN YOUR STOMACH

Do you enjoy fizzy drinks? And after a soft drink, perhaps you enjoy letting out a huge **burp**. That's because the bubbles in the drink get larger and larger in your stomach, and need to find a way out.

- Fizzy lemonade contains carbon dioxide, which is compressed and dissolved into the liquid. That puts the bottle under a lot of pressure, which you can hear being released when you open it – that hissing noise is the sound of the pressure escaping.

- The carbon dioxide molecules in the soft drink slowly start clumping together to form bubbles. If you drink it straightaway from a freshly opened bottle, the air bubbles will continue to form inside your stomach. As the amount of gas increases, your stomach will expand and send a message to your brain saying that it's getting uncomfortable. Your brain will relax the muscle (or 'sphincter' – see Fact 216) that separates your stomach from your oesophagus, allowing the air to escape as a loud burp!

LET IT ALL OUT

In China, a burp is often seen as a compliment to the chef, and a sign that you've enjoyed the meal.

← BURP!

BUBBLE BUBBLE

220 EVERYTHING IS MADE OF ATOMS (INCLUDING YOU)

- **Atoms** are building blocks, a little like tiny pieces of Lego. Just look around you: everything you see – flowers, plants, your body, even the air – is made of atoms. They are so small that they are impossible to see with the naked eye. However, there are microscopes that can allow humans to see atoms.

- Try to imagine the biggest beach you've ever been to. A single grain of sand contains more atoms than there are grains of sand on the entire beach.

- But if everything is made of atoms, then what are atoms made of? Well, in the centre of the atom is the 'nucleus', containing protons (with a positive electric charge) and neutrons (with no electric charge). Around the nucleus, many tiny dots are revolving called 'electrons'. Electrons have a negative charge. The positive and negative charges cancel each other out, making the entire atom neutral overall.

In between the electrons and the nucleus is empty space. So everything you can see is made up of a nucleus and the tiny particles revolving around it, but also a vast amount of empty space.

- **Molecules** are formed when two or more atoms bond together. Different types of atoms exist in nature, which can all be combined to produce anything you like: a racing car, a chicken or an apple. The millions and millions of ways atoms can be combined are what produce the different objects all around us. Although you and your best friend are both human beings, you are constructed from different sets of atoms, so you don't look exactly the same.

- In nuclear power stations, the minuscule nuclei of atoms are split apart in a reaction known as 'nuclear fission'. The process releases tremendous amounts of energy, which we call 'nuclear energy'.

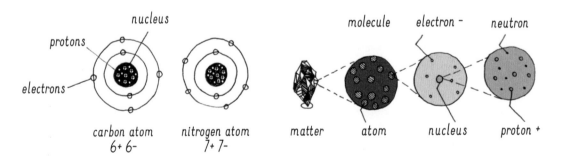

EVERYTHING'S MADE OF ATOMS

221 FLYING CARS ALREADY EXIST (YOU JUST CAN'T BUY THEM YET)

Ever ended up in a traffic jam, and imagined how wonderful it would be to just rise up off the ground and fly away over all the other cars? Then we've got good news for you: **flying cars** are a thing!

- They are being made by a company called Terrafugia (a combination of the words *terra*, meaning 'earth' and *fugia*, meaning 'flight') and have been in development since 2006 by a hardworking team of American engineers. The first test drives/flights have already been carried out.

- The Terrafugia Transition can be driven on roads and motorways and parked in a garage at night, just like an ordinary car. But if you need to get somewhere fast or travel large distances, then you can drive it to an airfield and take to the skies. This unique car can reach air speeds of up to 320 kilometres per hour.

- The company intends to sell the first flying cars in 2023, and they are expected to cost about as much as an expensive luxury car.

Flying cars seem like fun, but we're curious to see what the future will hold: will there be traffic lights and signs in the air? And will the police pull you over for reckless flying?

222 NO TWO SNOWFLAKES ARE EXACTLY ALIKE

When it snows, millions (or even billions) of **snowflakes** fall from the sky. It's quite a breathtaking sight, and is even more amazing when you realize that no two snowflakes are exactly alike.

Wilson Bentley discovered that snowflakes are unique at the end of the 19th century. Bentley lived in Vermont in the north of the United States, where the winters are cold and there is always plenty of snow. He tried to study the snowflakes under a microscope, but they melted too fast for him to draw their complex shapes.

To record his findings, he started taking photographs of the snowflakes. No specialized cameras existed in those days, so he had to invent one himself by fitting a camera to his own microscope. People found Bentley's fascination with snowflakes quite endearing, and gave him the nickname 'Snowflake Bentley'.

His photographs were beautiful in their own right but Bentley made another important observation: he noticed that no two of his photographed snowflakes were ever identical. They all had six 'arms' or points, but other than that, each one had a unique shape.

We now know more about how snowflakes are formed. Each one begins as a tiny ice crystal which flutters down to the ground, growing along the way as water vapour freezes onto it and forms new crystals. The snowflake's final appearance depends on many factors, such as levels of humidity and the wind. It is these factors that give each snowflake its unique structure.

Of course, it would be impossible to analyse and compare the billions upon billions of snowflakes that fall to the earth, so we can never say with total certainty that no two are alike.

BONUS SNOWFLAKE FACTS

Snowflakes and hailstones are very different. Snowflakes form when temperatures drop below freezing point: the water droplets in the clouds freeze into ice crystals, and grow as they fall due to water vapour freezing onto the six-sided shape of the original crystal.

Hail consists of frozen water droplets that form at very high altitudes. During warm but stormy weather, the hot, moist air is blown upwards where it meets the ice-cold clouds, and the water droplets freeze. As they churn around in the clouds, the frozen droplets clump together and form a hailstone.

The largest snowflake ever found was 38 centimetres wide and 20 centimetres thick. It fell in 1887 in Montana, USA. Be careful catching that one on your tongue!

223 YOUR HAIR CAN CARRY AN ELECTRIC CHARGE

When combing or brushing your hair, have you ever noticed that it sometimes stands on end? This phenomenon is known as **static electricity**.

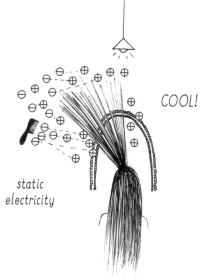

COOL!

static electricity

- Electricity is a kind of energy created by the movement of tiny particles inside atoms. Atoms consist of a nucleus made up of positively charged protons surrounded by a cloud of electrons, which are negatively charged. The positive and negative charges usually cancel each other out, giving the atom a neutral charge overall.

- Under normal circumstances, your body's electric charge is also neutral. But as you move around, you can develop a slight charge on your body in one direction or the other, which discharges when you come into contact with another object. Ever received a shock from grabbing a door handle? That's the static electric charge leaving your body.

- Static electricity can be created through rubbing or 'friction' – running a comb through your hair gives the hairs a positive charge, for example. And because they all have the same charge, the hairs repel each other like the poles of a magnet, standing on end and giving you that frizzy look.

224 ADDING SALT TO YOUR DRINK WILL COOL IT FASTER

Want to cool down a can or bottle of drink super-fast? There's a simple trick to it.

Fill a big bowl of water with ice blocks, and add a small handful of **salt**. Place the can inside the water, stir, then wait two minutes. Your drink should now be ice-cold!

How does it work? Well, salt makes ice melt more quickly, but to do this, the ice needs to draw thermal energy from another heat source. Since the only other thing nearby is your drink can, that's where it draws the heat from, making the can colder.

SSSS

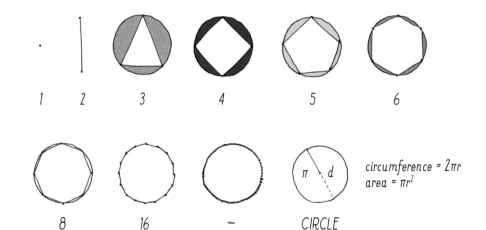

1   2   3   4   5   6

8   16   ~   CIRCLE

$$\text{circumference} = 2\pi r$$
$$\text{area} = \pi r^2$$

225 IT'S IMPOSSIBLE TO COUNT THE CORNERS ON A CIRCLE

A triangle has three sides, squares have four, pentagons have five, and so on. The more sides a shape has, the harder it is to make them out individually, and the shape will start looking more and more like a circle. That's why a **circle** is sometimes called a shape with an infinite number of sides.

In maths classes, you've probably heard about the number 'pi'. To calculate pi, you first need to measure the distance around the circle – this is called the 'circumference'. Then you measure the distance from one side of the circle through its centre to the other side. This is the circle's 'diameter'. Dividing the circumference by the diameter will always produce the same number: pi, whose value is 3.141592… something something. The number of digits after the decimal point is infinite, and the numbers never repeat. People even compete to see who can memorize the most digits of pi. The world record is currently held by Rajveer Meena from India, who can recite 70,000 digits from memory.

How many digits of pi can you remember?

226 THERE'S MATHEMATICS IN NATURE

1, 1, 2, 3, 5, 8, 13, 21, 34, 55…

Take a good look at the row of numbers above. Notice a pattern? That's right – each number in the series is the sum of the previous two numbers. The sequence is called the **Fibonacci series**, and is one of the most famous mathematical sequences in the world. Fibonacci was an Italian mathematician who lived from around 1170 to 1250. He is sometimes also called Leonardo of Pisa.

The Fibonacci series is also known as the 'rabbit sequence', since Fibonacci used it to develop a model for breeding rabbits. But the pattern can be seen everywhere in nature: in plants especially,

where the Fibonacci numbers appear in the petals of flowers, the arrangements of seeds or the branches of a tree.

The seeds of sunflowers and pinecones, for example, are arranged into pairs of spirals twisting in opposite directions. The numbers of spirals will often be pairs from the Fibonacci series, such as eight spirals turning clockwise and thirteen turning anti-clockwise.

227 YOU CAN CHARGE YOUR PHONE WITH A T-SHIRT

If researchers from Wake Forest University in the United States have their way, you'll soon be able to buy a T-shirt that generates enough **electricity** to charge your phone.

Scientists have developed a fabric that can generate electricity using differences in temperature. To do this, they melted carbon nanotubes into a layer of flexible plastic. If the temperature outside the T-shirt differs from the temperature inside, enough electricity is generated to charge up small devices, like an iPod or phone. Handy if you want to go for a run but your battery's flat.

Carbon nanotubes aren't the only way to generate electricity with clothing. A Dutch inventor, Pauline van Dongen, has made T-shirts with inbuilt solar cells that can charge a mobile phone within a couple of hours.

Sadly, these products aren't in the shops yet, as the production costs are still too high. But who knows: perhaps in the future your outfit will become a personal mobile charging station?

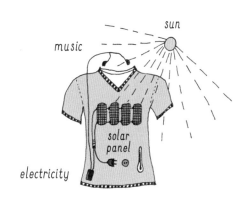

228 A FRIDGE CAN RUN ON COW FARTS

- Cows burp and fart like you wouldn't believe – so much so, in fact, that they are one of the main contributors to global warming. According to some scientists, they are responsible for up to one-quarter of all the world's methane emissions.

- Argentina has lots of cows. So Argentinian scientists found a way to put the methane gas to good use: by giving cows a backpack and inserting a tube into its intestines, they can successfully collect approximately 300 litres of methane gas per day.

- That amount of methane gas can be re-used for other purposes, such as powering a refrigerator for 24 hours. A large herd of cows can easily provide enough power a small village!

229 LOTS OF PEOPLE DON'T LIKE CLOWNS

Do you think clowns are no laughing matter? Maybe you even think they're a little bit creepy? Well you're not alone – lots of people are scared of clowns, even though it's their job to make people laugh. The phenomenon is so widespread, in fact, that scientists have given the fear of clowns a special name: **coulrophobia**.

Special websites exist for people who don't like clowns, such as www.ihateclowns.com. There is also a Facebook group of the same name, with several thousand followers.

But why do so many people dislike clowns? There are several possible explanations.

- Some experts say that humans don't like things that look like people but still aren't completely human. We have a similar reaction to robots that look like people, for example.

BOO!

AAH!

- Other researchers say that masks and other disguises are what unnerve people, as we cannot see what the person behind the mask is thinking or feeling. Usually we can read people's facial expressions to tell if they're trustworthy, angry or happy. But if the signals are covered by mounds of make-up, that information is hidden from us.

Filmmakers know that clowns creep people out, and often use them to portray scary or evil characters. Just look at Stephen King's *It*, or the Joker character in the Batman movies. If you go to a circus, be sure you have someone to cling to!

230 WATER DOESN'T COOL DOWN CHILLI PEPPERS

Biting into a **chilli pepper** is not a smart thing to do – it won't be long before it feels like your mouth is on fire. The culprit is capsaicin, a molecule found in the flesh of many chilli peppers. The capsaicin molecules bond with the pain receptors in your mouth, which tell your brain that something's not right. It also really, really hurts! Your brain responds by setting several reactions in motion: your eyes water, your nose starts running and you'll begin to sweat. All of these reactions are intended to 'flush' the capsaicin out of your body as quickly as possible.

Sometimes it's nice to speed up that process a little, so it's tempting to take a sip of water to cool things down. But that's a really bad idea! Water will only make things worse. What you need is another substance that can bind to the capsaicin and carry it away, and that means you need something fatty. Milk or yogurt will usually help soothe the burning, so next time your mouth's on fire, ask for a glass of milk instead.

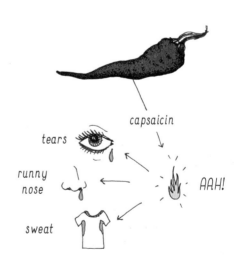

capsaicin

tears

runny nose

AAH!

sweat

231 TESLA IS BUILDING THE WORLD'S LARGEST FACTORY

The Boeing factory in Everett, Seattle is currently the biggest **factory** in the world. Fifty-five football fields could fit inside it, with 3.7 kilometres' worth of passageways below the ground. The factory builds enormous aeroplanes, so all this space is necessary. A Boeing 747 is one of the largest aeroplane models in the world, at an impressive 19 metres tall. Some parts of the factory even house twelve fully-assembled 747s, ready for painting. No wonder they need so much space.

Still, the record might be broken soon by a much bigger factory. Elon Musk is the head of a huge company called Tesla, and his factory manufactures the batteries used in electric cars. The batteries are what make electric cars so expensive.

Elon Musk has opened a factory, or Gigafactory (a unit of measurement meaning billions!) in the Nevada desert that is more than a square kilometre in size. And that's not all: he's purchased an additional six square kilometres in order to make room for seven factories capable of producing enough batteries for half a million electric cars, starting in 2020. Once complete, this factory's surface area will make it not just the world's biggest factory, but also the largest single building on earth.

Musk aims to mass-produce electric car batteries on a huge scale using the latest technologies. That will make them cheaper, allowing more cars to be equipped with them. The factories must also be able to recycle the batteries and re-use the most important components, to make them even more environmentally friendly.

232 SPIDER-MAN WOULD NEED SIZE 145 SHOES TO WALK ON THE CEILING

Have you ever been jealous of spiders, frogs and lizards that can walk on the walls and ceilings? Their special feet are what stop them from slipping and falling down. Bigger animals need bigger feet, and gecko lizards are about as big as an animal can get and still walk on the ceiling. If Spider-Man climbed the walls this way, he would need shoe size 145 – that means having feet 95 centimetres long!.

The soles of a gecko's feet are lined with sticky structures called lamellae, which allow the gecko to climb up almost any surface. Scientists took a long time to figure out exactly how it worked: the lamellae are covered in tiny hairs, which split into even more hairs at the tip. The molecules at the ends of the hairs and the molecules in the wall are attracted to each other by a force called 'Van der Waals force', which is what keeps the gecko stuck to the surface. Unfortunately, geckos aren't able to just turn the force off, so they need to curl their toes at a special angle to pull free from the wall. Luckily all geckos are born knowing how to do it!

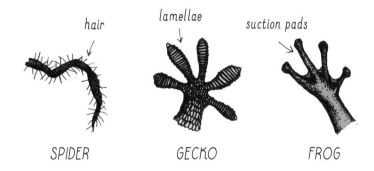

hair   lamellae   suction pads

SPIDER   GECKO   FROG

233 ONLY HUMANS DANCE

'Not true!' you might say, 'I once heard of a dancing bear!'

- That may be, but bears don't **dance** naturally in the wild – dancing circus bears learn it as a trick to earn rewards from their trainers.

this never happens in nature!

There is not a single wild bear that will move rhythmically to music of its own accord. Even other primates such as bonobos and chimpanzees don't dance. Animals just aren't interested in the rhythms of music.

- Humans do dance, of course, probably because dancing releases substances in our brains called endorphins that put us in a happy mood. They make us feel happy, cheerful and more social.

- Dancing also enables physical contact between people, and is comparable to how monkeys groom each other's fur. Dancing makes people seem less threatening, more open, and encourages social connections.

234 JET FIGHTERS CAN REFUEL IN THE AIR

Jet fighters are incredibly fast aeroplanes. They usually only seat one or two people, and are used mostly by the armed forces.

Jet fighters use a lot of fuel. So to avoid having to land all the time, a system was invented to allow them to refuel during flight. A second fuel tanker joins the jet fighter in the air, and a long tube is run between them to allow a fast transfer of fuel. It's a spectacular sight!

...AND A BAG OF CRISPS PLEASE

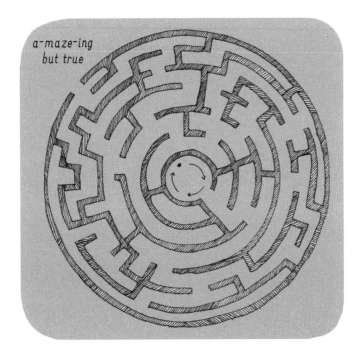

a-maze-ing
but true

235 LOST PEOPLE WALK IN CIRCLES

You see it in cartoons all the time: someone gets lost and starts running around in circles like a headless chicken. Funnily enough, people actually do the same thing in real life. If you were to lose your way in a snowstorm or thick fog, for example, you would soon start **walking in circles**.

As usual, our brains are to blame. Scientists once tested the phenomenon by dumping people in the desert and the woods, and attaching GPS trackers to them. While the sun was out, the people walked in relatively straight lines. But as soon as the sun disappeared, they started walking in circles, always returning to the same place without even noticing. Blindfolding people works even faster, reducing the circles to less than 20 metres in diameter.

Without any landmarks, people quickly lose their sense of direction. We are very reliant on our eyes to find our way. In this respect we are very different from pigeons, who can always find their way back home (see Fact 217).

236 E = MC²

You've probably heard this **formula** somewhere before. It's the most famous part of the theory of relativity developed by the scientist and mathematician **Albert Einstein**. The 'E' stands for energy, the 'm' for mass and 'c' for the speed of light. So the formula says that the energy contained in an object is equal to its mass times the square of the speed of light. Because the speed of light is very fast indeed (300,000 kilometres per second), the formula means that even a tiny bit of mass can generate vast amounts of energy.

The formula can be used to understand the workings of a nuclear reactor. The core of a nuclear reactor is where atoms are split to release energy. More explanation is given below.

- Every atom has a core or 'nucleus' consisting of protons (which are positively charged) and neutrons (which have no charge). Electrons orbit around the nucleus, and have a negative charge. Atoms normally contain protons and electrons in equal numbers.

- The number of neutrons can vary from atom to atom, and different numbers of neutrons produce different 'isotopes'. Some isotopes are stable, which allows the atom to stay in one piece. But others are unstable, and cause the nucleus to break apart.

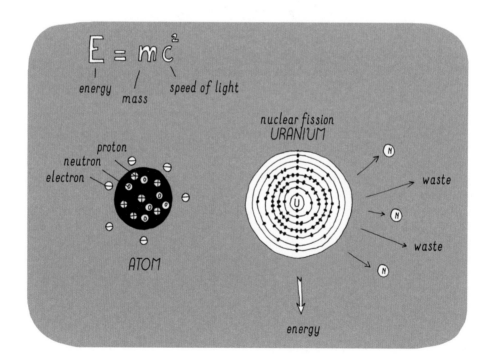

- Uranium is a metal with a very unstable nucleus, which can easily be broken by bombarding it with extra neutrons. When it splits, the nucleus divides into two lighter nuclei and several leftover neutrons.

- If you tried to put the nucleus back together again, you would notice there was a piece missing. That tiny piece of mass gets converted into a large amount of energy, which is what Einstein's formula is all about.

- The energy generated by splitting atoms is called 'nuclear power'. In a nuclear power plant, the energy released by splitting atoms is used to boil water. The resulting steam is used to drive a turbine attached to an enormous dynamo, generating electricity that can be used to power everything in your home, from the lights to your computer.

237 PAPER MONEY ISN'T MADE OF PAPER

Strange but true: the **banknotes** used to pay for things in shops are not made of wood pulp, like ordinary paper.

- Banknotes are traditionally made of cotton paper mixed with linen, a material that fades and wears out much more slowly than ordinary paper. The notes are also soaked in gelatine, making them even stronger. The lifespan of a banknote is usually around two years.

- The first banknotes were invented when the transportation of large amounts of gold and silver coins became too inconvenient. The notes were pieces of paper saying how much money somebody owed you, and could be cashed in at a bank. Notes of this type were called 'promissory notes', which comes from the word 'promise'. Giving one out was like making a paper 'promise' that the other person would receive their money.

- Different types of materials are now used to make modern banknotes, including special types of plastic. Plastic notes last even longer than cotton or linen, and are also harder to forge or counterfeit.

BONUS MONEY FACTS

In the late 19th century, the Russians ruled Alaska, and printed their banknotes on seal hides.

During the Boer War in Africa, money was printed on pieces of clothing.

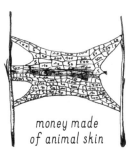

money made of animal skin

238 BLUE BLOOD DOES EXIST (BUT NOT IN HUMANS)

Kings and queens are often said to have **blue blood** running through their veins. But that's not true. Kings, queens, princes, princesses and all other (healthy) members of the nobility are red-blooded, just like you and me. Next time you run into one of them, just ask to prick their finger and you'll see.

Blue has always been considered a special colour.

- In many cultures, blue is used as an indication of social status. Nobles and aristocrats would wear blue clothing to show off how important they were, and in churches the Virgin Mary is often pictured wearing a blue cloak.

- There are other explanations too. The nobility didn't work in the fields and were less exposed to the sun, so their skin was much paler. That made it easier to see the blue-coloured veins beneath their skin.

- Lastly, rich people used a lot of silver, which can leave behind a bluish tint on your skin if you use it often enough.

So humans don't really have blue blood. The veins visible through your skin might look bluish, but that's just because your skin blocks red light while allowing blue light to pass through. Blood gets its red colour from a substance called **haemoglobin**, a molecule that transports the oxygen you breathe to all the cells in your body.

But some animals really do have blue blood, such as squid and some crabs, including horseshoe crabs. The octopuses that live in Antarctica have very blue blood, due to special substances that are capable of absorbing larger quantities of oxygen. Without the extra oxygen, they wouldn't survive.

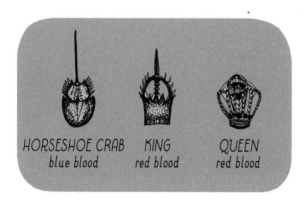

HORSESHOE CRAB
blue blood

KING
red blood

QUEEN
red blood

BONUS BLUE-BLOOD FACT

It's quite possible that your life has already been saved by a horseshoe crab. Horseshoe crab blood is used to test all kinds of drugs and vaccines. It's special, because while it doesn't contain any antibodies, it does contain a substance called LAL that causes bacteria and viruses to clump together. So to find out whether a drug or vaccine is contaminated, simply add some LAL. If no clumps form, you know it's okay to use!

SPLOSH!

239 YOU CAN WEIGH YOUR HEAD BY STICKING IT IN A BUCKET OF WATER

No, there's no need to hack it off first. That would be a pity, as it would be pretty useless after that.

Here's how it works: fill a bucket of water to the brim, place it inside a large tub, then dunk your head in it.

Pull your head back out, and remove the bucket from the tub. Weigh the water left in the bottom, and that will be approximately the same weight as your head, since the density of the matter inside your head is about the same as water.

This doesn't just work with your head – you can do it with any of your limbs, or even your whole body. All you need is a really big bucket, and an even bigger tub.

Do you want to know exactly how much your head weighs, down to the milligram? Then you'll need a CT scanner, or a machine that carves your brain up into extremely thin slices. Not physically of course, but as images. The scanner's computer can work out the density of every given point inside your head, create a 3D model and then calculate its weight.

To give you some idea of what to expect: a hairless adult head usually weighs somewhere between 4.5 and 5 kilograms.

240 BRIGHT LIGHT CAN MAKE YOU SNEEZE

Most people squint when looking at a bright light, but one in four will respond by **sneezing**. This reaction is called the **photic sneeze reflex**.

- Aristotle knew it was possible to make himself sneeze by looking at the sun. He thought it was because the sun warmed up his nose.

- Seventeenth-century scientist Francis Bacon also gave it a try, and noticed that he only sneezed when he kept his eyes open to see the sun. So he deduced that the sneezing was due to the sun's light, not its heat. According to Francis, the sun made his eyes water, which in turn irritated his nose.

- We now know that the real culprit is the nerve that transports sensory messages from the face. Light enters your eyes, causing signals to be sent to your brain. But a hiccup occurs somewhere along the way: something causes the brain to think that the nose is being stimulated instead of the eyes, and it responds by initiating a nasal reflex.

- The nasal reflex occurs mostly when moving from darkness into light. It normally only causes one or two sneezes, but some people can sneeze as many as forty times!

photic sneeze reflex

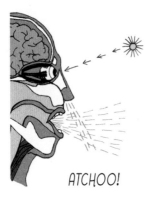

ATCHOO!

BONUS NOSE FACT

Your **nose** might not grow longer when you lie – but it does get warmer. Feeling guilty will cause more blood to flow to certain tissues in the nose, increasing its temperature. You might not notice it straightaway, but it can be measured with scientific instruments. That's why people often scratch their noses when telling a lie.

241 THE TELESCOPE WAS INVENTED ACCIDENTALLY BY A STUDENT OPTICIAN

There is a story that one day, an optician's apprentice in a workshop in the Dutch town of Middelburg was playing around with lenses. He held one lens up to his eye, and the other at arm's length. When he looked through them both at the same time, everything appeared much bigger and closer.

Master optician Hans Lippershey told the boy off for messing about, but afterwards began experimenting with the lenses himself. By 1608 he had invented the **telescope**, and news of the invention spread quickly through the village and beyond. When Italian inventor **Galileo Galilei** heard of it, he quickly set to work on his own model. One year later, he had built a telescope that could magnify objects by a factor of 30.

Galileo liked studying the stars with his new telescope. He discovered that the earth revolved around the sun, and not the other way around. The pope didn't like his conclusion, as he was convinced that the earth was the centre of the universe and that God had created the world and humankind in his image.

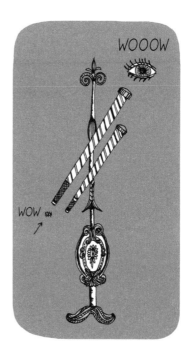

Galileo's work was examined, and he was forced to make some changes to it. He did so, but twenty years later he wrote a book that repeated his initial findings and ridiculed the pope. The pope wasn't happy, and put Galileo under house arrest. Galileo's theory later proved to be completely correct, and we have been sure for some time that the earth really does revolve around the sun.

9

WORDS AND LANGUAGE

242 A BLIND PERSON INVENTED BRAILLE

- **Louis Braille** was three years old when he lost an eye in an accident. He then got an infection in his other eye, and eventually went blind. His parents sent him to a school for the blind.

- At the age of fifteen, Louis invented a special alphabet for **blind** people. He made pinpricks in the paper that could be felt by the fingertips as small bumps. That way, blind people could read using their fingers instead of their eyes.

- Each character in the Braille alphabet is made up of three horizontal pairs of bumps. To form the letter 'A', only the top-left bump is formed – the rest are left flat. The letter 'B' consists of the top two bumps on the left. By using all the possible combinations, each letter and punctuation mark gets its own unique code.

- With enough practice, Braille can be read with the fingers just as quickly as printed text can with the eyes.

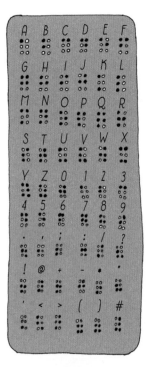

THE BRAILLE
ALPHABET

243 THE PATAGONIANS AND THE WELSH CAN UNDERSTAND EACH OTHER

Welsh is a Celtic language with many unique sounds and symbols. It is spoken by around 800,000 people around the world, most of whom live in Wales.

But Welsh is also spoken by 5,000–12,000 people in the Argentinian region of **Patagonia**. They are the descendants of the Welshmen who travelled to Argentina in 1865.

To this day, teachers are sent from Wales to Argentina to give language lessons. There are currently three bilingual Welsh-Spanish schools in Patagonia.

The dialects spoken by the Welsh and the Patagonians are slightly different, but they can still understand each other pretty well.

244 BABBLING BEGAN IN THE BIBLE

When a person talks nonsense, we often say they are 'babbling'. One possible explanation for this word comes from the Bible.

The first book of the Bible, **Genesis**, says that all people on earth used to speak the same language. The folk who settled in Shinar, near the Euphrates river, decided that they would build a tower reaching all the way to heaven, which would make them famous.

God saw them building the tower and didn't like the idea at all. So he descended to earth and made everybody start speaking different languages, which meant they could no longer communicate and had to stop building the tower. According to the Bible, the city and the tower were given the name of Babel or Babylon, based on a Hebrew word *balal*, meaning to jumble or confuse.

245 'BARBARIAN' HAS TWO MEANINGS

If you call someone a **barbarian** nowadays it usually means you think they are rude.

- The word comes from the ancient Greeks, who referred to foreigners as *barbaros*, or non-Greek speakers who could not be understood. The word 'bar-bar-os' was an imitation of the foreigner's unintelligible speech. Imitating sounds like this in language is called **onomatopoeia**. Other examples include words like 'meow', 'hiss' and 'whoosh'.

- The Romans used the same word but wrote it a little differently, spelling it *barbarus*. In Rome, a barbarus was someone who was unfamiliar with the local language and culture. So it was quite possible to have good manners, but still be called a barbarus.

- Today, the word 'barbarian' means something different. A modern-day barbarian is somebody who knows nothing about art or culture, and has little respect for other people. So be careful next time you call someone a 'barbarian'...

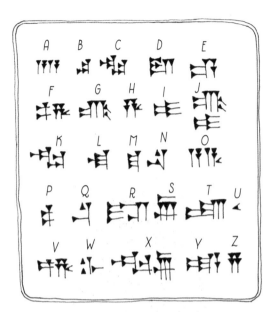

CUNEIFORM SCRIPT

246 EARLY WRITING WAS MADE USING PLANT STALKS

One of the world's oldest **writing** systems was invented by the **Sumerians**, a people who lived in Mesopotamia. The system was developed between 3,300 and 2,900 BCE.

The Sumerians made symbols by pressing reed stalks into clay tablets. Because this method gave many of the markings a triangular shape, today we call this writing system *cuneiform*, which is Latin for 'wedge-shaped'.

The Sumerians used the cuneiform script to keep financial records. They wanted to know exactly how much of each product they had in store, and who owed how much to whom.

247 WANT TO 'CLICK' WITH A LANGUAGE? TRY XHOSA

Xhosa is one of the 'click languages' spoken in South Africa and Lesotho.

- Around eight million people speak Xhosa as their native language, making it the second-biggest language in South Africa (after Zulu). Nelson Mandela, the anti-apartheid activist and president of South Africa, spoke Xhosa.

- Xhosa includes three basic clicking sounds: **C** sounds like 'tsk', **X** sounds like the click used to spur on horses while **Q** sounds like the popping of a champagne cork.

- There are six different versions of each click, and words can contain multiple clicks.

- In addition to the clicks, there are also vowel sounds and consonants that don't involve click sounds.

XHOSA

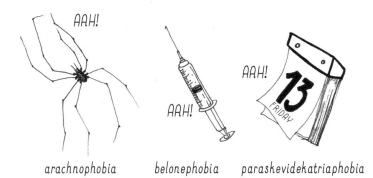

AAH!

arachnophobia

AAH!

belonephobia

AAH!

paraskevidekatriaphobia

BONUS FEAR FACT

If you want to skip school, you could try telling your parents you have **didaskaleinophobia**, which is the fear of going to school! Or **sophophobia**, which is the fear of learning.

248 YOU ARE NOT A BIBLIOPHOBE

How can we be so sure? Well, **bibliophobia** is a fear of books, so if you had bibliophobia, there's no way you would dare to touch this one – let alone open it or read it!

- A **phobia** is an irrational fear, or a fear of something without a good reason. It's normal, for example, to be a bit scared of spiders. But if you simply refuse to enter a room because a spider might be lurking there somewhere, there's a good chance you suffer from **arachnophobia**, or an irrational fear of spiders.

- Many phobias are harmless, but some can occasionally cause serious problems. **Belonephobia**, for example – an irrational fear of needles – often prevents people getting injections from the doctor when they're ill.

- Phobia-sufferers sometimes need special treatment from a therapist to help them overcome their fears.

- Some phobias have special names that you can use to impress your friends. Take **paraskevidekatriaphobia**, the fear of Friday the 13th. Or **sesquipedalophobia**: the fear of reading or pronouncing long words.

- People can develop phobias of almost anything, and there's usually a special scientific name for it.

249 LIBRARIES HAVE EXISTED FOR THOUSANDS OF YEARS

Libraries have been around for a long, long time.

- There is evidence that Mesopotamia had a library in 2,300 BCE. Of course it didn't look like the libraries we have now, with rows of neatly-ordered books on the shelves. It was more like a temple where priests were educated, and the books were clay tablets. They were arranged on shelves, however.

- Ebla, a city in the north-west of Syria, had a well-known library of clay tablets. The library itself was destroyed by a fire one day, but the blaze actually baked the clay tablets into hardened bricks, allowing them to be preserved for centuries. The tablets can still be read today – but you will need to learn cuneiform script first (see Fact 246).

- The library of Alexandria is the most famous of all the ancient libraries. It is said that all ships docking in Alexandria had to hand over all their books to the library, where they were copied by scribes. The original was then kept by the library, and the copy given back to the travellers to take away. Most of the books in the library of Alexandria were papyrus rolls – unfortunately, it too was destroyed by fire, and nothing of it remains today.

250 NOBODY COULD DECIPHER HIEROGLYPHS
(UNTIL A CODESTONE WAS FOUND)

In July 1799, French soldiers made an amazing discovery while digging in the Egyptian city of Rosetta. They found a dark-coloured stone tablet, roughly 112 by 76 centimetres, on which a text had been engraved.

- The special thing about the text was that it was written in three different languages: Egyptian **hieroglyphs**, Demotic script (a form of ancient Egyptian) and Greek.

- Scholars wasted no time, and soon figured out that the text was a decree issued by priests proclaiming the status of King Ptolemy V Epiphanes. It was written in the year 196 BCE.

- The stone – now known as the **Rosetta Stone** – was especially important in helping to decipher Egyptian hieroglyphs. Scholars had been trying to understand them for hundreds of years, and the text on the Rosetta Stone worked like a kind of dictionary, because there was a direct translation right beside it.

- Want to see the Rosetta Stone with your own eyes? Then head to the British Museum in London, where it has been kept since 1802.

251 THERE IS A FLY NAMED AFTER BEYONCÉ

The *Scaptia beyonceae*, or simply the Beyoncé fly, is a species of horsefly native to Australia. The back end of the fly is covered in a patch of bright, gold-coloured hair, which is probably what inspired its discoverer to name it after the singer Beyoncé Knowles.

Another singer, Shakira, lent her name to a species of wasp – the *Aleiodes shakirae*. The wasp lays its eggs inside the bodies of live caterpillars. When they hatch, they make the caterpillar dance around – just like Shakira does with her audiences.

Barack Obama has also been a great inspiration to biologists, who have used his name for two spiders (*Aptostichus barackobamai* and *Spintharus barackobamai*), several fish (*Etheostoma obama, Tosanoides obama* and *Teleogramma obamarum*), a beetle (*Desmopachria barackobamai*), a worm (*Paragordius obmai*), a bird (*Nystalus obamai*) and a bee (*Lasioglossum obamai*). Even an extinct reptile – the *Obamadon graciis* – has been named after the former US president.

Want an insect to be named after you too? Then the best thing to do is to become a biologist yourself and make new scientific discoveries. That's your best chance to have the Royal Institution name a new species after you. Alternatively, some charity organizations allow their donors to name new animals: at the Scripps Institution of Oceanography in San Diego, for example, you can name a newly-discovered marine species for a mere $5,000!

BZZZ

Scaptia beyonceae

252 THERE ARE OVER SIX THOUSAND LANGUAGES ON EARTH

MANDARIN — 你女子
ENGLISH — HI
SPANISH — hola
OTHER — ○ ○ ○

It's hard to say exactly how many **languages** there are on earth, but scholars believe it's somewhere between six and seven thousand. Some are spoken by many millions of people, others by only a handful. When the last remaining speakers of a language die, the language dies with them, which is why the number of languages on earth is steadily decreasing.

- Mandarin is the most widely-spoken language on earth, with 1.05 billion speakers. Although most of them live in China, Mandarin is also spoken in Taiwan and other parts of the world. The language has many different dialects, some of which are so different that the speakers cannot even understand one another.

- The world's second-biggest language is English, with 1.01 billion speakers. This figure is due mostly to all the people who speak English as a second language – in actuality, only 500 million people speak English as their mother tongue.

- Spanish also has 500 million native speakers, but fewer non-native speakers than English. In total, the world has about 570 million Spanish speakers.

253 'BIKINI ISLAND' IS A REAL PLACE

The **bikini** was invented in 1946 by French fashion designer Louis Réard. Until that time, all women's swimsuits were made in one piece. Many people objected to the new style, saying it was indecent and exposed far too much skin.

During the 1940s, atomic bombs were being tested on the island of Bikini in the Pacific Ocean. The terrible tests were all over the news, and everybody was talking about it. So to give his new invention some extra publicity, Louis Réard decided to name his new invention the bikini.

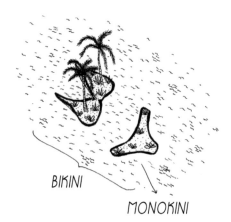

BIKINI

MONOKINI

He also explained that the start of the word, **bi**, is Latin for 'two', which made sense because his swimsuits consisted of two separate parts. Later came the monokini, a swimsuit that consisted only of the bottom half!

254 SIGN LANGUAGE IS NOT THE SAME EVERYWHERE

People with hearing difficulties can use **sign language** to communicate.

- Like spoken languages, not all sign languages are the same. There are different versions throughout the world. For instance, although the UK and the USA are both English-speaking countries, they use different sign languages.

- It's also possible to whisper and shout in sign language:

  To shout, straighten your back and make larger movements – instead of moving just your hand, for example, use your whole arm.

  To whisper, hold your hands close to your chest and make your movements as small as possible.

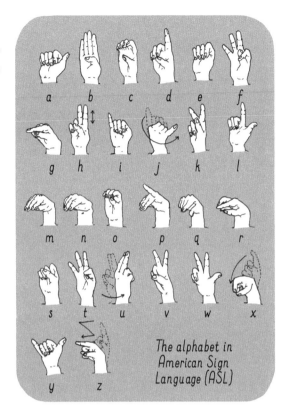

The alphabet in American Sign Language (ASL)

255 THE BIBLE IS THE WORLD'S MOST TRANSLATED BOOK

The entire **Bible** has been translated into more than 600 languages, and parts of it into over 2,500 languages. The Old Testament was originally written in Hebrew, but was translated very soon after. Translations were available as early as the second century BCE, when the Old Testament could be read in Greek. In the fourth century CE the entire Bible was translated into Latin, and many other translations soon followed.

The first full translation of the Bible into English that can still be read and understood today was made by an Oxford priest named William Tyndale in 1523. Many of the versions that followed borrowed heavily from Tyndale's work.

THE BIBLE

256 WE ARE STILL USING WORDS FROM THE TIME OF JULIUS CAESAR

I DICTATOR
II CAMPVS
III EXIT
IV CASEVM
V CASTELLVM
VI VIA STRATA
VII CAMERA

Many centuries ago, **Latin** was a world language. The Roman Empire covered vast expanses of Europe, so in order to be understood, the rulers communicated in Latin. Some of the words they used still appear in European languages today.

The word 'dictator' literally means 'he who speaks'. Also consider 'dictation', when the teacher reads a text aloud that you have to write down.
In Roman society, dictators were very important and well-respected people; only later did the word come to mean 'tyrant' or 'despot'.

In Roman times a 'campus' was a field or open space. Nowadays we use it as a name for the area surrounding university buildings.

If you want to leave a building, you will probably look for an 'exit' sign. In Latin, 'exit' literally means 'he/she walks out'.

Remnants of Latin can still be found in words we use every day: words like cheese (*caseus*), castle (*castellum*) or street (from *via strata* or 'paved road'). The full name for a 'camera' is actually *camera obscura*, Latin for 'dark chamber', and refers to the very first pinhole cameras made of a dark box with a hole in one side.

257 CHINESE SPEAKERS NEED GOOD MEMORIES

Written **Chinese** has than 100,000 characters! Each character depicts a separate object or idea, which is why Chinese writing is called *ideographic* (Greek for 'shape-writing'). However, only about 3,000 of the characters are used in everyday texts.

In the English alphabet, we use 26 letters to write all the words we need. Because each letter represents a certain sound, our writing system is called *phonetic*, after the Greek word *phonein* which means 'to speak'.

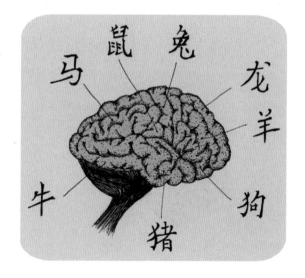

258 DONALD DUCK HAS MANY NAMES AROUND THE WORLD

You probably know him simply as Donald Duck – that's the original name given to the bumbling bird by his creator Walt Disney. In many of the world's countries, his name has been translated into something else. See which one you like most!

- Italy: Paperino
- Spain: El Pato Donald
- Sweden: Kalle Anka
- Denmark: Anders And
- Finland: Aku Ankka

Mickey Mouse has a few other names too:

- Finland: Mikki Hiiri
- Italy: Topolino
- Sweden: Musse Pigg

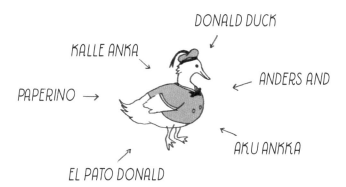

259 SOME PEOPLE EAT BOOKS

They don't just devour them by reading them. They literally eat whole books!

- People who do this suffer from a condition called **bibliophagia**. Bibliophagia also used to be a punishment: people who wrote books about religion or politics that went against the ideas of those in power were forced to eat their words, quite literally!

- There are also **biblioclasts**, people who want to destroy books. Usually they are against whatever the book says, and want the ideas to disappear. Their urge is so great that they often do it without thinking. Common biblioclast targets include the Bible and other religious writings.

- **Bibliokleptomaniacs** are those with an uncontrollable urge to steal books.

- Thankfully the world is also full of **bibliophiles**, or people who love books and are dedicated to looking after them.

10

ADVENTURES
IN BOTANY

260 THE GIANT SEQUOIA CAN GROW AS TALL AS A 25-STOREY BUILDING

Giant sequoias grow in California, on the west coast of the United States. They can grow up to 75 metres tall and weigh nearly 2,000 tonnes, making them the largest living things on earth.

- The world's tallest giant sequoia even has a name: General Sherman. It grows in the Sequoia National Park in California and is 83.8 metres tall, with a trunk 7.7 metres across. General Sherman is probably about 2,300–2,700 years old, making it not only the world's tallest sequoia, but also the oldest.

- In the 19th century, people sometimes carved tunnels into sequoia trunks in order to drive cars through them. This practice has thankfully died out, but some of the old tunnels can still be seen today.

- The bark of the giant sequoia is 90 centimetres thick! That means if ever there is a forest fire, the bark will be damaged but the tree itself will not go up in flames. Fire is even sometimes necessary for the trees to reproduce – their seeds will only fall when surrounded by extreme heat.

- The sequoia may be the largest tree on earth, but it isn't the tallest – that honour goes to the coastal redwood, which also grows in California and can reach heights of 115.5 metres. That's taller than most skyscrapers.

Rafflesia arnoldii

261 THE FLOWER THAT REEKS OF DEATH

Most flowers give off a pleasant smell, but not *Rafflesia arnoldii*.

- **Rafflesia** is also known as the 'corpse lily', and can be found in the jungles of south-western Asia. It is a parasite, and grows on vines.

- The plant produces the biggest blossoms on earth: enormous reddish-brown flowers with white speckles. They give off a scent similar to rotting meat, a terrible stink that attracts the flesh-eating flies and other insects needed to pollinate the flower.

- Pollination is a complicated affair, since it requires both a male and a female flower to bloom at the same time. Since the flowers only survive for 5–7 days, their chances of reproduction are very small. The effects of deforestation are also destroying the flowers' habitat, so the probability of both a male and female flower being close together *and* blooming at the same time is lower than ever. This is why the corpse lily is already an endangered species.

262 TOMATO PLANTS ARE POISONOUS

Tomatoes themselves are healthy and delicious – but be careful when dealing with the rest of the tomato plant!

- Tomato plants belong to the nightshade family. Their stems contain tomatine, a poison produced by the plant to protect itself against all kinds of dangers. Tomatine is also poisonous to humans.

- Unripe tomatoes still contain a little tomatine, but it disappears once the tomato has become red, sweet and juicy.

- Just like tomato plants, the potato plant, aubergine plant and bell pepper plant are also poisonous.

- Tomatine is only dangerous in large doses, but it can give you a stomach-ache, cause diarrhoea, or make you drowsy. So just stick to ripe tomatoes and there's no need to worry – you can keep eating all the spaghetti sauce you want!

deadly delicious?

263 THERE'S LOTS OF KISSING
IN CORAL REEFS

Coral is made up of millions of tiny creatures called polyps, living in large colonies on the ocean floor. The colonies are called coral reefs.

Scientists have discovered that at night, the polyps press their mouths against each other to kiss. They probably do so to exchange food as well as other useful substances.

The scientists first noticed the kissing in the Gulf of Aqaba. They were using a very special underwater microscope that was much more powerful than any microscope ever used before.

But there's not just kissing going on in the reefs – there's also the occasional tiff or two. If one coral's territory is invaded by another, it feels threatened and will stretch out tendrils that give off substances called enzymes. These enzymes attack the other coral, and can even kill it. But corals know how to tell friends from foes, so these attacks only ever occur between corals of different species.

264 TREES AND PLANTS ALLOW US TO BREATHE

Most living things on our planet need gases in order to survive. Most gases are invisible, but they are what make our beautiful blue-green planet so full of life. The main gases necessary for life are carbon dioxide, water vapour and oxygen.

- When you breathe in, you suck air into your lungs. That air contains oxygen, a gas that is needed by every living cell in your body. Your cells consume oxygen and produce carbon dioxide, which is sent back to your lungs for you to breathe out again.

- Plants, trees and flowers need carbon dioxide, water and sunlight in order to survive.

- Plants get their water (and certain minerals) from the ground via their root systems. Extremely thin tubes transport the water from the roots up the stem of the plant and into the tips of the branches and leaves.

- Plants breathe in carbon dioxide gas through tiny holes in their stems and leaves, just like you breathe in oxygen through your mouth. These special holes are called **stomae**.

- Sunlight enables carbon dioxide and water to be converted into glucose: a kind of sugar that the plant can use to fuel growth.

- A different set of tubes transports the glucose created during **photosynthesis** back down into the plant (see also Fact 274).

- As part of this process, oxygen is released back into the air, which is what allows us to breathe.

- For plants, it's important for their tube systems to stay full of water. Whenever water supplies drop too low, the stomae clamp shut to prevent the plant from drying out. As long as the stomae are closed, the plant cannot breathe in any carbon dioxide. If they stay closed for too long, the plant will die.

So next time you wander past an enormous oak tree, don't forget to say thank you!

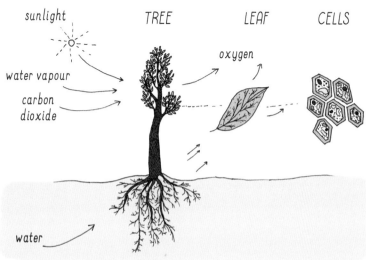

A GUIDE TO PHOTOSYNTHESIS

sunlight TREE LEAF CELLS

oxygen

water vapour

carbon dioxide

water

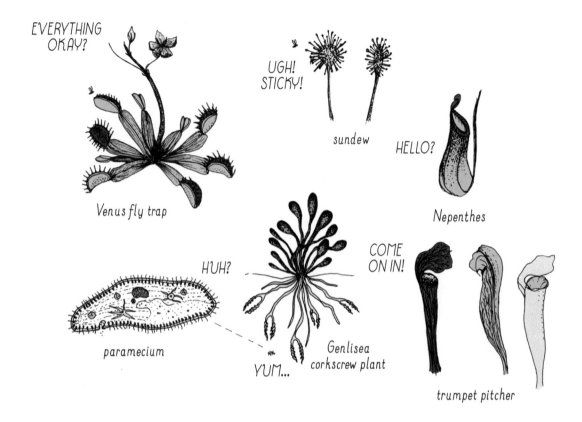

EVERYTHING OKAY?

UGH! STICKY!

sundew

HELLO?

Venus fly trap

Nepenthes

HUH?

COME ON IN!

paramecium

YUM...

Genlisea corkscrew plant

trumpet pitcher

265 SOME PLANTS ARE CARNIVOROUS

As well as carbon dioxide gas and water, plants also need certain minerals to survive – nitrogen, for example, is vital to plant growth. Most plants get their minerals from the ground, but some grow in regions that are quite low in minerals, and have found a clever way to obtain their nitrogen. They catch and eat insects!

Not all **carnivorous** plants work the same way, however.

- The Venus fly trap has jaw-like pairs of leaves that snap shut when an insect walks on them.

- Sundews are plants with sticky fronds that can trap insects.

- Pitcher plants in the *Nepenthes* family grow large vase-like leaves that are filled with digestive juices. When insects fall in, they drown and are slowly digested.

- Trumpet pitchers have hairs on the inside of their spouts that point inwards. When insects land on them, they can no longer escape and are digested whole by the plant.

- Corkscrew plants are extremely specialized carnivorous plants. They eat insects with their roots, which contain tiny holes just large enough for little insects to get inside. They crawl into the root, but small hairs prevent them from crawling back out again. The only direction they can travel is towards the plant's stomach, where they are eventually digested.

266 POTATOES ARE (A TINY BIT) POISONOUS

Potatoes contain **solanine**, a toxic chemical that forms in the potato plant's leaves and can cause serious illness in humans. When the potatoes themselves are exposed to sunlight, they turn green and start producing solanine.

- Potato plants came to Europe from South America in the 16th century. Their flowers, leaves and berries were extremely poisonous, and so people found it hard to believe that the roots were edible. It took two whole centuries before Europeans dared to peel and eat a potato.

- Solanine is only dangerous in quantities of 200 milligrams or more. One kilogram of potatoes contains only 40 milligrams of solanine – that means you would need to eat five kilograms' worth before suffering any ill effects. It would make you sick, but you still wouldn't die: solanine only reaches deadly strength at 400 milligrams.

- Found a potato with green blotches? Best thing to do is throw it away, as the solanine spreads throughout the whole potato, and isn't broken down by cooking.

- Does this mean you should stop eating chips? Not at all! All foods contain some substances that can be dangerous in large quantities, so just eat a varied and balanced diet and you'll be fine.

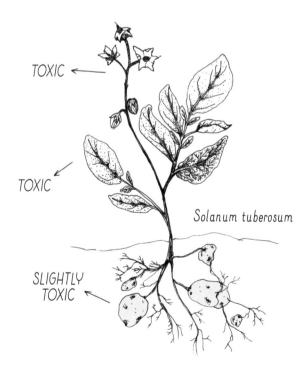

TOXIC ←

TOXIC ↙

Solanum tuberosum

SLIGHTLY
TOXIC ←

Lodoicea maldivica
or Coco de mer

♀
love nut

♂
fruit/pollen

leaf

267 SOME SEEDS CAN WEIGH UP TO 30 KILOGRAMS

If you're imagining a tiny seed like the ones inside an apple core, then we've got a surprise for you. The **coco de mer** or sea coconut is a tree that grows on the islands of Praslin and Curieuse in the Seychelles. Its seeds can reach up to 50 centimetres in diameter and weigh up to 30 kilograms, making it the largest known seed of any plant in the world. The fruit is sometimes called the 'love nut', since it resembles a shapely bottom! That's also why one of the plant's old scientific names contains the word *callipyge*, which is Greek for 'beautiful behind'.

Because the trees grow on islands, the seeds are often washed away by the tide and end up on faraway shores. But they never grow there, and scientists recently found out why. The seeds' enormous weight makes them sink to the ocean floor, where they can sometimes lie for a very long time. Eventually the nut begins to rot, releasing a gas that buoys it back to the surface. That's how the seeds float over to other islands, but because they are already rotten by that time, they can never grow.

Other islanders were amazed at the strange, washed-up objects, and didn't know what they were. They often believed they must have magical powers, and invented stories to explain them.

- Some seafaring explorers thought the seeds came from an enormous forest on the ocean floor, where giant birds built their nests. According to the legends, the birds were so large that they hunted tigers and elephants, and occasionally devoured an entire boat, crew and all!

- In the Maldives, it was compulsory for anyone who found a coco de mer to take it to the king immediately. Those who did not risked the death penalty.

- Even when people realized where the nuts were coming from, the legends continued to exist. One reason is the shape of the plant itself. Sea coconut trees are either male or female: the female trees bear the bottom-shaped nuts, while the male trees have long parts that stick out like penises. People would tell of how the male trees would uproot themselves to go in search of the female trees, and whoever saw the trees 'doing it' with each other would go blind!

- Because botanists still don't fully understand how the trees pollinate one another, the legends live on to this day.

268 OVER THE LAST TWENTY-FIVE YEARS, ONE-TENTH OF THE EARTH'S WILDERNESS HAS DISAPPEARED

Nature is having a hard time on earth right now. Over the last twenty-five years, around one-tenth of all the world's **wilderness** has disappeared. That's equal to 3.3 million square kilometres, or an area about the size of India.

Scientists define wilderness as areas that are untouched by human hands; places where there are no farms, cities or streets, and no trees are chopped down.

The earth has about 30 million square kilometres of wilderness left, or one-fifth of all the land on the planet. Most of it is located in North America, Australia, northern Asia and north Africa. But there is still wilderness in the United Kingdom too, such as the Scottish Highlands or the mountains of England and Wales.

Humans need to band together to take care of the earth's wilderness. Scientists and environmentalists have issued a call to preserve the last remaining regions that we have, because once it's gone, it's gone forever.

20–25 years

spider plant
1

bromeliad
2

sansevieria
3

269 NOT ALL PLANTS NEED LOTS OF SUNLIGHT

Fact 264 talks about how plants need sunlight to survive. But not all plants need the same amount of sunlight – some plants can grow and thrive in even the darkest room.

- **Spider plants**, for example, don't need sunlight – fluorescent lighting is enough. They are not demanding at all. Forget to water it for a week? Or even a month? No problem, the spider plant can take it, making it ideal for people without green fingers.

- Does your bathroom have a tiny window somewhere? Then the **bromeliad** will feel right at home. Bromeliads do best in dark, moist spaces. Just like spider plants, they need very little sunlight – any ordinary light bulb will do. This cousin of the pineapple also has stunning red flowers that will bring a delightful splash of colour to a bathroom!

- Lastly there's the **sansevieria**, or 'Grey Lady'. Give her a little sunlight and the occasional drop of water, and she'll grow wonderfully well. In fact, if you give her too much water, she may not even survive!

270 DO TREES SLEEP AT NIGHT?

Strange but true: at night, **trees** let their branches droop a little and seem to doze off. You know they're awake again when their branches spring back into shape.

However, you need to look very closely or you won't notice. A tree five metres in height will drop its branches approximately ten centimetres, which is barely visible to the naked eye. Researchers from Finland and Austria used special scanners to monitor the trees' smallest movements, and saw that they always lower their branches a little at sundown. The branches are lowest right before sunrise, and once the morning sun breaks through, they proudly stand to attention once more.

The trees probably aren't really asleep; the phenomenon is more likely to be related to the trees' sap circulation. When the sun goes down, the tree's pores, or stomae, close up and there is less tension in its twigs and branches. Once the light returns, the stomae open up again; water evaporates from the leaves, and the roots suck more water up from the ground. This cycle is what makes trees appear to 'sleep' and 'wake up'.

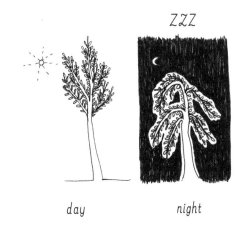

day   night

271 NOT ALL ORANGES ARE ORANGE

Oranges were invented by humans. A clever fruit grower once crossed a mandarin with a pomelo (a kind of Chinese grapefruit), and the result was what we now call an orange. In fact, oranges actually used to be green on the outside, and green oranges are still sold in many places today.

Orange oranges only grow in slightly cooler weather – the peel turns orange when the temperature drops below a certain point. In hotter countries, such as Honduras, oranges stay green. When oranges from Honduras are exported to the West, they are turned orange artificially by exposing them to ethylene, a harmless sweet-smelling gas. The green colour disappears, and the fruit becomes orange not only by name, but also by nature.

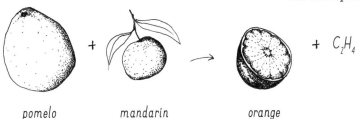

pomelo   mandarin   orange $+ \ C_2H_4$

272 MUSHROOMS CAN MAKE YOU SEE THINGS

Mushrooms and toadstools grow mainly in late summer and autumn, erupting out of the ground from mycelia, which are rather like fungus roots. Whenever male and female mycelia merge together, a mushroom can form.

- There are around five thousand different species of mushrooms and toadstools on earth. About one hundred of them are edible, but around a dozen are very poisonous to humans!

- Some mushrooms will make you see things that aren't really there. This is called hallucinating, and is caused by chemical substances called hallucinogens. Because of these effects, they are classed as an illegal drug in many countries, including the UK.

- One of the world's prettiest toadstools is called the **fly agaric**: it's bright red with white spots, and gnomes and other magical woodland creatures are often depicted sitting on them. To find one, look around where birch trees grow.

- Never eat mushrooms if you don't know exactly what they are! One of the world's deadliest toadstools, commonly known as the **death cap**, is actually quite delicious to eat, but can easily kill you.

273 THERE ARE 3,000 BILLION TREES ON EARTH

Of course, nobody has counted them all one by one. Scientists use satellite images and supercomputers combined with other data to estimate the **number of trees** on earth.

- Without trees, we would not survive. Trees pump out the oxygen we need to breathe, and remove the carbon dioxide that we breathe out.

- The densest forests in the world are in Russia, Scandinavia and North America.

- The largest forested areas are in tropical countries, where nearly half of all the world's tree species are found.

1   2   3   4   5   6

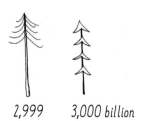

2,999   3,000 billion

274 PLANTS AND SOME BACTERIA MAKE THEIR OWN FOOD

in → out

green plant

After all, it's not like plants can go to the kitchen and fry themselves some sausages, is it?

- These special organisms use the sun's energy to turn carbon dioxide gas and water into carbohydrates. These starchy substances are important to all plants, as they form the building blocks for new cells.

- Once they have carbohydrates, the plants can also break them down into energy to power all their vital functions.

- Plants therefore use carbohydrates as both building blocks and as fuel.

- This conversion process is called **photosynthesis**. Photosynthesis can only happen if there are pigments (coloured cells) to capture the sun's rays. In green plants, the pigment is called chlorophyll, and that's what makes plants green. Bacteria and algae also use pigments to capture light.

275 ENORMOUS WATER LILIES GROW IN THE TROPICS

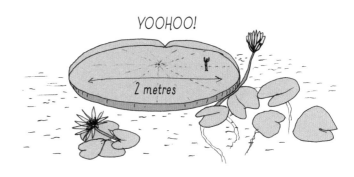

YOOHOO!

2 metres

- Ever heard of *Victoria amazonica*? This species of **water lily** grows leaves up to 2 metres in diameter, with edges that stand up like little fences. These 'lily pads' are attached to 8-metre-long underwater stems.

- The lilypads can carry up to 40 kilos in weight. You might even be able to stand on one!

- Each water lily blooms only for two nights. On the first night a white flower appears, attracting beetles that pollinate the plants.

The flower closes again during the day, and on the second night when the petals unfold, the flower is pink in colour.

- *Victoria amazonica* only grows in still or very slow-moving waters. It can be found in Bolivia, Brazil, Guyana and Peru.

- In other countries, it is often cultivated in botanical gardens. Maybe there's one near you?

276 BACTERIA CAN'T BE SQUASHED TO DEATH

Bacteria are literally everywhere, and are only 1–2 microns in length. A micron is one-thousandth of a millimetre, which means that ten thousand bacteria can fit into a single square centimetre. That's really, really small.

Bacteria aren't bothered by a whack from your hand – they have strong cell walls that protect them from outside forces. And you'll hardly touch the bacteria anyway, since the pressure of your hand is spread out over an enormous area relative to the size of each bacterium.

So how *do* you kill bacteria?

- To kill bacteria in food, special acids or preservatives are used that can break through bacterial cell walls and kill them.

- Cooking food will also kill most bacteria, but not all. They leave spores behind, which new bacteria can use to grow. To kill the spores, food must be heated to around 120–130 ˚C. This process is called **ultra-heat treatment** or **sterilization**, and is used on products such as milk to increase its shelf life.

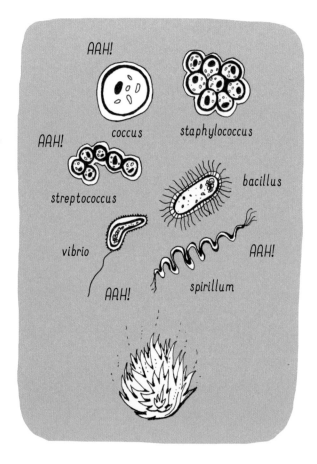

- At low temperatures, bacteria reproduce at a much slower rate. That's why we keep a lot of foods in the refrigerator.

277 DRAGON TREES DON'T BREATHE FIRE

The island of Socotra in Yemen is home to many unique species of plants and animals. Around one-third of all the species on Socotra cannot be found anywhere else on earth. That's because the island is 350 kilometres from the nearest coastline – it broke away from the mainland six million years ago, and just kept on drifting.

BONUS FACT

If an animal or plant is found in only one place on earth, it is said to be **endemic** to that place.

One of the most fascinating plants on Socotra is called the **dragon tree**, or *Dracaena cinnabari*. It looks like an enormous umbrella, and its bark contains a fiery red sap. The early inhabitants of Socotra were convinced the sap was made of dragon's blood, which is how the tree got its impressive name.

DRAGON TREE

278 YOU CAN SURVIVE ON A DESERT ISLAND

Scotsman Alexander Selkirk proved it.

Selkirk was an unruly type, and when the authorities threatened to punish him for his bad behaviour, he joined the crew of a buccaneer ship. **Buccaneers** were groups made up of European adventurers and slaves who had escaped from Africa. Just like pirates, they attacked other ships to steal from them.

In September 1704, the ship ran ashore on a **deserted island**. Alexander thought the ship was no longer seaworthy and needed repairs. The captain would hear nothing of it, and Alexander stubbornly yelled out: 'I'd rather stay here on this island than board a leaky rust-bucket like that!' The captain was already sick of Alexander's moodiness, and before Selkirk knew it, the ship set sail without him on board, leaving him marooned on the island.

Thankfully, there was enough food growing on the island for Selkirk to survive. He lived on edible plants, fruits, roots and berries. Now and again he would eat a lobster, a fish or a bird's egg. He survived all alone on the island for four years and four months.

On 2 February 1709 he was rescued by captain Woodes Rogers. Rogers wrote a book about his travels called *A Cruising Voyage Round the World*, which included a section on Alexander Selkirk.

It was these stories that later inspired Daniel Defoe to write the novel *Robinson Crusoe*.

In 1966, the island of Más Afuera was officially renamed Alejandro Selkirk, after its famous solitary visitor.

BONUS SURVIVAL FACT

In 1982, Steven Callahan's ship was badly damaged at sea. Thankfully he had an emergency boat, and managed to salvage some essentials from the ship before it slowly sank to the ocean floor.

When his food ran out, he fashioned a primitive spear in order to catch birds and fish. To drink, he collected rainwater. Callahan survived for 76 days before he was rescued: he was very thin and covered in sores, but he lived to tell the tale.

Bamboo can grow through anything!

279 BAMBOO GROWS FAST – VERY FAST!

Bamboo grows everywhere in the world, and there are lots of different varieties.

- Giant bamboo can grow as tall as 35 metres, with stalks 10–35 centimetres in diameter. But there are also plenty of bamboo species with stalks only a few centimetres wide.

- Bamboo is best-known as a tropical plant, but in fact it grows just as well in cold, mountainous regions.

- Bamboo roots can spread out underground incredibly quickly, and suddenly sprout new shoots in places you wouldn't expect.

- Some bamboo species grow amazingly fast – sometimes more than a metre per day – making bamboo one of the fastest-growing plant species in the world.

- Stories say that prisoners sentenced to death in Asia used to be tied down onto a patch of fast-growing bamboo stalks. Eventually the bamboo would pierce and stab through the poor soul's body. But researchers have found no evidence for these tales, so they're probably just an urban legend.

280 THERE ARE MYSTERIOUS CIRCLES IN AFRICA

The people of Namibia and South Africa sometimes find strange circular shapes in grassy areas. Although some people might see the circles and immediately think of aliens, the circles are probably created by a species of very smart sand **termites**.

The termites feed on the roots of young plants. Eventually the plants die, leaving a bare patch in the grass. What's so smart about that, you might think?

Well, when it rains, the water seeps down through the bare soil, creating a useful water reservoir for the termites. The water also means the grass around the bare circle will grow faster, producing seeds that the termites can snack on later.

Termites might not be the only things making the circles, however. Some smaller circles may result from plants competing for water amongst themselves, and drawing it out of the soil with their long roots.

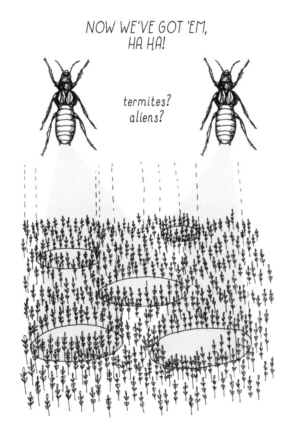

NOW WE'VE GOT 'EM, HA HA!

termites?
aliens?

11

FOOD, GLORIOUS FOOD

281 THE WORLD'S MOST EXPENSIVE COFFEE IS MADE OF WEASEL POO

Did you know that **kopi luwak**, or **civet coffee**, fetches between 125 and 400 pounds per kilogram?

- Normally, coffee beans are first dried and then roasted. After that, they are finely ground and then used to produce coffee.

- Kopi luwak is harvested in a very special way. Weasel-like animals called civets eat the raw coffee beans. The outer shells are digested by their intestines, but the seeds are pooped out whole and have a unique flavour. Workers collect the seeds, and process them like normal coffee beans.

- Very limited amounts of this unusual coffee are produced – only several hundred kilos per year worldwide.

- If you want to be really exclusive, seek out the coffee from the wild civets of Vietnam. You'll have to pay £2,000 per kilogram for their coffee. That's an expensive cup of weasel poo!

fizzzz

282 DYNAMITE HAS PEANUTS IN IT

Don't worry, you don't need to be afraid of **peanuts** exploding in your mouth. But it is true that peanuts are used as an ingredient in **dynamite**.

Like all nuts, peanuts are full of oil. Peanut oil is a common cooking oil, but it can also be used to make glycerol, the principal ingredient in nitro-glycerine. 'Aha!' some of you will say, 'Nitro-glycerine – that has something to do with explosives.'

You're right. Nitro-glycerine is a dangerous explosive. A stick of dynamite is made of nitro-glycerine mixed with other materials such as sawdust and clay, making it far safer to transport and work with than pure nitro-glycerine.

So, do you still feel like rummaging around in that bowl of peanuts?

283 FUGU IS A DELICACY THAT CAN KILL YOU

Fugu is a Japanese delicacy made from the **pufferfish**, also called the porcupine fish.

- These fish are extremely poisonous. Their internal organs contain a substance called tetrodotoxin, a poison hundreds of times more powerful than the deadly poison cyanide. If you consume any by accident, your muscles will become paralysed. First your lips and tongue will go numb, followed by the rest of your body. Eventually, you will stop breathing and suffocate.

- Despite this danger, fugu is actually a delicacy served in the very best Japanese restaurants. Before being allowed to include it on the menu, chefs first need to take a special training course. To prove the fish has been perfectly prepared, the chef must always take the first bite.

- Things do go wrong occasionally. One customer of Fugu Fukuji, a restaurant in Tokyo, once ended up in hospital. It wasn't entirely the chef's fault: the woman was intent on consuming the liver of the fish to prove how tough and brave she was. The chef should have refused, but eventually gave her what she wanted. The woman was taken to hospital, and survived her daring-do. The chef was fired.

- In Japan, the word 'fugu' is often pronounced 'fuku', which means 'happiness'. Seems a little strange … but okay.

BONUS FUGU FACTS

Fugu has been a delicacy in Japan for over 2,300 years.

Fugu is the only food that the Emperor of Japan is not allowed to eat.

The flavour of fugu meat is nothing special, and most connoisseurs say it's actually rather bland. So eating fugu is more about the thrill than the taste.

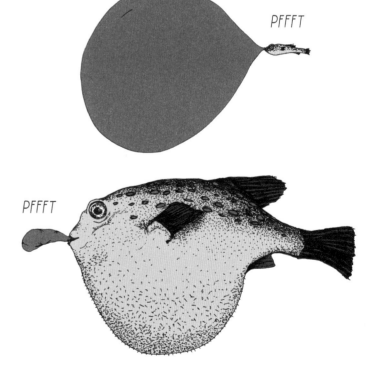

PFFFT

PFFFT

284 ONE MUSHROOM CAN BUY YOU A HOUSE

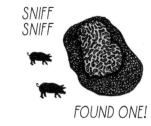

SNIFF SNIFF

FOUND ONE!

Chinese businessman Stanley Ho once paid $330,000 for a single piece of fungus. But not just any old mushroom: it was a one-and-a-half-kilo **truffle** that Cristiano Savini had unearthed near the Italian city of Pisa. Actually it was his dog Rocco that found the truffle. Hopefully Rocco got an extra-special treat that night!

Truffles grow on the roots of trees, usually oaks. Trained pigs or dogs are used to sniff them out. They have a very unique and pleasant flavour, but are generally only eaten in small quantities because they are so expensive.

285 KETCHUP USED TO BE A MEDICINE

Dr Miles' Compound Extract of Tomato! The name might sound glorious and fancy, but all it really means is **ketchup.**

During the early nineteenth century, ketchup was used as a medicine. The man selling it claimed that it could combat virtually any disease. But because it contained exactly the same ingredients as modern-day ketchup, its 'medicinal' effects were probably very limited.

It may not be a medicine, but ketchup is not bad for you either. It's made of tomatoes, which contain lycopene – a substance that helps your body protect itself against all kinds of diseases. The body does have trouble absorbing lycopene from raw tomatoes, but heat them up and it's much easier. So things like tomato soup, pasta sauce – and ketchup – will give you a delicious dose of healthy lycopene.

Cola was also invented by a pharmacist. It was created in 1886 by John Pemberton, who was not only a chemist but also a doctor. He had tried creating medicines before, but they weren't very successful or popular. So this time he changed

his strategy, and made a soft drink. It eventually became hugely popular, and today the recipe for Coca-Cola is one of the world's best-kept secrets.

So is Coke good for you? Not really – it contains a lot of sugar, so you should probably only enjoy it occasionally.

286 FRIED WORMS AND GRASSHOPPERS ARE GOOD FOR YOU

Cricket chips, mealworm burgers, grasshopper kebabs... are you starting to feel queasy? In a lot of countries, **eating insects** is considered very normal practice.

- Families in the Congo can easily eat up to half a kilogram of caterpillars per week.

- Just try to find a South-African who isn't crazy about mopane worms!

- Grilled bee larvae and fried silkworms are both considered delicacies in China.

- In Mexico, bowls of fried crickets are often put on the table instead of chips. Caterpillars, ants and worms are also every popular Mexican treats.

- In fact, there are over two billion people on earth who think that eating insects is not out-of-the-ordinary at all.

It would be a good idea for us to start including insects on the menu too. They are very high in protein, which is necessary for growing strong bones and muscles. Insects also need very little food to grow, since they are cold-blooded creatures and don't use energy to maintain their body temperature. That's why it's better for the environment to raise crickets instead of other animals like pigs, cows or sheep.

And lastly, beetles, grasshoppers, mealworms and other creepy-crawlies produce almost no greenhouse gases, especially when compared to mammals.

Scientists all over the world are currently researching the best methods for farming insects, as well as ways of encouraging more people to include them in their diet.

Maybe one day you'll sink your teeth into a cricket burger without even realizing it...

BONUS FOOD FACT

In Cambodia, fried **tarantulas** are a delicacy. These enormous spiders are served up whole, with a slice of lime and a bowl of dipping sauce. They're a real family favourite, with enough legs for everybody!

HEY THERE!

san-nakji   oyster   sea urchin

287 SOME ANIMALS GET EATEN ALIVE

- When holidaying in South Korea, you should think carefully before accepting an offer of **san-nakji**: raw octopus that is cut into pieces and served still alive, wriggling on the plate. Real fans of this dish will tell you they particularly love the feeling when the tentacles' suction cups cling to the inside of their mouth…

- It's not just the Koreans who enjoy eating live food. The Japanese eat **ikizukuri**, a fish that is filleted alive without being killed first. When the dish is placed on the table, the fish's heart is still beating.

- In China, occasionally a dish of **drunken prawns** is served. The little critters are first soaked alive in strong alcohol, making them 'drunk'. Then the bowl is covered with a plate to stop them all scampering off (wouldn't you?). The beasties are then eaten alive.

- Many Aboriginal Australians enjoy eating **witchetty grubs**, or large white caterpillars that apparently taste like almonds. To eat one, you suck it dry while it is still alive.

- Europeans don't need to travel very far for a live-food treat. Oysters and sea urchins are a delicacy in the West, and they are gobbled up alive too.

288 FEEL LIKE SOME ROTTEN CHEESE? VISIT SARDINIA

We don't mean ordinary stinky blue cheese here. No, we mean cheese that literally has maggots crawling out of it: the famous **casu marzu**, or 'rotten cheese' from the Italian island of Sardinia. Made of sheep's milk, it is ripened until little maggots start appearing. The maggots not only eat the cheese but also poop it back out again, giving casu marzu a distinctively strong, sweet flavour and creamy texture.

To eat it, the Sardinians break the cheese apart and spoon it into their mouths, maggots and all.

The **maggots** in casu marzu cheese are about 8 millimetres long. They can jump too, so when opening up a wheel of the cheese, it's a good idea to keep your eyes shut to avoid a worm ambush.

Unfortunately, it's illegal for the cheese to be sold in stores. To get a taste, you'll need to visit a farm where the cheese is made.

casu marzu   surströmming

289 THE SWEDISH EAT STINKY HERRING

- Swedish shops sell a product called **surströmming**, or fermented herring. To make it, the herring is lightly pickled and then allowed to ferment for three months at a constant temperature. The herring is then put into tins, where the fermentation continues. You can probably imagine the stink that comes out when a tin of surströmming is opened… from experience, we can tell you it's better to do it outdoors. The tins are sometimes even opened underwater or beneath a wet towel, which also helps prevent the brown liquid in the tin from spurting everywhere.

- Norway has a different delicacy: they make **rakfisk**, or salted trout. First the trout are smeared with salt and placed in the bottom of a tub. A big wooden plank goes on top, followed by another layer of fish, and so on. After three months, the tub is opened and the Norwegians happily gobble up their rakfisk. It's not rotten, but rakfisk is still certainly an acquired taste.

290 THE SPANISH MAKE VERY SPECIAL BISCUITS

Mmmm, biscuits… tasty right? Well maybe not. We're talking here about **criadillo**, a tasty treat that might look like a crunchy cookie, but is in fact something completely different. Here's a hint: another name for the criadillo is 'bull's eggs'. Can you guess what that might be?

That's right! Criadillo is made from the testicles of a bull. The little balls are first pounded lightly into a flat shape, then fried.

Bull's testicles are eaten in other parts of the world too. In the United States, the dish is called **Rocky Mountain Oysters**.

Incidentally, the bull is not the only animal whose testicles are eaten. Goat, sheep and rooster testicles are also often served as dishes.

291 HOW OLD DO YOU LIKE YOUR EGGS?

- **Hundred-year eggs** or **century eggs** are a very popular dish in China. The name is not entirely accurate, however: the eggs take only one hundred days to prepare.

- To make them, a Chinese chef takes raw duck eggs, smears them with lime, ash, tea and salt, then buries them in a container with soil. One hundred days later, they dig up the eggs, which have turned hard inside and gone completely black. Open one up and you'll see a green yolk surrounded by a gold or bronze-coloured egg white. It stinks like rotten egg – and that's precisely what it is – but it's still edible.

- An even stranger egg dish is **balut**: a fertilized duck egg containing a chick that is almost ready to hatch. The egg is boiled or steamed, and the contents eaten out of the shell, chick and all. First you slurp up the liquid surrounding the baby duck, then peel the egg away. Balut is a common snack in the Philippines. Sometimes the chick is eaten straight out of the eggshell, but it can also be fried or boiled first.

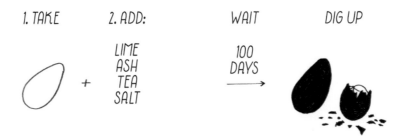

1. TAKE   2. ADD: WAIT   DIG UP

LIME
ASH
TEA
SALT

100 DAYS

292 NAPOLEON GAVE THE WORLD CHOCOLATE SPREAD WITH HAZELNUTS

- Do you like smearing **chocolate spread** on your toast in the mornings? How about the well-known brand that includes hazelnuts?

- The world has Napoleon to thank for this tasty treat. In the Italian city of Turin, chocolate was once very expensive due to the strict import taxes introduced by Napoleon. So the ingenious Italians started mixing the chocolate with a kind of hazelnut butter that they made themselves. Their name for the resulting chocolate-hazelnut paste was **gianduja**.

293 CHILDREN DRANK BEER IN THE MIDDLE AGES

And for a good reason!

- In the Middle Ages, **beer** was much healthier than water. Homes didn't have taps that delivered clean water like they do today – people needed to make special trips to collect water from rivers or wells. The canal water flowing through the cities was often highly contaminated with rubbish and other waste thrown into it. That included bodily wastes: people used to relieve themselves in the canals, making the water too dirty to drink. This polluted water caused many diseases and epidemics in past centuries.

- Although the same water was used to make beer, the breweries boiled it first, destroying most of the disease-causing germs. The 'hops' used to add flavour also killed many of the dangerous bacteria, and allowed the beer to be stored for longer. Hops even contain certain vitamins not usually found in water, making the beer even healthier.

- People in the Middle Ages drank around 300 litres of beer per year. It was less alcoholic in those days, so people didn't get drunk as quickly. Children were given 'small beer', which was beer made with a lower alcohol content. They often still drank the same beer as their parents, though.

BONUS BEER FACT

The inhabitants of the Czech Republic are officially the world's biggest beer drinkers. The average Czech drinks 572 beers per year, or 11 per week.

Cheers!

294 THE ROMANS WERE BIG EATERS

The Romans liked organizing lavish banquets with piles of food. Rich Romans led a very decadent lifestyle.

- When the Romans invited guests, they would do their utmost to put their wealth on display. Guests would enjoy enormous quantities of eggs, cheese, fish, olives, bread and meats and slaves stood constantly at the ready to serve new trays of delicacies. Whenever a platter emptied, it was replaced with a fresh one.

- Knives and forks weren't used. The Romans ate with their fingers, and rinsed them in small bowls of water.

- Wine was also drunk in vast amounts.

this didn't happen

- Throughout the banquet, the guests were entertained by musicians, dancers or storytellers reciting poetry.

- The Romans didn't sit on chairs, but instead they reclined on long couches, propped up on their elbows.

- Until recently, many people believed that the Romans would often eat a huge meal and then make themselves sick on purpose so they could go and eat more. But in fact, that's only a myth. Plenty of Romans had big appetites, however!

295 THE SANDWICH WAS INVENTED BY A CARD-PLAYING EARL

John Montagu was the Fourth Earl of Sandwich, and lived during the 18th century. He was a very keen card player – so keen in fact, that he never wanted to leave the card table to eat a dish of meat and potatoes.

Of course, the Earl did get hungry from time to time. So he would ask his servants to put some leftover meat between two slices of bread, enabling him to eat it with one hand at the table without needing any cutlery. And the cards never got greasy, because the Earl's fingers only ever touched the bread, not the meat.

While the Earl remained at the table, the other players couldn't leave either. So when their tummies started rumbling, they would always order 'the same as Sandwich'. The name stuck, and ever since then the famous combination of bread and filling has borne the Earl's name.

296 BONBON = YUM YUM!

Anybody who knows a little French can see that 'bon, bon' actually means 'good, good'. But 'good' in French also means 'delicious', making bonbons twice as nice!

A special type of bonbon is the 'praline'. These were originally named **prasline** after a French nobleman, Count César of Plessis-Praslin. To guests he would serve roasted almonds encased in a layer of sugar, a delicacy invented by his chef. His guests were so taken with the treat, they decided to call it a *prasline*, which later changed to praline. The name is now also used for small chocolates with a sweet nutty filling.

Boxes of chocolates as we know them today were probably invented by Jean Neuhaus, a Swiss baker who emigrated to Belgium and started a fancy patisserie, where he made filled chocolate bonbons. Even today, Belgium is world-famous for its delicious chocolates.

297 CROISSANTS AREN'T COMPLETELY FRENCH

NON, JE NE SUIS PAS FRANÇAIS!

What could be more French than a **croissant**?

- Even the name 'croissant' is French. It's derived from the French word for the 'crescent' moon, a reference to the pastry's shape.

- Even so, it was an Austrian named August Zang who invented the croissant. Originally from Vienna, he opened up a bakery in Paris called the Boulangerie Viennoise, or the 'Viennese Bakery', where he sold all kinds of baked goods. His famous fluffy, curved pastry was dubbed 'croissant' by the French, and the name stuck.

- There's also a nice legend about the croissant. The story goes that early one morning, all the Viennese bakers heard an enormous racket that seemed to be coming from underground.

When they investigated, they discovered that the Turkish were digging a tunnel under the city walls to invade the city. They warned the police, who launched a counterattack and drove the Turkish away. The Viennese were so happy that the bakers had saved them, the authorities gave them the right to bake Turkish bread rolls in the shape of a half-moon. The bakers called it a **Hörnchen**, meaning 'little horn', which is still the name used for a croissant in Germany and Austria today (although none of the story is actually true).

298 SEA CUCUMBERS ARE NOT RELATED TO LAND CUCUMBERS

Have you ever eaten a **sea cucumber**? A tad saltier than its land-dwelling cousin perhaps, but it can be just as delicious.

- Despite the name, a sea cucumber is not just a type of cucumber that grows in the sea! Sea cucumbers are actually animals, and crawl over the ocean floor like slugs. They do look a little bit like cucumbers, but that's where the similarities end.

- They can be eaten, however. First the cucumber's tentacles and guts are removed, and then the body is dried to preserve it.

- Before chowing down on a sea cucumber, you'll need to soak and boil it in water first. Then it will take on a slippery, slimy appearance, a little like squid. The taste is also very similar. *Bon appétit!*

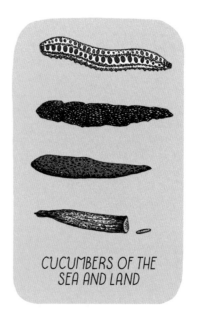

CUCUMBERS OF THE SEA AND LAND

299 CHEWING GUM IS MADE OF CRUDE OIL

Many people use **chewing gum** all the time to freshen their breath. But did you know that it's actually made of crude oil?

- Chewing gum is made by adding sugar or other flavourings to crude oil. The gum, scents, colours and flavours are heated up until they blend together and the mixture looks a bit like bread dough. Then it's pressed into flat sheets and cut into pieces.

- This type of chewing gum does not break down naturally. The leftover wads of gum that you spit out eventually find their way to seas, rivers, lakes and oceans, where they harden into tiny pieces of plastic. These are eaten by fish and other animals, so they end up back in our food chain.

- Thankfully, there is also chewing gum made from natural gum. To obtain it, a worker called a **chiclero** climbs into a sapodilla tree, makes a cut in the tree's bark and collects the sap or gum that flows out. This gum is called **chicle**.

No trees are cut down to produce it, which is another good reason to choose chewing gum that is bio-degradable.

made from crude oil

BONUS CHEWING-GUM FACT

Humans have always enjoyed chewing things. The Inuit people used to chew on whale skin, and Chinese people chewed ginseng root. Most often, however, hardened tree sap was used. A few years ago, Swedish archaeologists found a piece of chewing gum that was 9,000 years old!

300 HAMBURGERS REALLY DID COME FROM HAMBURG

Nowadays **hamburgers** are regarded as a typically American food. Even so, the famous meaty snack originated in the German city of Hamburg.

- Poverty was widespread in 19th-century Europe, and so many Europeans left for the United States to build better lives for themselves. There were no aeroplanes in those days, so the long journey was made by boat.

- That was also the time when the meat grinder was invented in Germany, which allowed meat to be minced into small pieces and combined with breadcrumbs and chopped onions. This type of meat was very popular in the city of Hamburg.

- Immigrants introduced this typical German dish to the New World. The meat became very popular with Americans, who would stuff it into a bread roll.

made from beef

- It is unknown who invented the hamburger as we know it today, and many people have claimed to be the first. In any case, the hamburger, or burger for short, is now popular around the world.

12

TO INFINITY
AND BEYOND

301 THERE ARE GIANTS IN SPACE

One of these giants is called VY Canis Majoris.

- VY Canis Majoris is a **red hypergiant**, an enormous type of star. Canis is an incredible 1,400 times larger than our sun, and has over twenty times the mass.

- 109 planet earths fit across the diameter of our own sun, and so Canis is really big. If VY Canis Majoris were at the centre of our solar system, it would swallow all the planets up to Jupiter.

- VY Canis Majoris is a red star, and produces about 500,000 times more light than the sun. That makes it half a million times brighter!

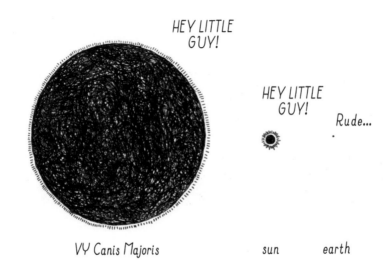

HEY LITTLE GUY!

HEY LITTLE GUY!

Rude...

VY Canis Majoris   sun   earth

302 SHOOTING STARS ARE THE SIZE OF COBBLESTONES

Have you ever seen a **shooting star**? A brief streak of light flashing across a dark sky, the type that fairy tales say you can make a wish on? They are easiest to see at night when there are no clouds.

A shooting star is actually nothing more than a chunk of rock no bigger than a cobblestone, flying through the earth's atmosphere at a very high speed. Its velocity creates a lot of friction with the air, so the rock – or meteor, as it should be called – literally evaporates. It is constantly colliding with tiny air molecules, causing its own particles to become electrically charged and break apart. When they meet each other again behind the meteor, they turn into sparks, producing the light that you see as a shooting star.

A POOPING STAR?

303 WE DON'T KNOW HOW BIG THE UNIVERSE IS

Despite the progress that science has made, we actually don't know all that much about the **universe**. From our vantage point on earth, we can only see a tiny section of it.

The universe is about 13.8 billion years old. Anything that's further than 13.8 light years away

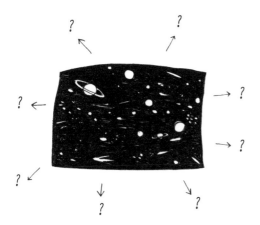

(see Fact 314) is invisible to us, since the light from those galaxies hasn't reached us yet.

The part of the universe that we *can* see contains about 350 billion galaxies, many of which hold millions upon millions of stars. This 'visible universe' measures ninety trillion light years from one side to the other. That's 90,000,000,000,000 – quite a dizzying figure. These are all figures that make your head spin, and even scientists have trouble grasping just how massive everything is. So sometimes comparisons are used to try to understand things. For example, it is often said that the visible universe contains more stars than there are grains of sand on a beach, or perhaps even on all the world's beaches.

The universe could be infinitely large – we just don't know. Our brains cannot fathom it. And if the universe *does* have a boundary, what might lie on the other side?

304 COMETS ARE BIG BALLS OF ICE

Comets are relatively small space objects: chunks of ice that orbit on the very outskirts of our solar system. Whenever a comet's orbit brings it closer to the sun, parts of the comet are turned into gas via a process called 'sublimation'. The solar wind blasts the gas away from the core, creating a long tail. Although the icy core usually only has a diameter of 10 kilometres or so, the tail can be millions of kilometres long, and is made up of wisps of glowing gas. The trail of dust and gas attached to a comet is called its 'coma'.

The coma of Comet Hyakutake, which passed by Earth in 1996, was an incredible 570 million kilometres long, and reached to the far edge of the asteroid belt.

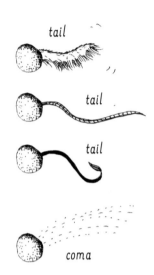

305 STARS DON'T LIVE FOREVER

When stars die, they go out with a bang. When red hypergiant VY Canis Majoris (see Fact 301) finally dies, it will explode with terrifying and tremendous force. When that happens to a large **star** (with at least eight times the mass of the sun) it becomes a **supernova**. Our sun is far too small, so it will never do that. Instead, its matter will be ejected into space as an enormous cloud of gas and dust. This leftover cloud is called a **nebula**.

At the very centre of an exploded supernova is what is called a **neutron star**. Imagine a red-hot ball about the size of a city (30 kilometres or so across). The temperature of a neutron star is above one million degrees Celsius, and a piece of it the size of a pinhead would weigh one million tonnes (or as much as three skyscrapers). These sizes are so huge, it's hard to even imagine them.

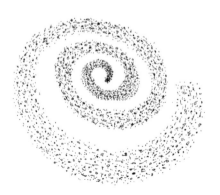

306 THE INTERNATIONAL SPACE STATION TRAVELS AT 27,600 KM/H

The **International Space Station** (or ISS) is made up of many different sections or 'modules' that were launched separately into space and then joined together. The first module was Russian, and left earth in 1998. There has been a continuous rotating crew of astronaut scientists living in the ISS since the year 2000.

The ISS is sometimes visible from earth, as a bright speck of light floating from west to east.

Although it seems to be moving slowly, in reality the ISS whizzes through space at a speed of 27,600 kilometres per hour, circling the earth once every 91 minutes. The space station is about 400 kilometres from the earth's surface. At such a high altitude, the atmosphere is so thin there is almost no air resistance. That is what allows the ISS to travel at such high speeds without burning up or being damaged.

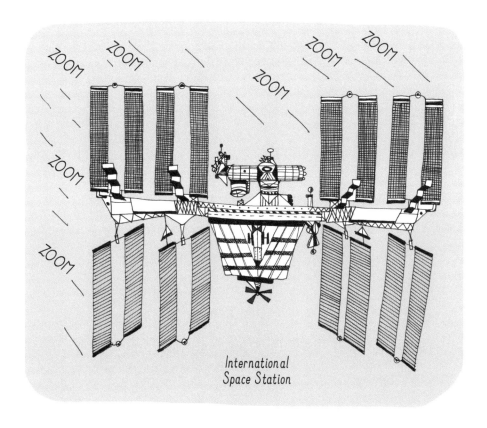

International
Space Station

307 BLACK HOLES
ARE TERRIFYING

POP!

- A **black hole** is a place in the universe where gravity is so great that nothing can escape. And we mean nothing: even light is trapped by the black hole's tremendous gravitational pull (that's why it's black).

- The inside of a black hole is not a particularly fun place to be. Any nearby material from space – like rocks, stones or gases – are sucked with huge force in the direction of the 'singularity,' which is the core or the very centre of the black hole. Once you get pulled in, there's no coming back out.

- As black holes age, however, they become less powerful. So it might be possible to survive the pull of an older black hole.

- Some scientists believe that black holes are gateways to other parts of the universe. There are movies and TV shows where spaceships fly through them and experience amazing adventures through time and space. But that's pure science fiction, and very unlikely. For the time being, there is only one known planet where humans can survive, and that's our very own earth.

308 THE EARTH IS NOT ROUND

Of course we don't mean that the earth is flat. But it isn't perfectly round either.

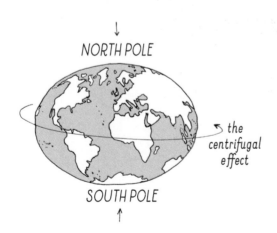

NORTH POLE

↘ the centrifugal effect

SOUTH POLE
↑

- A journey round the earth's equator is several dozen kilometres longer than a trip around the poles.

- This is because the earth has been spinning on its axis for an extremely long time, making it slightly wider at the equator and flatter at the poles. This effect is known as the 'flattening of the earth', or the **centrifugal effect**. So the earth is really shaped more like an oval than a perfect sphere.

- Scientists already suspected that the earth was an oval in the 17th century. But it took until 1735 to actually prove it, using land measurements taken in Lapland and Peru.

HEAVENLY BODY				
sun	Jupiter	Earth	Mars	moon
560	50.6	20	7.6	3.3
840	75.9	30	11.4	4.9
1120	101.2	40	15.2	6.6
1400	126.5	50	19	8.2
1680	151.8	60	22.8	9.8
1960	177.1	70	26.6	11.5
2240	202.4	80	30.4	13.1
2520	227.7	90	34.2	14.8
2800	253	100	38	16.4

WEIGHT in kg

less gravity

309 THINGS WEIGH LESS ON MARS THAN ON EARTH

- A person weighing 50 kilograms on earth weighs just 19 kilograms on **Mars**. That's because Mars is smaller and lighter than earth, and its gravity is weaker. To figure out how much you'd weigh on Mars, multiply your earth weight by 0.38. In the example above, that's 50 kg × 0.38 = 19 kg.

- You would weigh even less on the **moon**, since the gravity is even weaker there. Fifty kilograms on earth only weighs 8.2 kilograms on the moon.

- But on the largest planet in our solar system, **Jupiter**, everything is heavier than on earth. The same 50-kilogram example above would become 126.5 kilograms on Jupiter.

- The heaviest possible weights in our solar system occur on the **sun**, where an earth weight of 50 kilos turns into a massive 1.4 tonnes!

BONUS MARS FACT

In 2012, a robot landed on Mars that has been conducting scientific investigations ever since. It was given the name Curiosity. One year after landing on the red planet, the scientists controlling the robot celebrated by making it sing 'Happy Birthday' to itself.

310 THE SUN'S CENTRE IS SUPER HOT

- At the centre of the **sun** it's 15 million degrees Celsius. So it's quite interesting that the surface of the sun is far cooler, a 'mere' 5,700 °C. Of course that's still pretty scorching, considering that water boils at 100 °C.

- The sun is made of hydrogen gas, which becomes so compressed that it turns into another element: helium (*helios* is Greek for 'sun'). The fusion of the atoms produces an enormous amount of energy, which is why the centre of the sun is a mind-boggling 15 million °C.

- The area around the sun is also far hotter than the surface itself. That's because the sun has many active magnetic fields that cause gas explosions, making the surrounding atmosphere much hotter.

- Albert Einstein theorized about how it all worked. But now we can use satellites and special telescopes to measure the sun's phenomena directly.

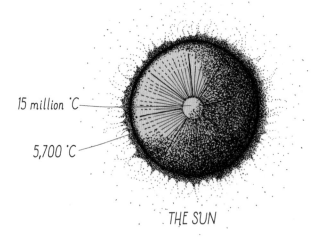

15 million °C

5,700 °C

THE SUN

311 IN SPACE, YOU CAN'T HEAR ... ANYTHING

Sound is made up of waves, or movements of particles through space. The best way to observe it is to place your hand on a loudspeaker – can you feel the vibrations? These cause waves in the surrounding air particles, which travel to reach your ears. Via your eardrums, they eventually reach your brain, where the vibrations are interpreted as sound.

Sound waves are constantly travelling all around us, which is why you can still hear many different sounds even when sitting perfectly still. Sound vibrations travel more easily through water, but even better through walls. That's why pressing your ear to the wall will allow you to hear the neighbours more clearly.

In space there's no air or water, and no walls. Sound waves cannot travel there, because there is nothing for them to travel through. So space is totally silent. That means that when the **Big Bang** happened, there actually wasn't much of a bang!

the neighbours

_____

space

312 PLUTO'S CORE IS MADE OF ICE

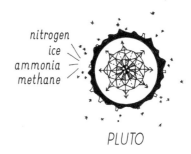

nitrogen
ice
ammonia
methane

PLUTO

Pluto is a **dwarf planet**.* It has a diameter of 2,370 kilometres, and orbits the sun once every 248 years.

Pluto's surface has mountains over 3 kilometres high, and some of them have holes in the top. They are probably some kind of volcano, but instead of spewing lava, they erupt with an icy mixture of nitrogen, frozen water, ammonia and methane.

The cause lies at Pluto's core, which is an enormous glacier about 4 kilometres thick and 1,000 kilometres wide. The glacier is made of frozen nitrogen, carbon monoxide and methane.

How do we know all this? Well, Pluto was studied by **New Horizons**, an unmanned space satellite that was launched in 2006. New Horizons examined the surface, composition and atmosphere of Pluto and its moons. The data collected was sent back to earth, and took around sixteen months to get here.

*Pluto's classification as a 'dwarf planet' has nothing to do with its size. The difference between a planet and a dwarf planet is that planets do not share their orbits with any other objects. Pluto's orbit around the sun contains many other dwarf planets and planetoids (see Fact 318), while the orbits of the 'real' planets have been wiped clean of any debris.

313 SPACE IS FULL OF ALCOHOLIC CLOUDS

In space, even in our own galaxy, there are enormous **clouds** full of **alcohol**. They are gigantic, sometimes covering a thousand times the distance from the earth to the sun. Some of the alcohol is the same as the type contained in beer or wine, called ethanol. Unfortunately, the alcohol would be undrinkable on earth, since it contains all kinds of other toxic substances.

All this alcohol is spewed out by a **comet** (see Fact 304) called Lovejoy – a strange but appropriate name.

Sometimes, Lovejoy sprays enough alcohol into space to make over five hundred bottles of wine per second. Who's up for a space cocktail?

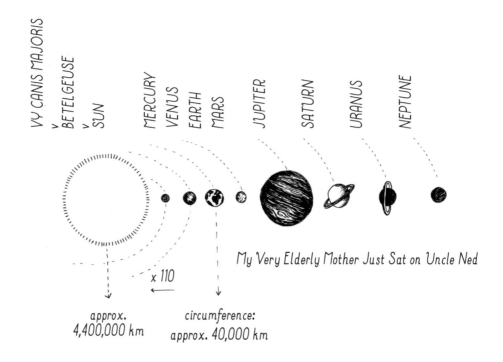

VY CANIS MAJORIS
BETELGEUSE
SUN
MERCURY
VENUS
EARTH
MARS
JUPITER
SATURN
URANUS
NEPTUNE

x 110

My Very Elderly Mother Just Sat on Uncle Ned

approx.
4,400,000 km

circumference:
approx. 40,000 km

314 THE SUN IS 110 TIMES LARGER THAN THE EARTH

The earth's circumference (that's the distance around the outside) is about 40,000 kilometres. The **sun** has a circumference of roughly 4,400,000 kilometres, making it a whopping 110 times bigger than the earth.

Despite its size, the sun is still a rather small star in the universe. There is a star around 600 light years away, for example, called **Betelgeuse**: a titan with a circumference of 900 million kilometres. Around 4,900 light years away is VY Canis Majoris, the largest star ever observed (see Fact 301). If you were to fly around VY Canis Majoris in an aeroplane, it would take you a thousand years!

BONUS FACT

In **astronomy**, light years are used to measure distances in space. A light year is the distance that light can travel in a vacuum in one year. Since light travels at 300,000 kilometres per second, in a year it can cover 9,460,730,472,580,800 metres, or just under 9.5 trillion kilometres.

The Milky Way Galaxy – our galaxy – is about 100,000 light years across.

315 STARS ARE NOT PLANETS (AND VICE VERSA)

When looking at the night sky, stars and planets often look very similar. Here's how to tell the difference.

- Close-up, **stars** and **planets** look nothing alike. A star is a huge ball of glowing hot gas: nuclear fusion reactions at its core produce massive amounts of light and heat, which are ejected out into the universe. Our sun is a star.

PLANETS — STARS

rock
ice
gas
metal

- Planets are smaller and colder, and are made of ice, rock, gases or metals. Any light or warmth on a planet comes from the star it orbits. The earth we live on is a planet.

- Looking into the night sky, planets and stars both look like tiny specks of light. But there is a way to tell the difference, even with the naked eye: planets are usually brighter, and don't twinkle or shimmer like stars do.

- Lastly, stars are always in the same place relative to the other stars in the sky. Planets move around as they orbit their stars, which is actually where their name comes from ('planet' is Greek for 'wanderer'). If you stare at the night sky for long enough, you will see which points stay put and which ones wander. In reality, the stars are moving too, but they are so much farther away from the earth than the planets that their movements are much harder to spot.

- From earth, five planets are visible with the naked eye. Venus is the brightest, and is often referred to as the 'Morning Star' or 'Evening Star', even though it's not really a star. These are the times of day when it is most visible.

- Mercury can usually only be seen during the twilight hours of dusk and dawn. Mars is clearly visible for a certain period once every two years, and can be recognized by its orange hue. Jupiter and Saturn can also be seen easily for several months a year.

316 THE SUN MAKES THE NORTHERN LIGHTS

Sometimes, close to the North and South Poles, an amazing phenomenon occurs: the dark sky will light up with a brilliant display of colours. They are called the **Northern Lights** and **Southern Lights**, or 'polar lights', but the Romans named them **aurora**, after their goddess of the dawn.

- Even though they happen in the dark, the polar lights are actually created by the sun. In addition to giving off light, the sun also sends out a stream of electrically charged particles into space, known as the 'solar wind'.

- When these particles arrive in our atmosphere, they collide with oxygen and nitrogen molecules. Their charge is transferred during the collision, producing tiny sparks of light.

- The colour of the polar lights depends on which molecules the particles collide with. The lights can be green, reddish-brown, blue or red.

- The lights only occur at the North and South Poles because these are the earth's magnetic poles and attract most of the solar wind.

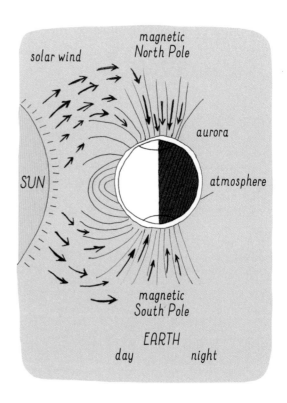

317 IT'S POSSIBLE TO GET HIT BY A METEORITE (BUT NOT VERY LIKELY)

The earth is constantly being bombarded with pieces of space rock. These **meteorites**, as they are called, usually land somewhere in the ocean, or in uninhabited parts of the world. But they do occasionally hit unlucky people too.

- In 1954, Ann Hodges was hit by a meteorite in her sleep. Luckily she survived, with only burns to her side.

- A cow in Venezuela wasn't quite so lucky, and was killed by a meteorite in 1972.

- In 1992, a little boy from Uganda was hit in the head by a meteorite weighing three grams.

- Things can sometimes be very serious, however. On 15 February 2013, a large meteorite exploded above Russia. The people of Chelyabinsk saw a massive fireball streak across the sky, accompanied by an ear-splitting supersonic boom that shattered many nearby windows. Thousands of people were injured by the shards of flying glass.

OUCH!

- But there's no need to be afraid: the probability of being hit by a meteorite is extremely small. In 2014, professor Stephen A. Nelson calculated that the chances of death by meteorite are one in 1.6 million.

- You don't need to be hit by a meteorite to die from one, however – the disastrous effects of a meteorite impact on earth can be deadly. But the probability of a piece of space rock actually landing on your head is so small, it's virtually non-existent.

318 SCIENTISTS ARE TRYING TO KNOCK A PLANETOID OUT OF ITS ORBIT

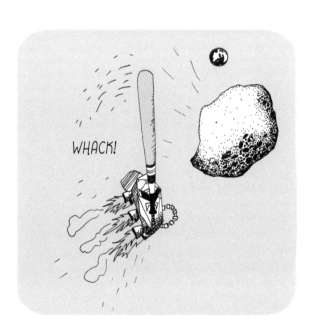

WHACK!

Aerospace agencies **NASA** and the **ESA** (European Space Agency) are working together to figure out how to stop a **planetoid** (also called an **asteroid**) from colliding with the earth. If this ever happened, it could mean the extermination of all life on earth. NASA and the ESA plan to send a space probe to the binary asteroid Didymos in 2022, to force a collision and knock it out of orbit. The probe will be sent to Didymos in summer 2021. A year later, after a journey of 11 million kilometres, it will smash into the planetoid, hopefully with enough momentum to send it off course, and away from the earth.

The main aim of the project is to see whether it's possible to knock a planetoid out of its orbit. With the information they collect, scientists can figure out what to do if a real space collision ever happens.

319 THE EARTH IS 4.57 BILLION YEARS OLD

That's a fascinating fact, but how do we know?

- For a long time, the **Bible** was used to work out when the earth was formed. Scholars studied the stories, and arrived at a date of 4,004 BCE. Since then, however, much more reliable information has become available.

- Scientific research into the age of the planet began in the 19th century, when many different methods were used. Biologists tried to apply Darwin's theory of evolution (see Fact 111): because Darwin assumed that it would take hundreds of millions of years for a single-celled organism to evolve into a human, the scientists surmised that the earth had to be at least as old as it took for humans to evolve.

- **Geologists** looked mainly at the rate at which the oceans became salty, or the time required for the sun to grow to its current size.

- But the scientists weren't done, and the discovery of radioactivity in 1896 offered a new breakthrough. By measuring how quickly uranium atoms break down, it's possible to calculate how long a uranium deposit has

1. Cut the earth in half

2. Count the rings

HOW TO WORK OUT THE
AGE OF THE EARTH

been trapped inside a rock. Using this method, scientists calculated that the oldest known piece of rock on earth was 4.4 billion years old.

- The oldest meteorite ever found was estimated to be 4.57 billion years old. If our planet is about as old as the rest of our solar system, logic says that the earth and the meteorite must be roughly the same age. Until an older meteorite is found, this remains the official figure.

320 THE BIGGEST LAKE IN THE SOLAR SYSTEM IS ON A MOON

Titan is the largest of Saturn's moons.

- A space probe discovered a **lake** on Titan that is 388,000 square kilometres in size. Titanic, you might say! Earth's largest lake is almost as big: the Caspian Sea near Russia covers 370,000 square kilometres.

- But Titan's lake isn't made of water. It's incredibly cold around the planet Saturn,

a chilly -181 °C, and any water would be frozen solid. So instead of water, the lake is made of liquid methane and ethane.

- Scientists suspect that long ago, the earth's atmosphere was similar to Titan's now, only the earth was much warmer. In any case, scientists are certain that there can be no life on Titan – it's far too cold, and there is no liquid water to be found.

- Titan was discovered in 1954 by a Dutch astronomer named Christian Huygens. He was a smart cookie: he wrote a book on how to calculate probabilities when rolling dice, built the first pendulum clock, and also wrote the first physics equations. All that, plus he discovered Titan!

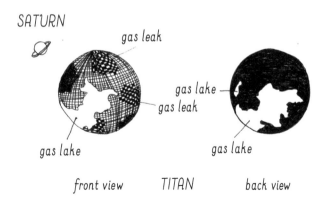

321 IF YOU KNOW WHAT A UFO IS, IT'S NOT A UFO

UFO stands for **unidentified flying object**. So if something whizzes by overhead and you don't know what it is, it's a UFO.

UFO sightings are quite common. Usually a little investigation will reveal the object's true identity: a satellite, a meteor, a sky lantern, a bird, a strange cloud, the planet Venus, a weather balloon, the ISS… All of these have once been reported as UFOs. But as soon as you know what it is, of course, it's not a UFO anymore.

Most UFO mysteries are solved eventually. But some do remain unexplained, and many people like to think we are receiving visitors from space. To these people, UFOs are spaceships full of weird-looking aliens, dropping in to see how the humans are doing.

We don't know for sure whether alien flying saucers have ever visited earth. But as long as the aliens don't announce themselves, there's no cause for concern. And until then, unidentified flying objects remain exactly that: unidentified.

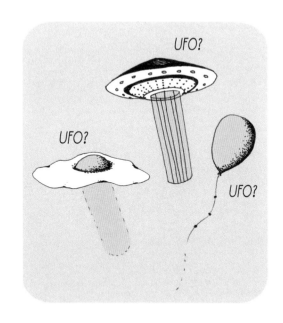

Translated from the Dutch *321 superslimme dingen die je moet weten voor je 13 wordt* by Brent Annable

First published in the United Kingdom in 2021 by Thames & Hudson Ltd, 181A High Holborn, London WC1V 7QX

Original edition © 2017, Uitgeverij Lannoo nv, Tielt www.lannoo.com

This edition © 2021 Thames & Hudson Ltd, London

This book was published with the support of Flanders Literature (flandersliterature.be).

FLANDERS LITERATURE

British Library Cataloguing-in-Publication Data

A catalogue record for this book is available from the British Library

ISBN 978-0-500-29602-8

Printed and bound in Italy

Be the first to know about our new releases, exclusive content and author events by visiting
thamesandhudson.com
thamesandhudsonusa.com
thamesandhudson.com.au

MIX
Paper from responsible sources
FSC® C015829